DATE DUE

			PRINTED IN U.S.A.

Authors & Artists for Young Adults

ISSN 1040-5682

12

Authors & Artists for Young Adults

VOLUME 31

Thomas McMahon
Editor

GALE GROUP

Detroit
San Francisco
London
Boston
Woodbridge, CT

Thomas McMahon, *Editor*

Joyce Nakamura, *Managing Editor*
Hal May, *Publisher*

Catherine Goldstein, *Contributing Editor*

Victoria B. Cariappa, *Research Manager*
Cheryl L. Warnock, *Project Coordinator*
Andrew Guy Malonis, Gary J. Oudersluys, *Research Specialists*
Patricia Tsune Ballard, Tracie A. Richardson, Corrine A. Stocker, *Research Associates*
Phyllis J. Blackman, Tim Lehnerer, Patricia L. Love, *Research Assistants*

Susan M. Trosky, *Permissions Manager*
Maria L. Franklin, *Permissions Specialist*
Sarah Chesney, Edna Hedblad, Michele Lonoconus, *Permissions Associates*

Mary Beth Trimper, *Production Director*
Cindy Range, *Production Assistant*

Randy Bassett, *Image Database Supervisor*
Gary Leach, *Graphic Artist*
Robert Duncan, Michael Logusz, *Imaging Specialists*
Pamela A. Reed, *Imaging Coordinator*

The paper used in this publication meets the minimum requirements of American National Standard for Information Sciences—Permanence Paper for Printed Library Materials, ANSI Z39.48-1984.

Library of Congress Catalog Card Number 89-641100
ISBN 0-7876-3231-7
ISSN 1040-5682

10 9 8 7 6 5 4 3 2 1

Printed in the United States of America

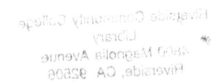

Contents

Introduction

Authors and Artists for Young Adults is a reference series designed to serve the needs of middle school, junior high, and high school students interested in creative artists. Originally inspired by the need to bridge the gap between Gale's *Something about the Author*, created for children, and *Contemporary Authors*, intended for older students and adults, *Authors and Artists for Young Adults* has been expanded to cover not only an international scope of authors, but also a wide variety of other artists.

Although the emphasis of the series remains on the writer for young adults, we recognize that these readers have diverse interests covering a wide range of reading levels. The series therefore contains not only those creative artists who are of high interest to young adults, including cartoonists, photographers, music composers, bestselling authors of adult novels, media directors, producers, and performers, but also literary and artistic figures studied in academic curricula, such as influential novelists, playwrights, poets, and painters. The goal of *Authors and Artists for Young Adults* is to present this great diversity of creative artists in a format that is entertaining, informative, and understandable to the young adult reader.

Entry Format

Each volume of *Authors and Artists for Young Adults* will furnish in-depth coverage of twenty to twenty-five authors and artists. The typical entry consists of:

—A detailed biographical section that includes date of birth, marriage, children, education, and addresses.

—A comprehensive bibliography or filmography including publishers, producers, and years.

—Adaptations into other media forms.

—Works in progress.

—A distinctive essay featuring comments on an artist's life, career, artistic intentions, world views, and controversies.

—References for further reading.

—Extensive illustrations, photographs, movie stills, cartoons, book covers, and other relevant visual material.

A cumulative index to featured authors and artists appears in each volume.

Compilation Methods

The editors of *Authors and Artists for Young Adults* make every effort to secure information directly from the authors and artists through personal correspondence and interviews. Sketches on living authors and artists are sent to the biographee for review prior to publication. Any sketches not personally reviewed by biographees or their representatives are marked with an asterisk (*).

Highlights of Forthcoming Volumes

Among the authors and artists planned for future volumes are:

Douglas Adams	Thomas Harris	Jackson Pollack
Allen Appel	S. E. Hinton	Tom Robbins
Robert Aspirin	Edward Hopper	William Shakespeare
Nevada Barr	John Jakes	Neil Simon
Olive Ann Burns	Francisco Jimenez	Isaac Bashevis Singer
Jane Campion	Trudy Krisher	Sheri S. Tepper
Grace Chetwin	Lois Lowry	Studs Terkel
Arthur C. Clarke	George R. R. Martin	Jean Ure
Robin Cook	Henri Matisse	Vivian Vande Velde
Charles de Lint	Anne McCaffrey	Joan D. Vinge
Gabriel Garcia Marquez	Robin McKinley	Oprah Winfrey
Allen Ginsburg	Nick Park	Frank Lloyd Wright

Contact the Editor

We encourage our readers to examine the entire *AAYA* series. Please write and tell us if we can make AAYA even more helpful to you. Give your comments and suggestions to the editor:

BY MAIL: The Editor, *Authors and Artists for Young Adults*, 27500 Drake Rd., Farmington Hills, MI 48331-3535.

BY TELEPHONE: (800) 347-GALE

Authors
& Artists
for Young
Adults

Emma Bull

■ Personal

Born December 13, 1954, in Torrance, CA; daughter of Volney R. and Dorothy (Harris) Bull; married Will Shetterly (a writer and editor), October 17, 1981. *Education:* Beloit College, B.A., 1976.

■ Addresses

Home—Studio City, CA. *Agent*—Valerie Smith, 1746 Route 44/55, Modena, NY 12548.

■ Career

Writer. Performer with Cats Laughing, a Minneapolis psychedelic jazz/folk band, and with the Flash Girls, a Celto-Goth acoustic duo; co-owner of SteelDragon Press, specializing in hardcover fantasy and comic books. Worked variously as an editor of corporate publications, a rubber stamp maker, a car parker at a summer resort, a security guard, a folksinger, and a car saleperson. *Member:* Minnesota Science Fiction Society, Minneapolis Scribblies, Writers Guild of America, West.

■ Awards, Honors

Inclusion among three hundred best books for young adults, New York Public Library, and Best First Novel designation, *Locus* magazine poll, both 1987, both for *War for the Oaks;* Nebula Award nomination, and Hugo nomination, both 1991, both for *Bone Dance.*

■ Writings

War for the Oaks, Ace/Berkley, 1987.
Falcon, Ace, 1989.
Bone Dance, Ace, 1991.
(With husband, Will Shetterly) *Double Feature,* NESFA Press, 1994.
The Princess and the Lord of Night (picture book), illustrated by Susan Gaber, Harcourt, 1994.
Finder: A Novel of the Borderlands, Tor, 1994.
(With Steven Brust) *Freedom and Necessity,* Tor, 1997.

Contributor to anthologies, including *Sword and Sorceress,* DAW, 1984; *Liavek,* Ace/Berkley, 1985; *Liavek: The Players of Luck,* Ace/Berkley, 1986; *Bordertown,* New American Library, 1986; *Hidden Turnings: A Collection of Stories through Time and Space,* edited by Diana Wynne Jones, Greenwillow Press, 1990; *Life on the Border,* Tor, 1991; *After the King: Stories in Honor of J. R. R. Tolkien,* edited by

Martin H. Greenberg, Tor, 1992; and *The Armless Maiden and Other Tales for Childhood's Survivors*, Tor, 1995.

■ Work in Progress

Territory, an historical fantasy set in Tombstone, Arizona, in the early 1880s; with Will Shetterly, *Virtual Meltdown*, a feature-length, animated science-fiction movie, in development with Perfect World Entertainment.

■ Sidelights

Emma Bull is a storyteller with a love of language. From a pool of remembered people, places, and events, impressions of the things she sees around her, and the creations of her vivid imagination, she has fashioned a body of fiction praised for its creativity and appeal, particularly to teen science-fiction and fantasy buffs. With the publication of her first book, 1987's *War for the Oaks*, Bull has commanded critical attention and, according to *Booklist* contributor Carl Hays, "forged a stellar reputation for sharply original storytelling." Since beginning her career as a novelist, Bull has expanded into the picture-book genre, and has also collaborated with her husband and fellow writer Will Shetterly on screenplays.

Bull was born in Torrance, California, in December of 1954. The daughter of a salesman specializing in steel products, young Emma recalled being fascinated by the product samples her father would bring home from work. "He sold large things made of steel that made larger things made of steel . . . [and] brought home such a splendid collection of magnets, ball bearings, cocktail swords . . . artifacts from a distant world, one where adults did powerful adult things beyond my understanding or skill," she recalled in an autobiographical essay. Because of her father's job, the family moved frequently, and Bull saw a great deal of the United States.

It would be Bull's early experience of California culture, however, that she would credit with shaping her lifelong love of the fantastic. "Everyone grows up in the land of make-believe, of one sort or another," Bull noted. "Mine was a golden age of amusement parks." Disneyland was part of her neighborhood, rather than a special place far from home. Her early memories of being pushed, in her stroller, through Tomorrowland and the Magic Kingdom, where she could see and hear such storybook characters as Peter Pan and the Lost Boys, caused Bull to learn to view everything around her with an accepting, imaginative gaze. From that point on, wherever she lived, amusement parks, tourist traps, and other artificially created worlds dotted her landscape. "Maybe I grew up thinking that people were supposed to reinvent reality," Bull later pondered.

Reinvented Realities

In addition to her constant exposure to the imagined worlds of others made real, Bull was also

Police officer Sunny Rico teams up with Orient, a young man with a sixth sense for finding things, to track down a deadly drug dealer in 1994 novel.

fortunate to be exposed to stories that allowed her to create her own imaginary people and places. Her mother, Dorothy, read to her young daughter constantly, providing the soundtrack for such arduous tasks as room-cleaning and bathtime, her voice bringing life to everything from *Treasure Island* to *Through the Looking Glass*. And the Bull family's constant relocation made each new town library a fresh adventure, its books new treasures waiting to be discovered during Bull's explorations of the shelves. Librarians were, to her, like "goddesses. . . . They knew everything, or could find it out." They possessed the answers to Bull's questions, and channelled her childish curiosity into the pages of books on everything from Grand Prix auto racing courses to mythology.

But Bull did not always have her head buried in a book in some quiet corner of her family's home. During the 1950s and 1960s the medium of television was coming into its own, and a host of programs, ranging from spy thrillers to westerns to serious dramas, were available at the turn of a knob. *The Man from U.N.C.L.E.* made perhaps the biggest impression on Bull, with its exotic locale and its dashing heroes and their super-spy capers, and she began to make up stories involving the television series' characters. Comic books, too, combined intriguing stories with illustrations of the impossible, from superheros to friendly ghosts to hulking monsters, all of which captured Bull's attention. As she grew older and moved into the adult section of the library, Bull discovered that fantasy and science-fiction literature best captured her own sense of the fantastic: the possibilities presented as average people were suddenly whisked into a magical world or faced with some planetary disaster that they must overcome. Her vivid imagination set her apart in high school; by college, it began to dictate her future.

A Commitment to Writing

Enrolling at Beloit College in 1972, Bull realized that writing would be her future. But that knowledge was intimidating to a young woman faced with the works of so many other talented writers. "If there were all those people who could write better than me out of 750 people at a small Midwestern college, how many more were there in the rest of the world?" she wondered, and her confidence was shaken by another possibility. As she recalled: "Did that mean that I'd found what

I wanted to do when I grew up . . . only to learn that I wasn't good enough at it?"

Determined not to give up on herself, Bull began an arduous "catch-up" regimen. Days were devoted to the serious pursuit of a degree in English literature: reading the works presented to her by her professors with an eye toward serious analysis, breaking them down into pieces and seeing how they worked, why they were considered "great." Nights were spent at the other end of the literary spectrum, as she discovered New Wave science fiction—works by authors like Samuel R. Delany. Finally, she enrolled in a series of classes that combined imaginative, untraditional fiction with writing, and discovered her own writer's voice. During this time, Bull also met her husband-to-be, Will Shetterly.

Puts Down Writer's Roots in Minnesota

After graduation from college, Bull moved to Minneapolis, and eked out a living as a freelancer by writing for several local newspapers. After attending her first science-fiction (SF) convention, she began to realize how accessible science-fiction authors were, and she began to gain a feeling of confidence that she too might be that successful in writing someday. Forming a writers' group with other aspiring SF novelists was also a help. Called the Interstate Writers' Workshop but known informally as the Scribblies, the group proved to house a vast store of talent which was honed through constant meetings, critiques of each others' work, and encouragement. When the film *Star Wars* was released in the mid-1970s, the popularity of the genre suddenly exploded, and the market for SF novels expanded. Bull and her fellow Scribblies, which included Shetterly, Patricia Wrede, Steven Brust, and Pamela Dean, were asked by Ace Books editor Terri Windling to write a "shared world" anthology: a collection of short stories by different authors, each taking place in the same fantasy world. The group got together and invented Liavek, a city-state whose leaders vie for power against other rulers along its borders. Bull contributed short stories to several *Liavek* anthologies, including 1985's *Liavek*, and the following year's anthology *Liavek: The Players of Luck*.

Bull, an aficionado of many types of modern music and a musician who performed in rock and folk bands in and around her adopted home of

Minneapolis during the 1980s, was inspired by both her current band, Cats Laughing, and the other-worldly scene at a local night club to set her first novel in that city. *War for the Oaks* takes place in contemporary Minneapolis as two competing courts of fairies—the Seelie and the Unseelie—do battle, unseen by most humans amid the hustle and bustle in the city's streets, parks, and playgrounds. The novel's mythic characters are invisible to almost everyone except the book's heroine, rock guitarist Eddi McCandry. The "war for the oaks," as the conflict between the rival courts is called, requires each group to have a human ally, and Eddi is chosen to help the Seelie Court. With the help of a phouka—a fairy charged with keeping her safe during the battle—she learns the formalities of fairy warfare and attempts to assist the Seelie fairies in vanquishing their opposition, both on and offstage. In fact, her band becomes a vehicle for the final showdown between the rival fairy factions. *Booklist* contributor Roland Green called Eddi McCandry among the "better female fantasy protagonists" of the 1980s, while in *Voice of Youth Advocates* Barbara Evans called *War of the Oaks* "exciting reading."

A member of a royal family living on the fictional and very Wales-like planet Cymru is the subject of Bull's second novel, *Falcon,* which finds the novelist straying, like her princely protagonist, into the interplanetary realm. Divided into two parts, the novel introduces the young hero, Falcon, and the kingdom over which his family rules as he defies royal dictates regarding the suppression of "a few damned unemployed malcontents" in favor of preserving justice among his people. Political intrigues include assassination attempts and a successful coup masterminded by the sinister Central Worlds Concorde that ultimately breaks Falcon's family's hold on the reins of power. One of the few family members to survive the political uprising, Falcon is forced to flee from his homeland. The novel's concluding chapters find Bull weaving elements of high-tech science fiction into her fantasy plot as her hero, now with his nervous system reengineered to accommodate the faster-than-light speeds he must attain in outer space, finds a new vocation as a daring space pilot whose task of saving worlds from oppression causes him to encounter adventure, discover a love interest, and navigate more than a little intrigue while also uncovering secrets about his family's past that prove eye-opening. Praising Bull's ability to "pull off this sort of thing with

such facility," *New York Times Book Review* contributor Gerald Jonas compared her work to her writer-hero Samuel R. Delany, finding "the same love of language that finds expression in well-formed descriptive sentences inlaid with an occasional flamboyant metaphor."

Minnesota after the Apocalypse

Bull also set her next novel, *Bone Dance,* in Minnesota, but this time the city, as well as the planet, has been in the process of rebuilding in the wake of a nuclear Armageddon. Her protagonist, an androgynous teen named Sparrow, has suffered from blackouts for most of his short life. Making a living seeking out and then selling the few remaining videos and CDs in existence to rich folks who have the money to spend, Sparrow has also accumulated a secret stock of prized video and audio equipment that he wishes to keep despite the outrageous price it would bring in the marketplace. He also works as a volunteer at a local nightclub called the Underbridge but, despite this attempt to keep active, his intermittent blackouts continue to disturb the young man, and he feels somehow detached from both his customers and the people at the club.

Ultimately, after taking the advice of a tarot-card reader that he get more involved in those around him, the reason for Sparrow's sense of not belonging becomes known when he meets a woman identifying herself as one of the two remaining members of the Horsemen, agroup that spied for the U.S. government before the nuclear disaster and whose members possess the power of mind control. Before the war sparking the holocaust, she explains to Sparrow, the Horsemen were all-powerful, and the government, realizing the need to curtail their power if necessary, constructed clones for their eventual habitation. Meanwhile, factions among the powerful Horsemen developed, resulting in the war that brought on Earth's environmental disaster. After the nuclear war, the Horsemen's clones were left abandoned and unattended, and several of these clones wandered away from their storage locations, taking on the semblance of humans, albeit without much in the way of personality. After his initial shock at the discovery that he is one such clone and that the ruler of the City is himself a Horseman, Sparrow finds himself drawn into a new feud that once again threatens the future of the planet.

STEVEN BRUST
AUTHOR OF *THE PHOENIX GUARDS*

& EMMA BULL
AUTHOR OF *WAR FOR THE OAKS*

FREEDOM & NECESSITY

Set in Victorian England, this romance-mystery novel features a young man trying to piece his life together after a bout of amnesia stemming from a boating accident.

Reviewing Bull's 1991 novel in *Publishers Weekly*, a critic found that, while the novel gets off to a slow start, "Bull keeps the focus on the people and their relationships, and eventually the off-beat characters draw the reader in." The reviewer also had praise for Bull's "sharp ear for relaxed dialogue and conversational humor," and noted that her setting and characters are wholly believable. Writing in *Analog Science Fiction/Science Fact*, reviewer Tom Easton commented that, while *Bone Dance* has a "mystic component" that is difficult for the reader to fully accept, he found the novel "interesting and significant," and "worthy of ap-

plause" for its imaginative plot and the ethical dilemma inherent in the use of such creatures as the Horsemen by governments. "If there is any justification for or value in their use," noted Easton, "there must come a time when they are no longer needed. How do you retire them? Do you—*can* you—destroy them?"

The Borderlands Grows Up

In addition to inspiring Bull and her writers' group to create the Liavek shared world anthologies, Ace editor Windling also sparked the group's work on the "Borderlands" series, a collection of fictions that posit the consequences of a world wherein the land of faerie and the commonplace meet. Beginning with the short story collection *Bordertown* in 1986, Scribblies have also contributed full-length novels to the growing annals of their shared world. Bull's novel *Finder*, the sixth installment in the Borderlands chronicles, expands on a character she introduced to the series in a story several years previously. A detective, science fiction, and fantasy novel all in one, *Finder* is set in the magical city of Bordertown, where young elves and humans mingle, and where a new drug called Passport is rumored to transform humans into elves, enabling those who ingest it to cross into the lands surrounding Bordertown. While many attempt to get the drug, lured by the promise of the Elflands, in reality the drug kills those who use it.

Into this tragic scenario comes Sunny Rico, a female police officer. Determined to find the dealer of this deadly and seductive drug, she calls upon the help of Orient, one of a rare group of humans called "finders" who, possessing a sixth sense, are able to discover the location of anything or anyone they seek. While tracking down one of the city's most dangerous drug lords does not sound like a healthy occupation to Orient, he agrees to help Rico because the officer threatens to reveal Orient's criminal past if he refuses. Together, Rico and Orient attempt to put an end to the spread of Passport, as well as to discover the source of a virus that threatens the elf population, including Orient's friend Tick-Tick, a female motorcycle mechanic. Praising Bull's attention to building realistic relationships between her characters, *Voice of Youth Advocates* contributor Paula Lewis praised *Finder* as an "excellent choice for sophisticated YA readers."

A critic in *Kirkus Reviews* described the novel as a "refreshing [and] ingenious hardcover debut" for author Bull, while Faren Miller of *Locus* commented that Bull's work "brings new maturity" to the teen-focused Borderlands series. While the series had been an "adolescent mingling of cool and excitement in the shared world of punk elves and human wannabees," according to Miller, Bull's depiction of the city reveals a new vision. As her character Rico states, Borderlands "is a scary place, an angry place, and sometimes you'll see it reach out and crush somebody." Clearly, Bull intends to interject reality into the magical mix, but does so without dispelling "all the glamor, or romance, or sheer fun of being young and alive in an exotic place touched with magic," according to Miller.

Collaboration Results in Winning Fiction

Bull's 1997 book, *Freedom and Necessity*, is an epistolary novel—a novel told through letters, journal entries, and articles from newspapers and magazines. Written with fellow Minneapolis writers' group member Steven Brust, the saga is set in Victorian England, and opens as a young Englishman named James Cobham is feared to have perished in an accident while out boating, although his body is never actually recovered. Eventually, suffering from amnesia, Cobham resurfaces at an inn in the south of England, although he cannot remember how he got there. With the memory of events leading up to the boating accident intact, Cobham writes to his cousin, beginning what Roland Green in *Booklist* calls "an exceptional page-turner . . . a mass of Victorian virtues, vices, and settings." Referring to the book as a "romantic mystery-adventure that alternates bloody fights and breathless chases" with polite conversation and social restraint, a *Publishers Weekly* critic praised both Bull and Brust for their creation of "engaging characters" and a "clever and horrific twist" of an ending.

"Collaboration is not a thing one takes on lightly," Bull explained, and she should know, having worked with, not only Brust, but several other authors, including her husband, on fictional works. While she also admits that collaboration requires a great deal of planning, communication, and structure, *Freedom and Necessity* marks an exception to that rule. Indeed, Bull and Brust treated it more like a game during most of the writing pro-

---

If you enjoy the works of Emma Bull, you may also want to check out the following books and films:

Clive Barker, *Weaveworld*, 1987.
Charles de Lint, *Jack the Giant-Killer*, 1987.
Joan D. Vinge, *Catspaw*, 1988.
Photographing Fairies, a film starring Toby Stephens and Ben Kingsley, 1997.

---

cess, Bull writing letters from Cobham and Brust responding as Cobham's cousin, allowing the story to unfold only slightly with each new letter. "That's now it went on: no planning, no discussion of what we were doing or where we were going, . . . [until] we thought there were things that the reader would want explained and we needed to agree on what the explanations were. . . . We dropped hints in our letters, knowing that our collaborator would pick them up and do something with them. . . . There was tremendous excitement in waiting for the next installment, or the reaction to it. It was the most fun I've ever had writing a book." Brust, whose own fantasy career has been built on novels inspired by Hungarian legends, has published novels in the "Vlad Talos" series and authored several works of science fiction.

Explores New Fictional Genres

In addition to her novels and short fiction, Bull has branched out into the world of picture books with 1994's *The Princess and the Lord of Night*. Illustrated by Susan Gaber, the story presents what *School Library Journal* contributor Lauralyn Persson deemed "an intriguing premise": The bad-tempered Lord of Night casts a spell over a newborn princess requiring that her parents give her everything she wants or else they will die and their kingdom fall into ruin. While the young princess endeavors to be generous in all things and covet nothing, on her thirteenth birthday she awakens with the terrifying knowledge that she wants something. Not knowing what that something is, she goes in search of it, giving away all of her possessions as she travels to ensure that the spell is not activated. Bull's fanciful tale concludes as the princess's good deeds, good intentions, and quick thinking release her from the

Night's curse. Calling *The Princess and the Lord of Night* a "cleverly plotted story with an interesting mix of folkloric elements," Persson praised Bull's prose as both "elegant" and "vivid." A *Publishers Weekly* critic described the book's heroine as "spunky and intelligent," and noted that Bull captures the essence of the traditional fairy tale "without compromising the originality of her own voice."

In recent years, Bull and Shetterly have abandoned the northern Midwest city of Minneapolis for warmer, West Coast climes, namely, California, following the couple's interest in screenwriting and writing for television. A fan of television shows such as *Highlander* and *The X-Files,* Bull has become increasingly fascinated with the technical aspects of film production—everything from special effects and costumes to camera angles—but even more fascinated with writing for the medium. After she and Shetterly authored a script for the *X-Files* series and sent it off to Hollywood, they decided to move their household out to the West Coast in pursuit of future film-related opportunities. As she noted, Bull has in a sense come full circle, having been born in a magical world, "the land of the amusement parks." With several screenplays to their credit, the couple continues to work on collaborative projects, as well as independent works that allow each of them to follow their interests and imagination.

■ Works Cited

Review of *Bone Dance,* in *Publishers Weekly,* April 12, 1991, p. 54.

Bull, Emma, *Falcon,* Ace, 1989.

Bull, Emma, *Finder: A Novel of the Borderlands,* Tor, 1994.

Bull, Emma, essay in *Something about the Author,* Volume 103, Gale, 1999.

Easton, Tom, review of *Bone Dance,* in *Analog Science Fiction/Science Fact,* November, 1991, p. 164.

Evans, Barbara, review of *War for the Oaks,* in *Voice of Youth Advocates,* February, 1988, p. 286.

Review of Finder, in *Kirkus Reviews,* December 15, 1993, p. 1555.

Review of *Freedom and Necessity,* in *Publishers Weekly,* January 27, 1997, p. 77.

Green, Roland, review of *War for the Oaks,* in *Booklist,* September 15, 1987, p. 112.

Green, Roland, review of *Freedom and Necessity,* in *Booklist,* March 15, 1997, p. 1231.

Hays, Carl, review of *Finder,* in *Booklist,* February 15, 1994, p. 1064.

Jonas, Gerald, review of *Falcon,* in *New York Times Book Review,* October 1, 1989, p. 40.

Lewis, Paula, review of *Finder,* in *Voice of Youth Advocates,* June, 1994, pp. 96-98.

Miller, Faren, review of *Finder,* in *Locus,* February, 1994, p. 19.

Persson, Lauralyn, review of *The Princess and the Lord of Night,* in *School Library Journal,* May, 1994, p. 89.

Review of *The Princess and the Lord of Night,* in *Publishers Weekly,* February 28, 1994, p. 87.

■ For More Information See

PERIODICALS

Booklist, October 1, 1989, p. 265.

Horn Book Guide, fall, 1994, p. 299.

Kirkus Reviews, March 1, 1994, p. 300.

Kliatt, September, 1995, p. 18.

Locus, December, 1991, p. 51.

School Library Journal, December, 1991, p. 152; June, 1995, p. 143.

Science Fiction Chronicle, June, 1994, p. 42.

Voice of Youth Advocates, December, 1990, p. 269; December, 1991, p. 320.

—Sketch by Lynn MacGregor

John Feinstein

■ Personal

Surname pronounced "Fine-steen"; born July 28, 1956, in New York, NY; son of Martin (an opera director) and Bernice (a college professor; maiden name, Richman) Feinstein; married Mary Clare; children: Daniel, Brigid. *Education:* Duke University, B.A., 1977. *Politics:* Democrat. *Religion:* Jewish.

■ Addresses

Home—9200 Town Gate Lane, Bethesda, MD 20817. *Agent*—Esther Newberg, 40 West 57th St., New York, NY 10019.

■ Career

Journalist. *Washington Post*, Washington, DC, sportswriter, 1977-88; *Sports Illustrated*, New York City, staff writer, 1988-89; *National Sports Daily*, New York City, sportswriter, 1989-91; television commentator for ESPN and National Public Radio. *Member:* U.S. Basketball Writer's Association (former president), U.S. Tennis Writer's Association (former president), National Sportscasters and Sportswriters Association, Golf Writer's Association of America, Newpaper Guild.

■ Awards, Honors

Awards from U.S. Basketball Writer's Association, 1981, 1982, 1983, 1984, 1985, 1988, 1989, 1990, 1992, 1993, 1994, 1995, 1996, and 1997; National Sportscasters and Sportswriters Association, best sports stories awards, 1982, 1985, and 1986, D.C. writer of the year award, 1985; best event coverage award, Associated Press Sports Editors, 1985; Ron Buckman Award, U.S. Tennis Writer's Association, 1991.

■ Writings

NONFICTION

A Season on the Brink: A Year with Bob Knight and the Indiana Hoosiers, Macmillan, 1986.
A Season Inside: One Year in College Basketball, Villard, 1988.
Forever's Team, Villard, 1990.
Hard Courts: Real Life on the Professional Tennis Tours, Villard, 1992.
Play Ball: The Life and Troubled Times of Major League Baseball, Villard, 1993.
A Good Walk Spoiled: Days and Nights on the PGA Tour, Little, Brown, 1995.

A Civil War: Army vs. Navy: A Year inside College Football's Purest Rivalry, Little, Brown, 1996.

A March to Madness: The View from the Floor in the Atlantic Coast Conference, Little, Brown, 1998, with new afterword, 1999.

The First Coming: Tiger Woods, Master or Martyr?, Ballantine, 1998.

The Majors: In Pursuit of Golf's Holy Grail, Little, Brown, 1999.

Also editor of *The Best American Sports Writings 1996*, 1996. Contributor to periodicals, including *Golf*, *Washington Post Sunday Magazine*, *Sporting News*, *Basketball America*, *Basketball Times*, *Golf*, *Inside Sports*, *Tennis*, *Outlook*, and *Eastern Basketball*.

Feinstein has recorded four books as audiocassettes: *A Good Walk Spoiled*, Time Warner Audio-Books, 1998, *A Season on the Brink*, *A Season Inside*, and *The Majors*.

NOVELS

Running Mates, Villard, 1992.
Winter Games, Little, Brown, 1995.

■ Sidelights

Praised by many as America's favorite sportswriter, award-winning journalist John Feinstein first gained national prominence with his best-selling *A Season on the Brink: A Year with Bob Knight and the Indiana Hoosiers*. A chronicle of the 1985-86 basketball season at Indiana University—from the first pre-season meetings through practices, games, and strategy-mapping sessions, to the team's surprise upset during the first round of the National Collegiate Athletic Association (N.C.A.A.) championship tournament in early 1986—the book was a result of Feinstein's relationship with well-known Hoosiers head coach Bobby Knight, whose reputation combined an amazing winning streak and an Olympic gold medal victory with stories of a hot temper and tough coaching tactics that some maintained bordered on abusive. Cemented by the journalist's career as a sportswriter for numerous publications—and his reputation for being hard-edged and persistent in his quest for interviews—*A Season on the Brink* was praised by several critics for its author's knack for portraying the personalities behind the game, a characteristic that Feinstein has continued to cultivate in his nonfiction writing. Reviewing the book for the

Atlanta *Journal and Constitution*, contributor Kim Gagne noted of its author that "Feinstein offers an insider's perspective that brings the reader to an appreciation of both the genius and the madness of the coach." A publishing success, *A Season on the Brink* remained among the top bestsellers in the sports genre even a decade after its publication; on the down side, it marked the end of continued communication between Feinstein and his recalcitrant subject.

Feinstein was born in New York City, the son of Martin Feinstein, director of the Washington Opera, and Martin's wife, Bernice, a music history professor. Feinstein inherited his love of at least one sport from his mother, who was an enthusiastic golfer, while a love of basketball was instilled

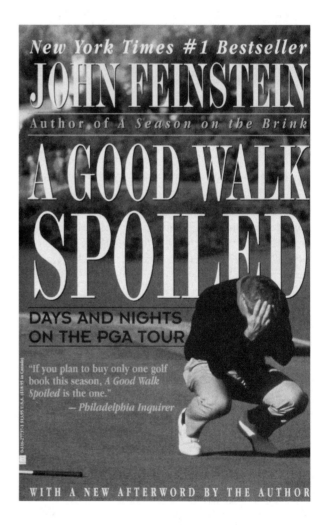

This 1995 bestseller delighted golf fans with its detailed account of the 1993-94 PGA Tour.

by the hours of play he and friends would engage in after school. Tennis, swimming, and baseball would also capture the young man's interest, although his competitive nature sometimes resulted in bouts of temper during the frustrating beginner phase. That competitive nature was inherited, in part, from his parents, both musicians devoted to their craft, who instilled their own enthusiasm and their demand for perfection in their son. As he told Mitchell Bard in an article for *Writers' Digest*, "I think the thing my parents passed on to me was being passionate about what you do. . . . My personality is to be passionate whether I'm talking about sports or politics."

From Participant to Chronicler

While Feinstein enjoyed writing as a teen and was particularly successful in his creative writing endeavors, his major love was always athletics. Enrolling at Durham, North Carolina's Duke University in 1973, Feinstein swam competitively during his freshman year until he was sidelined by a knee injury. As a way of filling up his free time to avoid the frustration of not competing, he signed on as a sports reporter and news reporter with the newspaper at his high-profile college, and was promoted to sports editor during his junior year, eventually becoming assistant managing editor and sports editor as a senior. Graduating in 1977 with a degree in history, he used the connections he had made while serving as a college intern to win a stint at the *Washington Post*, where Feinstein covered the police beat and politics before moving on to his favorite subject: sports. Although he took a leave of absence in 1985 to work on his first book, Feinstein stayed at the *Post* until 1989, when he joined the staff of *Sports Illustrated*.

One of the more notable aspects of Feinstein's journalism career has been the access he has been able to gain to the coaches and players in the events he has covered, both as a reporter and as an author. For some coaches, the key to access is to sell them on the idea that allowing a journalist to spend time with the players will promote their school's program, whether the resulting publicity is good or bad; if the news is bad it will hit the press anyway. In-depth press coverage, Feinstein routinely argues, highlights the more positive, noble aspects of athletic competition, which often get overlooked in briefer coverage.

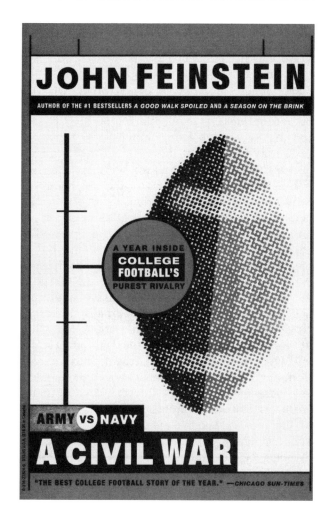

Feinstein's critically acclaimed 1996 work about college football shows how two legendary football rivals play for sport and school honor rather than fame or fortune.

But the most important thing, he maintains, is that reporters make a request for team access in person, and be specific about what they intend their focus to be. "If you have a good story and make a good case, people will listen," Feinstein told Bard, adding that if a coach won't talk to you, the comeback is that to tell them if you have no access, you cannot tell their side of the story. And Feinstein advises would-be journalists to do their homework before conducting an interview. His own interviews begin with the easy questions, questions that show he has researched his subject's career, has made himself familiar with stats, and remembers his subject's best efforts on the playing field, as well as those efforts that didn't come off quite as well.

Knack for Interviewing

Beginning his nonfiction career with *A Season on the Brink,* Feinstein continued with several other books about basketball. *A Season Inside: One Year in College Basketball* expands upon his first book by recounting the highlights of the 1987-88 season that saw coach Larry Brown boost University of Kansas to a win at the 1988 N.C.A.A. championships. Through interviews with coaches like Kansas's Brown and reports of the less communicative John Thompson of rival Georgetown University, as well as a large cast of assorted players on and off the court, the book was praised as enjoyable reading "not just for sports fans, but for readers interested in the people of contemporary America," in the opinion of Gordon A. Martin Jr. in *Wilson Library Bulletin.* Enthusing about the book in the *Washington Post,* journalist Robert D. Novak exclaimed: "Feinstein has attempted a tour de force and pretty well pulled it off. He has managed to convey the excitement, intrigue, confrontation, hysteria and sheer intoxication of college basketball." *Forever's Team* is a more intimate work, as Feinstein chronicles the 1978-79 season of the men's basketball team at his alma mater, Duke University. The Blue Devils, once cellar-dwellers in the Atlantic Coast Conference, fought their way to the N.C.A.A. championship game, losing by only six points to powerful Kentucky. That Duke team—with just one senior player—captured the attention of a nation, but Feinstein does not end his story with the loss to Kentucky. The story has a far more poignant ending than the loss of a game, as the personal tragedies of several of the players over the next dozen years—heart attack, automobile accident, cancer, and other setbacks—are recounted during a reunion, setting their athletic and academic accomplishments within a more human perspective. Noting that Feinstein is "too much the fan" to present an account the average reader can relate to, *New York Times Book Review* contributor Helene Elliot maintained that while *Forever's Team* "provides an illuminating thought, a telling phrase, a moving moment," there is "not enough to last forever."

Feinstein would return to basketball later in his writing career with 1998's *A March to Madness: The View from the Floor in the Atlantic Coast Conference,* a work of nonfiction that opens a window onto the hard-driving competition among the upper echelons of college basketball. Focusing on the nine member-teams of the Atlantic Coast Confer-

The author wrote about the fierce competition among college basketball coaches and players of the Atlantic Coast Conference in this 1998 work.

ence—Duke, North Carolina, North Carolina State, Clemson, Georgia Tech, Virginia, Maryland, Wake Forest, and Florida State—the book shows the techniques and strategies of college coaches and describes the performance of the contest's top-notch players. Interested in the personal dramas playing out in the lives of individual players and other participants in the high-pressure, high-stakes athletic competition, Feinstein posits these individual stories against an orderly backdrop that includes a profile of each of the nine schools, their coaches, their history, and their expectations going in to the season. *People* reviewer Alex Tresniowski maintained that the "Feinstein formula"—"pick out a sport, pal around with its superstars for a solid year, then write an incisive, engaging, behind-the-scenes bestseller"—paid off yet again in *A March to Madness*. A *Kirkus Reviews* contributor praised Feinstein for "pull[ing] off the difficult feat of keeping nine narratives moving relatively seamlessly," and cited his skill at "finding the telling moment or detail [and] reading the mindset of participating athletes and coaches with uncommon astuteness."

From Collegiate to Professional Sports

Tennis, as well as basketball, has come under Feinstein's scrutiny. His 1992 work, *Hard Courts: Real Life on the Professional Tennis Tours*, introduces readers to the realities of the life of a tennis pro. Interviewing one hundred and forty athletes, coaches, and agents, and following the pro tour throughout 1990, Feinstein was able to gain enough inside information to make this work as revealing as his volumes about basketball. However, his reverence for professional tennis players like Martina Navratilova, Andre Agassi, and John McEnroe does not appear to run as deep as it runs for collegiate athletes and their coaches. While noting the abnormal life that many professional tennis players experience, Feinstein characterizes many in the pro tennis circuit as motivated more by money and love of attention than love of the game itself. This conclusion brought disagreement from several critics, including *Time* contributor John Skow, who commented of *Hard Courts:* "there's more to world-class tennis than posturers and connivers, and Feinstein . . . misses the joy of the game almost completely." However, *Sports Illustrated* contributor Ron Fimrite maintained that the criticism lobbed at tennis pros and their sometimes excessively ambitious parents was balanced by a generous perspective. "Feinstein is perhaps at his best in describing their very human plight," Fimrite noted of the less well-known players who barely earn enough money on the tennis circuit to pay their expenses. "And this book is not without its heroes and heroines," the reviewer added, citing Feinstein's portrayal of African American tennis pro Zina Garrison among others.

From the courts of basketball and tennis, Feinstein has also travelled to the fields of baseball and football. 1993's *Play Ball: The Life and Hard Times of Major League Baseball* reviews the 1992 season, analyzing the relationship between the business of baseball and the strategies on the mound. From

If you enjoy the works of John Feinstein, you may also want to check out the following books:

William Gildea, *Where the Game Matters Most: A Last Championship Season in Indiana High School Basketball,* 1997.
David Halberstam, *Playing for Keeps: Michael Jordan and the World That He Made,* 1999, and *The Best American Sports Writing of the Century,* 1999.
David Owen, *The Making of the Masters,* 1999.

spring training to the World Series, Feinstein sees American's favorite pastime asprimarily a business, and his examination of the economics of baseball franchises yields a questionable future, in his opinion. In his 1996 work *A Civil War: Army vs. Navy: A Year inside College Football's Purest Rivalry,* Feinstein resumes his focus on the personal rather than financial elements of athletic competition. In recording a year in the life of the student athletes who double as cadets at both the Naval Academy and at West Point, he recognizes that there is more to this traditional game than an athlete's defense of his alma mater. In addition to the fact that, as *Library Journal* contributor William O. Scheeren noted, the players are all "true scholar-athletes in the sense that they have no aspirations of moving on to the pros": the Army-Navy game is a game of honor, grounded in a military tradition forged of a rigid academic and athletic discipline that makes this particular football rivalry unique. Profiling both the athletes and the schools from which they will soon graduate, Feinstein "builds a sense of excitement and anticipation throughout the book," despite the fact that the outcome of the game is already a matter of sports history, according to a contributor to *Publishers Weekly.*

A Lifelong Love of the Links

While Feinstein has covered almost every sport professionally played in the United States, the competition closest to his heart is the one that takes place on a golf course. After fifteen months' work taking in thirty-three tournaments in almost as many cities during the 1993-94 season, he produced *A Good Walk Spoiled: Days and Nights on the PGA Tour,* the drama of one year on the Professional Golfers Association (PGA) circuit, where the world's top golfers compete. The title is taken from a quip by American humorist Mark Twain; while Feinstein clearly holds the game and its players in high esteem, his growing intimacy with the sport would give him a more realistic perspective on the highs and lows of the game—as well as the corresponding ups and downs of the careers of some of the nation's top professionals. "I never knew just how hard golf is for great players," Feinstein explained in an interview with Peter Castro for *People.* "They go through times when they think they're never going to hit another good shot. It's difficult because you make your own calls. Nobody tackles you, nobody dunks on you. So when you fail, there's no excuse. That's very hard to deal with mentally." Following players such as Paul Azinger, Greg Norman, John Daly, and Nick Faldo around the links, Feinstein shares with readers some of the most personal aspects of the game, and provides an intimate perspective on its public, as well as private, moments. While *People* reviewer Tony Chiu concluded that the book's seventeen protagonists—golfers that Chiu maintained "seem to be clueless about life beyond the country-club gate"— are "as charismatic as a ball marker," other reviewers agreed with Feinstein in his obvious respect for the decorum of the sport. Commenting on his impressions after reading *A Good Walk Spoiled, New York Times Book Review* contributor Michael Bamberger noted: "Feinstein admires professional golf and the people who play it. . . . He describes a game that values tradition and fair play and dedication. If he had found something less, he surely would have written about it."

New Genres and Good Advice

Given his lengthy career as a sportswriter, it is not surprising that when Feinstein turned his hand to fiction writing in the early 1990s, his plots turned around competition. The mystery novel *Winter Games,* which Feinstein published in 1995, finds college basketball recruiters resorting to some desperate—and illegal—measures to ensure the success of their team in a book that contains what Chicago *Tribune Books* reviewer Gary Dretzka dubbed "an intriguing plotline." And in 1992's *Running Mates,* Feinstein's first novel, the sportswriter shows politics to be as much a team sport as football. Within the arena of state politics, the untimely death of Maryland's governor precipitates the drawing of battle lines in the state legislature, where a group of feminists who back the former lieutenant governor find themselves pitted against a conservative camp, forcing reporter Bobby Kelleher to turn sleuth and solve the crime. While noting that certain aspects of Feinstein's plot strain credulity, a *Publishers Weekly* contributor added that *Running Mates* "delivers on its promise despite its protagonist's occasional larger-than-life heroism and incredible luck."

Feinstein incorporates a strict writing regimen into his daily life, editing during the first part of the writing day, and then writing for an additional six hours. In addition to continuing his valuable contribution to the annals of professional sports, Feinstein has also taught his trade as a journalist to others. "I tell kids who want to be sportswriters they should get experience in hard news," he told Bard in *Writers' Digest.* "For one thing, it gives you a perspective on sports. . . . My experience covering police, sports and politics helped shape me in terms of recognizing a story that has something to do with something other than games. If you read my books, I write very little about the games themselves or the events. I use them as an excuse to write about people."

■ Works Cited

Bamberger, Michael, "The Grand Tour," in *New York Times Book Review,* June 11, 1995, p. 62.

Bard, Mitchell, "A Passion for the Game," in *Writers' Digest,* December, 1997, p. 36.

Castro, Peter, "Fore the Record," in *People,* August 28, 1995, p. 69.

Chiu, Tony, "Bogie, Birdie, Par," in *People,* June 19, 1995, p. 36.

Review of *A Civil War,* in *Publishers Weekly,* September 16, 1996, p. 61.

Dretzka, Gary, "Art and Crime, by One Who Knows," in *Tribune Books* (Chicago), November 5, 1995, p. 7.

Elliott, Helene, "The Year of the Blue Devil," in *New York Times Book Review,* January 7, 1990, p. 12.

Fimrite, Ron, "Tattletales of the Tennis Racket," in *Sports Illustrated,* October 14, 1991, p. 6.

Gagne, Kim, review of *A Season on the Brink,* in *Journal and Constitution* (Atlanta), March 1, 1987.

Review of *A March to Madness*, in *Kirkus Reviews*, November 15, 1997, p. 1683.

Martin, Gordon A., review of *A Season on the Brink*, in *Wilson Library Bulletin*, March, 1989, pp. 111, 124-25.

Novak, Robert D., review of *A Season Inside: One Year in College Basketball*, in *Washington Post*, November 28, 1988.

Review of *Running Mates*, in *Publishers Weekly*, March 2, 1992, p. 52.

Scheeren, William O., review of *A Civil War*, in *Library Journal*, October 1, 1996, p. 87.

Skow, John, "Balls and Brats," in *Time*, September 2, 1991, p. 69.

Tresniowski, Alex, review of *A March to Madness*, in *People*, March 16, 1998, pp. 34-35.

■ For More Information See

PERIODICALS

Booklist, November 15, 1986, p. 466; March 15, 1992, p. 1340.

Chicago Tribune, November 16, 1986.

Commentary, September, 1993, p. 61.

Kirkus Reviews, September 15, 1996, p. 1371.

Library Journal, December, 1988, p. 127; May 15, 1995, p. 76; January, 1998, p. 109.

Los Angeles Times Book Review, October 6, 1991, p. 6; April 4, 1993, pp. 1, 10.

New York Times, November 3, 1996, p. 18.

New York Times Book Review, February 8, 1987, p. 25; January 22, 1989, p. 14; August 18, 1991, p. 7; May 10, 1992, p. 23; April 4, 1993, p. 24; February 11, 1996, p. 22; March 22, 1998, p. 16; May 2, 1999, p. 16.

Publishers Weekly, September 25, 1995, p. 46; December 1, 1997, p. 38; March 29, 1999, p. 76.

School Library Journal, August, 1993, p. 206.

Sporting News, February 16, 1987.

Sports Illustrated, November 19, 1986.

Time, February 23, 1987, p. 78.

Voice of Youth Advocates, June, 1989, p. 122; August, 1990, p. 174.

Washington Post, January 26, 1990.

Washington Post Book World, November 23, 1986, p. 6; April 4, 1993, p. 8; January 18, 1998, p. 6.

Wilson Library Bulletin, November, 1990, p. 6.

—Sketch by Nancy Rae Tarcher

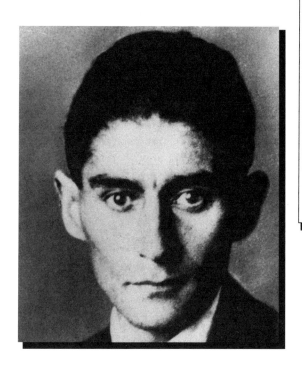

Franz Kafka

■ Personal

Born July 3, 1883, in Prague, Bohemia (now Czechoslovakia); died of tuberculosis of the larynx, June 3, 1924, in Kierling, Klosterneuburg, Austria; buried in Jewish cemetery in Prague-Straschnitz, Czechoslovakia; son of Hermann (a merchant and manufacturer) and Julie (Loewy) Kafka; children: one son. *Education:* Ferdinand-Karls University (Prague), earned doctorate in law, 1906; also attended technical institute in Prague. *Religion:* Jewish.

■ Career

Writer. Worked for attorney Richard Loewy drafting legal notices, Prague, Bohemia (now Czechoslovakia), 1906; intern in law courts, Prague, 1906-07; staff member of insurance company Assicurazioni Generali, Prague, 1907-08; Workers' Accident Insurance Institute for the Kingdom of Bohemia, Prague, specialist in accident prevention and workplace safety, 1908-22. Worked at Prague Asbestos Works Hermann & Co. (manufacturers), Zizkov, Bohemia, 1911-17.

■ Writings

SHORT FICTION

Der Heizer: Ein Fragment (title means "The Stoker: A Fragment"; also see below), Kurt Wolff (Leipzig), 1913, limited edition, illustrated by Elisabeth Siefer, Mary S. Rosenberg, 1985.

Betrachtung (title means "Meditations"; includes stories later translated as "Children on a Country Road," "Unmasking a Confidence Trickster," "Excursion into the Mountains," and "The Street Window"; also see below), Rowohlt, 1913.

Die Verwandlung (also see below), Kurt Wolff, 1915, new edition edited by Marjorie L. Hoover, Norton (New York City), 1960, translated by A. L. Lloyd as *The Metamorphosis*, Parton, 1937, Vanguard Press, 1946, expanded as *Metamorphosis and Other Stories*, translation by Willa and Edwin Muir, Penguin, 1961.

Das Urteil: Eine Geschichte (title means "The Judgement: A Story"; also see below), Kurt Wolff, 1916.

In der Strafkolonie, Kurt Wolff, 1919, translated by Willa Muir and Edwin Muir and C. Greenberg as *The Penal Colony: Stories and Short Pieces*, Schocken (New York City), 1948.

Ein Landarzt: Kleine Erzaehlungen (also see below), Kurt Wolff, 1919, translated by Vera Leslie as *The Country Doctor: A Collection of Fourteen Stories*, Counter-Point, 1945.

Ein Hungerkunstler: Vier Geschichten (includes stories later translated as "A Hunger Artist," "A Little Woman," "First Sorrow," and "Josephine the Singer; or, the Mouse Folk"; also see below), Die Schmiede (Berlin), 1924.

Beim Bau der Chinesischen Mauer, Ungedruckte Erzaehlungen und Prosa aus dem Nachlass (short stories; also see below), 1931, translated by Willa and Edwin Muir as *The Great Wall of China and Other Pieces*, Secker & Warburg, 1933, published as *The Great Wall of China: Stories and Reflections*, Schocken, 1970.

Parables in German and English, translation by Willa and Edwin Muir, Schocken, 1947.

Selected Short Stories, translation by Willa and Edwin Muir, Modern Library, 1952.

Description of a Struggle (also see below), Schocken, 1958.

Parables and Paradoxes: Parabeln und Paradoxe (bilingual edition), Willa and Edwin Muir, Schocken, 1958.

Erzaehlungen und Skizzen, edited by Klaus Wagenbach, Moderner Buch-Club (Darmstadt),1959.

Die Erzaehlungen, edited by Klaus Wagenbach, S. Fischer (Frankfurt), 1961, edited by Charles W. Hoffman, Norton, 1970.

Er: Prosa, edited by Martin Walser, Suhrkamp (Frankfurt), 1963.

Short Stories, edited by J. M. S. Pasley, Oxford University Press, 1963.

Der Heizer; In der Strafkolonie; Der Bau, edited by J. M. S. Pasley, Cambridge University Press, 1966.

Saemtliche Erzaehlungen, edited by Paul Raabe, S. Fischer, 1970.

The Complete Stories, translation by Willa and Edwin Muir, Tania Stern and James Stern, and Ernst Kaiser and Eithne Wilkins, postscript by Nahum N. Glatzer, Schocken, 1971, special centennial edition, edited by Glatzer, foreword by John Updike, illustrated by Adele Grodstein, 1983.

Shorter Works, edited with translation by Malcolm Pasley, Secker & Warburg (London), 1973.

The Bridge, illustrated by Henri Galeron, Schocken, 1983.

The Metamorphosis, The Penal Colony, and Other Stories, translation by Willa and Edwin Muir, Schocken, 1988.

The Sons (contains "The Metamorphosis," "The Judgement," and "The Stoker"), Schocken, 1989.

Give It Up!: And Other Short Stories, NBM Comics, 1995.

Stories also published in English translation independently and in additional collections and anthologies.

NOVELS

Der Prozess, edited by Brod, Die Schmiede, 1925, translation by Willa and Edwin Muir published as *The Trial*, Gollancz (London), 1935, Knopf (New York City), 1937, revised edition with additional chapters translated by E. M. Butler, Secker & Warburg, 1956, definitive edition, with illustrations by George Salter, Knopf, 1957, with drawings by Kafka, Schocken, 1968.

Das Schloss, edited by Brod, Kurt Wolff, 1926, translation by Willa and Edwin Muir published as *The Castle*, Knopf, 1930, new edition with introduction by Thomas Mann, Knopf, 1941, definitive edition with additional material translated by Wilkins and Ernst Kaiser and introduction by Mann, Secker & Warburg, 1953, Knopf, 1954, revised edition, Schocken, 1974.

Amerika, edited by Brod, Kurt Wolff, 1927, translation by Willa and Edwin Muir with preface by Mann, afterword by Brod, and illustrations by Emlen Etting, Routledge (London), 1938, New Directions (New York City), 1946, with foreword by John Updike, Schocken, 1983.

Novels also collected in single-volume editions.

NONFICTION

The Diaries of Franz Kafka, edited by Brod, Volume 1: *1910-1913*, translated by Joseph Kresh, Schocken, 1948, Volume 2: *1914-1923*, translated by Martin Greenberg and Hannah Arendt, Schocken, 1949, published as one volume, 1989.

Brief an den Vater, S. Fischer, 1953, bilingual edition with translation by Ernst Kaiser and Wilkins published as *Letter to His Father/Brief an den Vater*, Schocken, 1966.

I Am a Memory Come Alive: Autobiographical Writings, edited by Glatzer, Schocken, 1974.

COLLECTED WORKS

Gesammelte Schriften, edited by Brod and Heinz Politzer, Volumes 1-4, Schocken (Berlin), Volumes 5-6, Mercy (Prague), 1935-36, portions translated by Kaiser and Wilkins as *In the Penal Settlement: Tales and Short Prose Works*, Secker & Warburg, 1973, other portions translated by Willa and Edwin Muir and Tania and James Stern as *Description of a Struggle; and The Great Wall of China*, Secker & Warburg, 1960.

Gesammelte Werke, 11 volumes, edited by Brod, S. Fischer, 1950-74, Volume 4: *Briefe an Milena* translated by Tania and James Stern as *Letters to Milena,* Farrar, Straus, 1953, Volume 7: *Hochzeitsvorbereitungen auf dem Lande und andere Prosa aus dem Nachlass* translated by Kaiser and Wilkins as *Dearest Father: Stories and Other Writings,* Schocken, 1954, and as *Wedding Preparations in the Country, and Other Posthumous Papers,* Secker & Warburg, 1954, Volume 9: *Briefe 1902-1904* translated, with additional material, by Richard Winston and Clara Winston as *Letters to Friends, Family, and Editors,* Schocken, 1977, Volume 10: *Briefe an Felice und andere Korrespondenz aus der Verlobungszeit* translated by James Stern and Elisabeth Duckworth as *Letters to Felice,* Schocken, 1973, Volume 11: *Briefe an Ottla und die Familie* translated by Richard and Clara Winston as *Letters to Ottla and the Family,* Schocken, 1982.

The Basic Kafka (omnibus volume), edited by Heller, Pocket Books, 1983.

Fiction and nonfiction also published together in other collections.

OTHER

(Contributor) Harry Steinhauer and Helen Jessiman, editors, *Modern German Stories* (contains "A Hunger Artist"), Oxford University Press, 1938.

Contributor to periodicals, including *Arkadia, Bohemia,* and *Hyperion.*

■ **Adaptations**

The Trial was adapted by writer-director Orson Welles as a film of the same title in 1963, and by writer Harold Pinter and director David Jones in 1993; *Amerika* was adapted by writer-directors Jean-Marie Straub and Daniele Huillet for a film released in the United States as *Class Relations* in 1984; works adapted for the stage include *The Metamorphosis* and "The Hunger Artist."

■ **Sidelights**

One of the most influential writers of the twentieth century, Franz Kafka penned novels and short stories that portray the bewildered alienation of modern society. His characters frequently find themselves in threatening situations for which

there is no explanation and from which there is no escape. Writing in the *Bookman,* Edwin Muir found that "the four main ideas which run through Kafka's work may be condensed into four axioms. The first two are that, compared with the divine law, no matter how unjust it may sometimes appear to us, all human effort, even the highest, is in the wrong; and that always whatever our minds or our feelings may tell us, the claim of the divine law to unconditional reverence and obedience is absolute. The other two are complementary: that there is a right way of life, and that its discovery depends on one's attitude to powers which are almost unknown."

In an article for the *New Yorker,* John Updike explained: "The century since Franz Kafka was born has been marked by the idea of 'modernism' a self-consciousness new among centuries, a consciousness of being new. Sixty years after his death, Kafka epitomizes one aspect of this modern mind-set: a sensation of anxiety and shame whose center cannot be located and therefore cannot be placated; a sense of an infinite difficulty within things, impeding every step; a sensitivity acute beyond usefulness, as if the nervous system, flayed of its old hide of social usage and religious belief, must record every touch as pain. In Kafka's peculiar and highly original case, this dreadful quality is mixed with immense tenderness, oddly good humor, and a certain severe and reassuring formality. The combination makes him an artist; but rarely can an artist have struggled against greater inner resistance and more sincere diffidence as to the worth of his art." Among Kafka's most-studied works are the novels *The Trial* and *The Castle* and the short stories "The Metamorphosis," "The Hunger Artist," and "In the Penal Colony."

Experiences Social Prejudice Early in Life

Kafka was born into a Jewish family in the city of Prague in 1883. Prague was a part of the Austro-Hungarian Empire at that time, and Jews were expected to live apart from gentiles in a ghetto area. Kafka's father operated a dry goods store in the ghetto, assisted by his wife, Kafka's mother. The elder Kafka's domineering manner with his son led to the boy's resentment. His mother tried to intervene but, as Richard H. Lawson noted in the *Dictionary of Literary Biography,* "she proved unable to mediate the estrangement between her brusque, domineering husband

and her quiet, tyrannized, oversensitive son." In 1901 Kafka entered the Karl-Ferdinand University, an act in open defiance of his father, who wished him to work in the family store. When he turned to the study of law, however, Kafka met with his father's approval. During his college years he met his close friend and future literary executor Max Brod.

Following his graduation from college in 1907, Kafka took a position at an insurance office in Prague. The next year he moved to a government job handling workmen's compensation claims. At this time he also published his first short fiction in a literary magazine. He soon began writing stories drawing on elements from his own life. Lawson found that this early fiction possessed "narrative features . . . typical of Kafka: a first-person narrator as a persona of the author, an episodic structure, an ambivalent questor on an ambiguous mission, and pervasive irony." During his lifetime Kafka was to publish short stories in various literary magazines. But his novels, including *The Trial* and *The Castle*, were never completed. In fact, Kafka left orders with his friend Brod to destroy the unfinished manuscripts upon his death. This was something Brod decided not to do following Kafka's death in 1924 from tuberculosis; instead the literary executor published these novels posthumously, assembling the loosely organized manuscripts as he thought best.

Kafka wrote *The Trial* during 1914 in the months following his breakup with his fiancee, Felice Bauer. The couple had met in 1912 and became engaged, but before the engagement was officially announced Kafka had backed out. He became romantically involved with one of Felice's friends, Grete. Despite having broken the engagement himself, Kafka felt rejected by Felice and was soon imploring her to return to him. When she did so, and the two again became engaged, Kafka vowed that his love for Grete would continue despite his engagement. The unsettled emotional entanglements eventually led Felice, her sister, Grete, and Kafka's friendErnst Weiss to confront the writer in a hotel room to sort out the tangled situation. Kafka would later call the long session a kind of "law court" in which he was put on trial for his confused behavior. With the engagement finally canceled for good, Kafka began writing *The Trial*, a novel based in part on some of the events of his unhappy relationship with Felice. The novel remained out of print until Brod decided to re-

lease it a year after Kafka's death. It was published in 1925.

The Trial begins with the mysterious arrest of Joseph K., a bank clerk celebrating his thirtieth birthday. K. has apparently done nothing wrong, but two members of a mysterious Court arrive at his lodgings first thing one morning and place him under arrest. Although arrested, K. is not taken to jail. He is allowed to go on with his life as before, while his efforts to determine just what crime he is supposed to have committed lead nowhere. K.'s ordeal over the course of a year is told in a series of brief, unrelated chapters. Those bureaucrats he meets cannot explain the charge to him, the lawyer he hires to handle his case is equally in the dark, and the judges of the Court remain inaccessible. When K. gains access to the Court's law books, he finds them to be filled with obscenities. K.'s attempts to unravel the mystery of his dilemma are hindered by the contradictory information he receives from those he consults and by the confusing nature of the legal system in which his life has become entangled. At times the court itself seems only a figment of K.'s imagination; it holds its proceedings in such unlikely places as the attics of disreputable buildings.

The Trial Prompts Diverse Critical Commentary

Many critics of *The Trial* have seen it, at least in part, as a story about guilt. In *Reference Guide to World Literature*, B. Ashbrook noted: "Josef K.'s actions betray a recognition on his part that the court does have a claim upon him. . . . Whatever his words may indicate, his behaviour is that of a man who feels guilty. . . . Josef K.'s sense of guilt cannot be attributed to any one specific action; nor can it be characterized as universal human guilt. There are other accused men in the story but, equally, there are many who do not stand accused by the court. Josef K.'s failing may be found in his lack of humility and self-understanding, in his aggressive impatience and stubbornness." Commenting on the work in an essay collected in his *Gesammelte Werke Volume 12*, Hermann Hesse described the novel's ongoing, mysterious trial as being about "none other than the guilt of life itself. The 'accused' are the afflicted ones among the unsuspecting, harmless masses that have a dawning awareness of the terrible truth of all life, an awareness that is gradually strangling their hearts."

The chapter titled "In the Cathedral" offers some support for the idea that *The Trial* is concerned with a kind of universal guilt. In this chapter, K. visits a priest to seek his advice on what to do. The priest reveals that he is a chaplain for the Court and can help explain its enigmatic workings. He relates to K. the parable "Before the Law," a story about a man seeking the Law. When the man arrives at the door leading to the Law, the doorkeeper explains that he cannot let the man in "at present," and so he sits and waits. Years go by and the man is still waiting to be let into the Law. He tries bribing the doorkeeper, pleading with him, and questioning him about the Law's nature, all to no avail. Finally, as the man is dying, he asks the doorkeeper why he has been the only one to ever come seeking the Law. The doorkeeper explains: "No one but you could gain admittance through this door, since this door was meant for you alone. I am now going to shut it." Following the story, the priest discusses the parable's meaning with K., who ends up as baffled as before about the Law he faces and the Court passing judgment upon him. Erich Heller, in his study *Franz Kafka,* interpreted "Before the Law" as possessing a "terrible charm"; it shows "all the characteristic features of Kafka's art at its most powerful," continued the critic; "— possessing, that is, the kind of power that is in the gentle wafting of the wind rather than in the thunderous storm, and is the more destructive for it. Parodying Biblical simplicity, . . . it expresses the most unholy complications of the intelligence and raises hellish questions in the key of the innocently unquestionable. Its humor is at the same time tender and cruel, teasing the mind with the semblance of light into losing itself in the utmost obscurity."

The parable "Before the Law" encapsulates *The Trial*'s fundamental paradox as well. As K. continues in his efforts to discover the nature of his legal problem with the Court, he comes to realize that the Court has violated its own Law. The priest has told K. that "The Court wants nothing from you. It receives you when you come and dismisses you when you go." But as Heinz Politzer explained in his *Franz Kafka: Parable and Paradox:* "if it is the law of the Law to receive those who come, dismiss those who desire to go, and otherwise remain unmoved and unmovable, then the Court has broken this Law by the very act of arresting K." This fundamental paradox explains the confusion of all the Court officials K.

The Castle

FRANZ KAFKA

A NEW TRANSLATION BASED ON THE RESTORED TEXT

One of Kafka's most studied novels, this work was never completed but published posthumously against the author's wishes in 1926 as *Das Schloss.*

meets who attempt to reconcile the mistake made by the Court with the proper role of the Law.

K.'s growing confusion, disorientation, and desperate attempts to make sense of his situation make *The Trial* a powerful symbol of alienation. "*The Trial*," wrote Rene Dauvin in *Franz Kafka Today,* "is so mysterious, so vague, that many interpretations are possible. As we stand on the threshold of Kafka's work, we feel uneasy, disoriented. The very form and structure of the novel amaze us, for it escapes all classification and transports us into an atmosphere of hallucination and strange disquiet." Many critics interpret K.'s alienation as that of modern man in a society where traditional values have broken down or as that of every man in a fundamentally mysterious universe. Hesse, for example, argued that *The Trial* was a religious text. Speaking of the brief, unconnected chapters comprising the novel, he wrote: "This oppressive and fearful nightmare image persists until gradually the hidden significance dawns on the reader. Only then do [Kafka's] wilful and fantastic evocations radiate their redemption, only then do we understand that contrary to their appearance as carefully wrought miniatures their significance is not artistic but religious. They are expressions of piety and elicitations of devotion, even reverence."

Ultimately, K.'s confusion is never fully explained. On the eve of his thirty-first birthday, a year after his enigmatic arrest took place, he is knifed to death by two representatives of the Court. He is never given an explanation of the charges made against him, nor provided with knowledge as to the nature of the Court which has had him executed. "Ultimately," Ashbrook concluded, "it is impossible to ascribe any one single meaning to *The Trial*. It presents a double image: an innocent man destroyed by a despotic authority and a guilty man rightly condemned. We are not forced to choose between these possibilities; they co-exist and interpenetrate each other. Kafka's novel constantly challenges the reader to supply his own interpretation of its elusive substance." Similarly, Alvin J. Seltzer, writing in *Chaos in the Novel, the Novel in Chaos*, found that "*The Trial* is surely one of the most unrelenting works of chaos created in the first half of this century, and critics have done it the honor of interpreting it on many levels of significance. . . . But while the book certainly invites interpretations of a social, political, and religious nature, Kafka seems to have wanted it to evade any facile explanation. . . . It seems to have been his intention to create a world in which things happen arbitrarily to people whose only fault is in being there at the time."

Brod recounted how Kafka read from the manuscript of *The Trial* to several of his friends. "When Kafka read aloud himself," Brod recalled in *Franz Kafka: A Biography*, "this humor became particularly clear. Thus, for example, we friends of his laughed quite immoderately when he first let us hear the first chapter of *The Trial*. And he himself laughed so much that there were moments when he couldn't read any further. Astonishing enough, when you think of the fearful earnestness of this chapter. But that is how it was. Certainly it was not entirely good, comfortable laughter. . . . I am only pointing out the fact that is otherwise so

If you enjoy the works of Franz Kafka, you may also want to check out the following books:

Albert Camus, *The Stranger*, 1946, and *The Plague*, 1948.
Jean-Paul Sartre, *No Exit and Three Other Plays*, 1955.

easily forgotten in studies of Kafka—the streak of joy in the world and in life."

Same Name, Different Character

A character named K. also appears in Kafka's novel *The Castle*, published in 1926, although he is far different from the character of the same name in *The Trial*. One evening while traveling in the country, K. stops at an inn. In the middle of the night he is awakened and informed that he cannot stay at the inn without permission from the nearby castle. K. claims that he is in fact a land surveyor working for the castle. His claim is at first denied by those in the castle, but later confirmed. At this point K. realizes that those in the castle were "taking up the challenge with a smile." As Ashbrook explained: "This opening establishes a fundamental ambiguity in the relationship between K. and the castle. It is never clear whether K. has really been summoned by the castle or whether he invents the story to try to justify his presence. In either case his purpose is to penetrate into the castle and to obtain absolute confirmation of the position he claims for himself."

K. finds that the castle is run by Count Westwest and is a dilapidated building on the edge of town. "It houses a vast hierarchy of officials who are constantly engaged in frenetic bureaucratic activity," Ashbrook wrote, "all to no apparent purpose. They are obscene and immoral, regarding the women of the village as their rightful prey while the village sees it as the highest honour for a woman to be the mistress of an official. The castle has absolute dominion over the village. The villagers treat it with awe, devotion, and obedience. To them it is omnipotent and infallible. It seems to assume the qualities which they project onto it."

K.'s efforts to contact those in the castle, and even to visit the building, are consistently blocked. Like his namesake in *The Trial*, K. spends his time trying to gain access to a mysterious bureaucracy which holds unnatural power over his society. But in *The Castle*, he tries unsuccessfully to push the bureaucracy into validating his place in society. "Despite all of K.'s movement and activity," explained Frederick R. Karl in *Journal of Modern Literature*, "he never leaves the periphery of the village, he never finds the path or road that leads to the castle or the castle compound, and he never finds clues to the labyrinthine process in which he finds himself."

The castle sits on a hill near the town. "Its tower belongs to a private house and is of uncertain significance," critic Charles Bernheimer maintained in *The Kafka Debate: New Perspectives forOur Time*. "It is pierced with windows that glitter in an 'insane' manner and is topped with battlements of 'unsure, irregular, broken' design. Confused by his perceptive faculties, K. finally resorts to a metaphor to describe the appearance of the Castle. But the image he chooses, of a deranged . . . tenant breaking through the roof and lifting himself up to show himself to the world, is clearly a reflection of his own deranged state of mind." "The castle is, of course, the central symbol of the novel," wrote Peter Mailloux in *A Hesitation before Birth: The Life of Franz Kafka*, "and it is presented much more fully than its obvious counterpart, the court in *The Trial*. But it nonetheless seems just as vague, mysterious, and ultimately ambiguous as the court is."

Ashbrook concluded: "The castle contains an unfathomable bureaucratic authority but, at the same time, the text repeatedly insinuates that it is the seat of some transcendental principle. However, the nature of this principle is not spelled out. It might equally well be argued that it is the principle of divine truth or the principle of evil and negation. The ultimate mystery at the heart of the castle remains a mystery; neither K., nor the reader, can ever know the unknowable."

Short Fiction Captures Public Interest

Among Kafka's most widely studied short stories are "The Metamorphosis," "A Hunger Artist," and "In the Penal Colony," which were included in anthologies of his stories published between 1914 and 1919. As Dennis Vannatta wrote in the *Reference Guide to Short Fiction*, "No writer has more memorably dramatized the alienation of the individual in a fathomless world than Kafka in his short fiction. Kafka's short stories writhe with strain and struggle, with seeking, searching, questing, asking. They almost never resolve themselves by answering, finding, arriving. Inevitably the struggle ends in death . . ., in the realization that the struggle is endless . . ., or in the even more bitter conclusion that the concept of 'goal' or 'end' is itself a deception. . . . In the hands of another writer the very intensity of the struggle might imply a certain existential affirmation, but not so in Kafka, where the greater the struggle, the more cruel the 'punch line' at the end."

One of the most frequently studied stories in all of literature, "The Metamorphosis" concerns Gregor Samsa, an ordinary man who wakes one morning to discover himself inexplicably transformed into a giant insect. Although Gregor and his family try to deal with this horrific situation, things do not improve and Gregor is eventually killed during an argument with his father. While the story is fantastic, Kafka relates the tale in a realistic manner. Only the fact of Gregor's transformation is at all unusual; all of the other incidents in the story are ordinary and believable. Beginning from its outlandish premise, "The Metamorphosis" develops logically to a rational conclusion.

"The Metamorphosis," wrote Susanne Klingenstein in the *Reference Guide to Short Fiction*, "centers on a son who takes over the role of the father as caretaker of the family, finds himself transformed into an enormous insect, and is left to die in his room by his visibly revived family. In much of the critical literature Gregor Samsa's transformation into a giant bug is taken one of three ways: to signify his sense of guilt and desire for punishment for having usurped the role of the father, to symbolize both a libidinous rebellion and the condemnation of such a rebellion, or to represent a rebellious assertion of unconscious desires and energies that are identical with the primitive and infantile demands of the id."

More important to the story than how Gregor has become an insect—no explanation is even offered as to how such a thing occurred—is how others react to his unfortunate condition. The story is divided into three parts, with each part dealing with Gregor the insect emerging from his room and being confronted by someone. In the first part, it is his employer, who has come to Gregor's apartment because he is late for work. Gregor works as a salesperson for a company to which his family owes a large debt. His employment is helping to pay off this debt. Although he despises his work, Gregor has continued with the firm on his family's behalf. The first part of the story deals with Gregor's efforts to come to terms with his transformation, to find a way to climb out of his bed, and finally to summon the courage to open the door to his room so that his family and his boss will see him in this hideous state. "The story's first part," noted Klingenstein, "is desperate slapstick. . . . When Gregor finally manages to open the door of his room and reveals himself to his assembled family and his boss, their horrified reaction confirms that he is indeed a giant cockroach." Gregor's father drives him back into the room using a cane and a newspaper.

The second part of the story deals with Gregor's family and their attempts to live with him in his current condition. His sister brings him food and treats him as an invalid who needs special care. She decides that it is best that all the furniture and other human decorations in the room be removed. But while she and the mother are removing the items, Gregor reacts strongly to their taking down a particular print off his wall. Politzer wrote: "For the insect, the print becomes the one of his possessions to which he is determined to adhere both physically and metaphorically. He creeps up to the picture and covers it with his body when mother and sister threaten to remove it." Gregor's defiance leads to a fight with his father, who chases him around the room and finally throws apples at his hapless insect-like progeny. One of the apples cracks the shell of Gregor's back.

In the story's third and final part Gregor is again isolated in his room, suffering from the damage caused by the thrown apple. His family "no longer see in Gregor a transformed family member," noted Klingenstein, "but primarily an animal." Left alone, Gregor is forced to confront the transformation he has undergone, realizing that he is no longer human. When he makes one final attempt to emerge from his room, drawn by the sound of his sister playing the violin, his appearance scares the family's three new boarders. His sister, whom he had relied upon until then, de-

cides that Gregor must be gotten rid of. "As if to indulge and oblige his family one more time," Klingenstein wrote, "Gregor dies during the following night and is thrown out into the garbage by the charwoman the next morning. The remaining family members celebrate their liberation by taking a day off from their jobs and embarking on a train ride into the countryside."

Lawson called "The Metamorphosis" "one of the most widely read and discussed works of world literature: a shocking and yet comic tragedy of

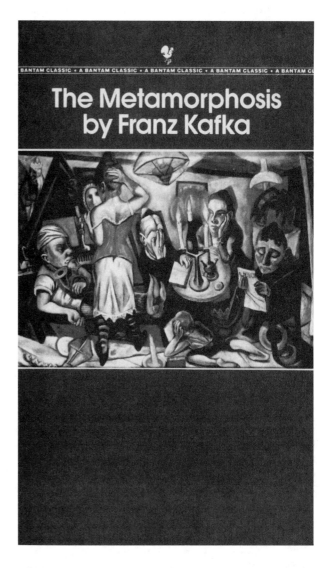

Gregor Samsa, a hard-working man who wakes up one morning to find that he has been transformed into a large beetle-like insect, is the protagonist of Kafka's widely read short story.

modern man's isolation, inadequacy, and existential guilt. . . . [The story] is compact, artistically and formally structured." According to John Updike, writing in the *New Yorker*, "The Metamorphosis" "alone would assure [Kafka] a place in world literature. . . . an indubitable masterpiece."

Literary Reputation Enhanced after Death

"A Hunger Artist" was one of the works Kafka had instructed his friend Max Brod to burn upon the writer's death. Instead, Brod arranged for the story's publication. The work of short fiction details the career of a hunger artist, a man who makes a living in a sideshow by going on prolonged, even dangerous, fasts. At first, the public is enthralled with the idea and the hunger artist prospers. He tours the major European cities. But after a time his audience loses interest, and the hunger artist finds that he is so dedicated to his art that he does not mind. No longer able to fill major halls, he instead joins a traveling carnival where he goes on fasting as a novelty act. Because there is no longer an audience interested in what he is doing, the hunger artist is finally able to fast as long as he wants, until he achieves a lonely and unremarked-upon death. "At the end," noted Lawson, "he dies unnoticed in a pile of dirty straw. His dying reply to the question of why he pursued his unusual—but in nineteenth-century Europe not unique— profession is that he could not find the food he liked; if he had, he would have made no fuss but would have eaten just like anyone else." The hunger artist fails to make known to either his audience or the reader exactly what manner of food he would have accepted, an omission that Lawson noted "has given rise to the critical suggestion that it is spiritual provender that he is talking about."

Kafka's character of the hunger artist has been interpreted by some critics as a symbol of the creative artist whose efforts were once appreciated by society but are now scorned. As Grace Eckley explained in the *Reference Guide to Short Fiction*, "The artist, then, lives an existence trapped in his own nature and between two worlds of pleasing others and pleasing himself. If he were not an artist, no system could make him one; because he is an artist, no system can prevent his being so." Politzer commented: "The art of this Artist is a negative performance. His fasting represents a passive act, which is a paradox. Running counter to human nature, it may, at least in the minds of a curious crowd, have proved attractive, so long as it was performed as a show of self-denial and a feast of sacrifice. Our Artist, however, was cheating even when he thought that he was working honestly; he could not help starving himself; he was forced into his fanatically pursued profession by the absence of the unknown nourishment appropriate to him and his tastes. His art is produced by a deficiency, and the question whether he is at fault for not finding the right food or whether the world is to be blamed for not providing him with it, this question aims ultimately at the meaning of the role that the artist performs in any kind of human context." Frederick R. Karl, in his *Franz Kafka: Representative Man*, argued that the hunger artist represents even more than the artist, but that of a spiritual man as well. Once the hunger artist left behind his glamorous days as a popular entertainer and joined the carnival, he was able to devote his energies exclusively to fasting. At this stage "the hunger artist," Karl wrote, "is becoming a shaman, a clairvoyant, a seer. . . . He has questioned the very foundation of the existence of the ordinary. He opens up questions of existential experience, of the individual edging toward the abyss, of a creature attempting to move ever closer . . . toward that forbidden borderline between life and death where the ultimate mysteries lie." Robert W. Stallman, writing in *Accent*, concluded: "'The Hunger Artist' is one of Kafka's perfections and belongs with the greatest short stories of our time."

Creates Vivid Images of Violence, Captivity, and Death

Kafka's story "In the Penal Colony" was written in 1914, published in German in 1919, and translated into English in 1948. It takes place in a prison camp on a remote island. The story opens with an officer of the camp showing a visiting explorer a machine used to execute prisoners. The complicated apparatus is fixed with needles that pierce the condemned man's flesh, writing into his skin the law he has been charged with breaking and killing the man in the process. While preparing the machine for use, the officer complains to the explorer that the present commandant of the camp shows no interest in this remarkable machine. The former commandant had built the machine and enjoyed using it frequently, while the new commandant is more interested in women.

Anthony Perkins portrays bank clerk Joseph K. in this 1963 adaptation of *The Trial*, directed by Orson Welles.

The officer tries to enlist the explorer's aid in persuading the new commandant of the machine's value. When it comes time to execute the prisoner, the explorer finally speaks out against the proceedings. This moves the officer to realize that his last chance of using the explorer to gain the commandant's favor is lost. He releases the prisoner and climbs onto the execution machine himself, setting it to write the law "Be Just" into his body. The machine breaks down while operating, however, and the needles move about crazily, tearing the officer apart. Following this the explorer, seemingly unmoved by the events he has witnessed, leaves the island.

Criticism of "In the Penal Colony" often focuses on its religious themes. As Klingenstein noted in *Reference Guide to Short Fiction,* "The novella can be read as an allegory of the transition from the stern, purifying notion of Justice in Judaism to the softer, seemingly more charitable and humanitarian attitude in Christianity. Like Yahweh the old commandant, who had always been remote and has now been superseded, was 'soldier, judge, mechanic, chemist and draughtsman,' whereas the new commandant is surrounded by women like Christ."

In contrast to this view, Douglas Angus in *Criticism,* who called "In the Penal Colony" "a remarkable story about a diabolical machine," saw the execution machine as a symbol for the Godless, mechanistic nature of the universe itself. He drew a parallel between the machine of the story with "those dangerous factory machines which so mutilated the workers in Kafka's day and which his work with the Insurance Institute made him so conscious of. These machines were a part of that very real and monstrous world in which Kafka found himself; they were a part of, and a symbol of, that total mechanistic universe in which he lived. From this system too God had departed. If you sought Him for explanation, pity or recompense, you were likely to end up in the red tape of The Workers' Accidental Insurance Institute."

Writing in his *Of War and War's Alarms: Fiction and Politics in the Modern World,* Paul J. Dolan saw "In the Penal Colony" as a story with personal and political dimensions. It is, he wrote, "Kafka's artistic statement of his sense of self-torture and the fantasies of self-destruction with which he lived. The story is also a prophecy of the horrors of German National Socialism in Europe from 1933 to 1945. The two visions, personal and public, psychological and political, are, in fact, one. The two are united because Kafka attempted no prophecy. He wrote of his own nightmare feelings so completely and so honestly that he wrote the history of the future when others made those feelings of guilt and self-torture motives for public policy and the nightmare became everyday reality."

Subject of Literary Study and Debate

In the years since his death in 1924, Kafka has served as the focus of study of numerous critics, who have attempted to penetrate the seemingly impenetrable works he composed duringhis brief life through use of psychoanalytic, theological, and political analysis. A reflection of the age in which he lived, a time and place marked by immense social and political upheaval poised on the verge of a social and cultural evolution that often was enacted through violent means, Kafka's body of work can be seen to reflect turn-of-the century Europe and prefigure a bellicose nation poised on the brink of declaring war on the world.

Summing up the variety of criticism "In the Penal Colony" has generated, Arnold Weinstein wrote in *Studies in Twentieth-Century Literature:* "Like all of Kafka's best stories, 'In the Penal Colony' is maddeningly rife with multiple and contradictory interpretations. Some have made it announce Auschwitz and Dachau; others have seen in it a grim reminder of harsher Old Testament values, according to which our modern liberal world stands either condemned or threatened; the brief tale has been read psychologically, psychoanalytically, anthropologically, historically, paradoxically and parabolically. No matter how one reads it, however, the story's resolution, i.e., the explorer's response to the penal colony, appears so ambivalent that it becomes effectively impossible to do the very thing that is central here and happening everywhere in Kafka: pronounce judgment."

"If one were to judge the worth of an author solely according to the amount of critical commentary which his works have generated," wrote A. P. Foulkes, summing up the German writer's body of work in *Reference Guide to World Literature,* "then there is no doubt that Franz Kafka has already earned his place beside Shakespeare, Goethe, and Cervantes. The primary attraction and challenge for the critic lie in the strange and enigmatic quality of the fiction, its disturbing capacity to invite and yet resist interpretation, and at the same time the intuitive belief of many readers that they are being addressed by a writer who has managed to capture in words the very essence of 20th-century experience and angst."

"Kafka is one of the founders of modern literature," wrote Lawson in his description of the author's overall accomplishment. "His claim to greatness includes his service in completely collapsing the aesthetic distance that had traditionally separated the writer from the reader. . . . Finally, in an age that celebrates the mass, Kafka redirects the focus to the individual. His characters stand for themselves as individuals; in the case of the male protagonists—and almost all of his protagonists are male—they stand for Kafka himself."

■ Works Cited

Angus, Douglas, "The Existentialist and the Diabolical Machine," in *Criticism*, spring, 1964, pp. 134-143.

Ashbrook, B., "Franz Kafka," in *Reference Guide to World Literature*, St. James Press (Detroit), 2nd edition, 1994.

Bernheimer, Charles, "Symbolic Bond and Textual Play: Structure of 'The Castle,'" in *The Kafka Debate: New Perspectives for Our Time*, edited by Angel Flores, Gordian Press, 1977, pp. 367-384.

Brod, Max, *Franz Kafka: A Biography*, Schocken, 1947.

Dauvin, Rene, "'The Trial': Its Meaning," in *Franz Kafka Today*, edited by Angel Flores and Homer Swander, University of Wisconsin Press, 1958, pp. 145-160.

Dolan, Paul J., "Kafka: The Political Machine," in his *Of War and War's Alarms: Fiction andPolitics in the Modern World*, Free Press, 1976, pp. 125-144.

Eckley, Grace, "Franz Kafka," in *Reference Guide to Short Fiction*, St. James Press, 1993, p. 867.

Foulkes, A. P., "Franz Kafka," in *Reference Guide to World Literature*, St. James Press, 2nd edition, 1994.

Heller, Erich, *Franz Kafka*, edited by Frank Kermode, Viking, 1974.

Hesse, Hermann, "Eine Literatur in Rezensionen und Aufsaetzen," in *Gesammelte Werke Volume 12*, Suhrkamp, 1970.

Karl, Frederick R., "Space, Time, and Enclosure in 'The Trial' and 'The Castle,'" in *Journal of Modern Literature*, September, 1977, pp. 424-436.

Karl, Frederick R., *Franz Kafka: Representative Man*, Ticknor & Fields, 1991.

Klingenstein, Susanne, entries in *Reference Guide to Short Fiction*, St. James Press, 1993.

Lawson, Richard H., "Franz Kafka," in *Dictionary of Literary Biography*, Volume 81: *Austrian Fiction Writers, 1875-1913*, Gale (Detroit), 1989, pp. 133-168.

Mailloux, Peter, *A Hesitation before Birth: The Life of Franz Kafka*, University of Delaware Press, 1989.

Muir, Edwin, "A Note on Franz Kafka," in *Bookman*, November, 1930, pp. 235-241.

Politzer, Heinz, *Franz Kafka: Parable and Paradox*, Cornell University Press, 1966.

Seltzer, Alvin J., *Chaos in the Novel, the Novel in Chaos*, Schocken, 1974.

Stallman, Robert W., "Kafka's Cage," in *Accent*, winter, 1948, pp. 117-125.

Updike, John, "Reflections: Kafka's Short Stories," in *New Yorker*, May 9, 1983, pp. 121-126, 129-133.

Vannatta, Dennis, "Franz Kafka," in *Reference Guide to Short Fiction*, St. James Press, 1993, pp. 286-287.

Weinstein, Arnold, "Kafka's Writing Machine: Metamorphosis in the Penal Colony," in *Studies in Twentieth-Century Literature*, fall, 1982, pp. 21-33.

■ For More Information See

BOOKS

Anders, Gunther, *Franz Kafka*, translation by A. Steer and A. K. Thorlby, Bowes & Bowes, 1960.

Bauer, Johann, *Kafka and Prague*, Praeger, 1971.

Boa, Elizabeth, *Kafka: Gender, Class, and Race in the Letters and Fictions*, Oxford University Press, 1996.

Buber-Neumann, Margarete, *Mistress to Kafka*, Secker & Warburg, 1966.

Camus, Albert, *The Myth of Sisyphus, and Other Essays*, translation by Justin O'Brien, Knopf, 1955.

Canetti, Elias, *Kafka's Other Trial: The Letters to Felice*, translation by Christopher Middleton, Schocken, 1982.

Carrouges, Michel, *Kafka versus Kafka*, translation by Emmet Parker, University of Alabama Press, 1968.

Dodd, W. J., *Kafka: "The Metamorphosis", "The Trial", and "The Castle"*, Longman, 1996.

Dowden, Stephen D., *Kafka's Castle and the Critical Imagination*, Camden House, 1995.

Eisner, Pavel, *Franz Kafka and Prague*, Arts, Inc., 1950.

Emrich, Wilhelm, *Franz Kafka*, Ungar, 1968.

Flores, Angel, editor, *The Kafka Problem*, New Directions, 1946.

Frynta, Emanuel, *Kafka and Prague*, Batchworth Press, 1960.

Gilman, Sander L., *Franz Kafka, the Jewish Patient*, Routledge, 1995.

Gray, Richard T., *Approaches to Teaching Kafka's Short Fiction,* Modern Language Association of America, 1995.

Gray, Ronald, *Kafka: A Collection of Critical Essays,* Prentice-Hall, 1962.

Gray, Ronald, *Franz Kafka,* Cambridge University Press, 1973.

Greenberg, Martin, *The Terror of Art: Kafka and Modern Literature,* Basic Books, 1968.

Greozinger, Karl-Erich, *Kafka and Kabbalah,* Contimuum, 1994.

Hall, Calvin S., and Richard E. Lind, *Dreams, Life, and Literature: A Study of Franz Kafka,* University of North Carolina Press, 1970.

Hayman, Ronald, *Kafka,* Oxford University Press, 1982.

Heidsieck, Arnold, *The Intellectual Contexts of Kafka's Fiction, Philosophy, Law, Religion,* Camden House, 1994.

Heller, Erich, *Franz Kafka,* edited by Frank Kermode, Viking, 1974.

Heller, Erich, *The Disinherited Mind,* Harcourt, 1975.

Herman, David, *Universal Grammar and Narrative Form,* Duke University Press, 1995.

Howe, Irving, *Modern Literary Criticism: An Anthology,* Beacon Press, 1958.

Hsia, Adrian, editor, *Kafka and China,* P. Lang (New York City), 1996.

Hughes, Kenneth, *Franz Kafka: An Anthology of Marxist Criticism,* New England University Press, 1981.

Janouch, Gustav, *Conversations with Kafka,* translation by Goronwy Rees, New Directions, 1971.

Kazin, Alfred, *The Inmost Leaf: A Selection of Essays,* Harcourt, 1955.

Kempf, Franz R., *Everyone's Darling: Kafka and the Critics of His Short Fiction,* Camden House, 1994.

Krauss, Karoline, *Kafka's K. versus the Castle: The Self and the Other,* P. Lang, 1996.

Kuna, Franz, editor, *On Kafka: Semi-Centenary Perspectives,* Harper, 1976.

Nabokov, Vladimir, *Lectures on Literature,* edited by Fredson Bowers, Harcourt, 1980.

Pascal, Roy, *Kafka's Narrators: A Study of His Stories and Sketches,* Cambridge University Press, 1982.

Pawel, Ernst, *The Nightmare of Reason: A Life of Franz Kafka,* Farrar, Straus, 1984.

Politzer, Heinz, *Franz Kafka: Parable and Paradox,* Cornell University Press, 1966.

Robert, Marthe, *Kafka,* Gallimard, 1968.

Robert, Marthe, *The Old and the New: From Kafka to Don Quixote,* University of California Press, 1977.

Robert, Marthe, *As Lonely as Franz Kafka,* Harcourt, 1982.

Rolleston, James, *Kafka's Negative Theater,* Pennsylvania State University Press, 1974.

Short Story Criticism, Gale, Volume 5, 1990, Volume 29, 1998.

Sokel, Walter H., *Franz Kafka,* Columbia University Press, 1966.

Spann, Meno, *Franz Kafka,* Twayne, 1976.

Spilka, Mark, *Dickens and Kafka: A Mutual Interpretation,* Indiana University Press, 1963.

Stern, J. P., *The World of Franz Kafka,* Holt, 1980.

Stringfellow, Frank, *The Meaning of Irony: A Psychoanalytic Investigation,* State University of New York Press, 1994.

Suchoff, David Bruce, *Critical Theory and the Novel: Mass Society and Cultural Criticism in Dickens, Melville, and Kafka,* University of Wisconsin Press, 1994.

Sussman, Henry, *Franz Kafka: Geometrician of Metaphor,* Coda Press, 1979.

Tauber, Herbert, *Franz Kafka: An Interpretation of His Works,* Kennikat, 1968.

Thorlby, Anthony, *Kafka: A Study,* Heinemann, 1972.

Tiefenbrun, Ruth, *Moment of Torment: An Interpretation of Franz Kafka's Short Stories,* Southern Illinois University Press, 1973.

Twentieth-Century Literary Criticism, Gale, Volume 2, 1979, Volume 6, 1982, Volume 13, 1984, Volume 29, 1988, Volume 47, 1993, Volume 53, 1994.

Unself, Joachim, and Paul F. Dvorak, *Franz Kafka, A Writer's Life,* Ariadne Press, 1994.

Urzidil, Johannes, *There Goes Kafka,* Wayne State University, 1968.

Wagenback, Klaus, *Kafka's Prague,* Overlook Press, 1996.

West, Rebecca, *The Court and the Castle: Some Treatments of a Recurrent Theme,* Yale University Press, 1957.

Ziolkowski, Theodore, *Dimensions of the Novel: German Texts and European Contexts,* Princeton University Press, 1969.

PERIODICALS

Approach, Fall, 1963.

Bookman, November, 1930.

Commonweal, September 4, 1964.

Comparative Literature, fall, 1959.

Criterion, April, 1938.

German Life and Letters, January, 1953.

Jewish Heritage, summer, 1964.

Journal of English and Germanic Philology, January, 1954.

Journal of Modern Literature, September, 1977.

Kenyon Review, winter, 1939.

Literary Review, summer, 1983.

Literature and Psychology, Volume 27, number 4, 1977.

Modern Fiction Studies, summer, 1958.

Modern Language Notes, October, 1970.

Mosaic, spring, 1972.

Nation, December 7, 1946.

New Republic, October 27, 1937.

New Yorker, May 9, 1983.

New York Times, April 12, 1989; April 16, 1989; August 9, 1989.

Publishers Weekly, June 5, 1995, p. 53.

Quarterly Review of Literature, Volume 2, number 3, 1945; Volume 20, numbers 1-2, 1976.

Reconstructionist, April 3, 1959.

Studies in Short Fiction, summer, 1965; spring, 1973.

Symposium, fall, 1961.

Thought, summer, 1951.

Tri-Quarterly, spring, 1966.

Washington Post, January 15, 1989.

—Sketch by Chas. M. Lowdith

Victor Kelleher

■ Personal

Born Victor Michael Kitchener Kelleher, July 19, 1939, in London, England; son of Joseph (a builder) and Matilda (a dressmaker; maiden name, Newman) Kelleher; married Alison Lyle (a potter and sculptor), January 3, 1962; children: Jason, Leila. *Education:* University of Natal, B.A., 1961; University of St. Andrews, Diploma in Education, 1963; University of the Witwatersrand, B.A. (with honors), 1969; University of South Africa, M.A., 1970, D.Litt. and Phil., 1973. *Religion:* Atheist. *Hobbies and other interests:* Travel, film, architecture, bush walking.

■ Addresses

Home—1 Avenue Rd., Glebe, New South Wales 2037, Australia. *Agent*—c/o Margaret Connolly, 16 Winton St., Warrawee, New South Wales 2074, Australia.

■ Career

Writer. University of the Witwatersrand, Johannesburg, South Africa, junior lecturer in English, 1969; University of South Africa, Pretoria, lecturer, 1970-71, senior lecturer in English, 1972-73; Massey University, Palmerston North, New Zealand, lecturer in English, 1973-76; University of New England, Armidale, Australia, lecturer, 1976-79, senior lecturer, 1980-83, associate professor of English, 1984-87. *Member:* Australian Society of Authors.

■ Awards, Honors

Patricia Hackett Prize, *Westerly* magazine, 1978, for story "The Traveller"; senior writer's fellowship, Literature Board of the Australia Council, 1982, 1988-90, 1995-99; West Australian Young Readers' Book Award, West Australian Library Association, 1982, for *Forbidden Paths of Thual*; West Australian Young Readers' Special Award, West Australian Library Association, 1983, for *The Hunting of Shadroth*; Australian Children's Book of the Year award, Children's Book Council of Australia, 1983, for *Master of the Grove*; Australian Science-Fiction Achievement Award, Australian Science Fiction Association, 1984, for *The Beast of Heaven*; Honour Award, Children's Book Council of Australia, 1987, for *Taronga*, and 1991, for *Brother Night*; Australian Children's Peace Literature Award, 1989; Koala Award, 1991; Hoffman Award, 1992, 1993, 1996; Cool Award, 1993; West Australian Young Readers' Award, 1993.

■ Writings

FOR YOUNG ADULTS

Forbidden Paths of Thual, Penguin (New York City), 1979.

The Hunting of Shadroth, Penguin, 1981.

Master of the Grove, Penguin, 1982.

Papio: A Novel of Adventure, Penguin, 1984, published as *Rescue!: An African Adventure,* Dial, 1992.

The Green Piper, Penguin, 1984.

Taronga, Penguin, 1986.

The Makers, Penguin, 1987.

Bailey's Bones, Penguin, 1988, Dial, 1989.

The Red King, Penguin, 1989, Dial, 1990.

Brother Night, Walker, 1990.

Del-Del, illustrated by Peter Clarke, Random Century, 1991, Walker, 1992.

To the Dark Tower, Random Century, 1992.

Where the Whales Sing, Penguin, 1994, Dial, 1995, published as *Riding the Whales,* illustrated by Vivienne Goodman, Dial, 1999.

Parkland (first novel in trilogy), Viking/Penguin, 1994.

Earthsong (second novel in trilogy), Viking/Penguin, 1995.

Fire Dancer (third novel in trilogy), Viking/Penguin, 1996.

Slow Burn, Viking/Penguin, 1997.

The Ivory Trail, Viking, Penguin, 1999.

FICTION

Voices from the River (novel), Heinemann (London), 1979.

Africa and After (stories), University of Queensland Press, 1983, published as *The Traveller: Stories of Two Continents,* University of Queensland Press, 1987.

The Beast of Heaven (novel), University of Queensland Press, 1984.

Em's Story (novel), University of Queensland Press, 1988.

Wintering (novel), University of Queensland Press, 1990.

Micky Darlin' (interconnected stories), University of Queensland Press, 1992.

(As Veronica Hart) *Double God,* Mandarin, 1994.

(As Veronica Hart) *The House that Jack Built,* Mandarin, 1994.

Storyman (novel), Random House (New York City), 1996.

Johnny Wombat (for young children), illustrated by Craig Smith, Random House Australia, 1996.

Into the Dark, Viking/Penguin, 1999.

Work represented in anthologies, including *Introduction 6,* Faber, 1977. Contributor of articles and stories to magazines.

■ Adaptations

A number of Kelleher's works have been translated into Spanish, Japanese, German, Swedish, and Danish.

■ Sidelights

The winner of numerous awards in Australia, where he makes his home, Victor Kelleher writes for both juvenile and adult audiences. While younger fans enjoy the elements of fantasy, science-fiction, and high adventure to be found in such novels as *The Hunting of Shadroth* and *Taronga,* more mature readers are intrigued by the author's darker side, both through such futuristic fantasy as Kelleher's *The Beast of Heaven* and his contributions to the horror genre. "In fact," observed Steven Paulsen and Sean McMullen in their essay in *St. James Guide to Horror, Ghost, and Gothic Writers,* "Kelleher has never shied away from horror and terror, and there have been elements of it in his work since his early young-adult fantasy novels." Such early novels include *The Hunting of Shadroth* and *The Green Piper,* the latter which was cited by Paulsen and McMullen as "the first-ever Australian children's horror novel." Whatever his genre, Kelleher is viewed by many as a writer of considerable intellectual depth. As Leonie Tyle noted in a *Magpies* profile, "He is a storyman: a writer dedicated to structure and technique, but onewho also knows the power of narrative. . . . Kelleher's work is a journey for the truth."

Born in London, England, in 1939, Kelleher did not spend a traditional "writer's" childhood immersed in books and enthralled by the sound and power of words. Instead, raised as part of a large, poor family with strong roots leading to Ireland, he had few academic ambitions and quit school in favor of work by age sixteen. Moving with his family to Zambia in 1955, he found work wherever he could, including as a miner and as a hunter. Within three years Kelleher grew to abhor the killing of wild animals, put down his gun, and became an advocate of wildlife and the environment, as well as a vegetarian.

Enrolling at the University of Natal, Kelleher graduated in 1962 with a bachelor's degree in English, which, along with marriage, whetted his taste for academic life. Accumulating several more advanced degrees at universities in South Africa, he attained his first academic position—as junior lecturer in English—at the University of the Witwatersrand in 1969. A move to New South Wales, Australia, by way of New Zealand during the 1970s found Kelleher serving as senior lecturer in English at the University of New England by 1979. 1979 would also see the release of his first two books, published when their author was forty.

Spins Vast Life Experiences into Fiction

Kelleher had begun writing in 1973, after leaving Africa. While it began as a way of dealing with his sadness at leaving a country he had spent so

In this award-winning 1984 novel, the lives of a group of peaceful people living on Earth long after a nuclear holocaust are increasingly disturbed by Houdin, also known as the Beast of Heaven, and two powerful supercomputers.

much of his life in, the practice of putting pen to paper soon went from therapy to habit, with the novel *Voices from the River* and the children's fantasy novel *Forbidden Paths of Thual* the result. *Voices*, a novel for mature readers, focuses on racism and the search for universalities in human nature that transcend barriers of color and ethnicity. Its themes would be taken up in several other adult novels, as well as in the short story collection *Africa and After*, which was first published in 1983. *Forbidden Paths* was a response to the dearth of good novels for young people, a situation Kelleher encountered in trying to find books of interest to his son.

In *Forbidden Paths of Thual* teen protagonist Quen comes of age in the process of a quest in search of a token that would free his people from the grey Mollags, an army of ruthless soldiers that continues to terrorize Quen's village. Because his youth and his strength of character enable the lad to overcome his personal weaknesses and resist the temptings of greed and cruelty, he is selected to go in search of the Great Eye, the mystical token said to consume all evil. Aided by a friendly fox, the heroic Quen saves his friends and family from destruction, although, as he discovers along the way, overcoming temptation isn't always easy. Praised as an "interesting, refreshing, worthwhile" young adult book by Norman Culpan in a review for *School Librarian*, *Forbidden Paths of Thual* was summarized by *Times Educational Supplement* contributor Audrey Lasky as "one boy . . . dar[ing] everything that is necessary to defeat the conquerors."

Kelleher's next two books echo the plot and setting of *Forbidden Paths of Thual* in their focus on a hazardous quest that parallels the heroic but very human protagonist's own inward journey toward understanding. In 1981's *The Hunting of Shadroth* readers are introduced to Tal, a boy with psychic talents who can see into the future. The recently released Shadroth, the destruction of which is the object of Tal's quest, is a beast that embodies the violent tendencies of Tal's clan. Mistakenly brought to life by the clan's new and overly enthusiastic leader, Kulok, the Shadroth proves hard to defeat. However, with help from a wild cat known as the Feln, the ultimately repentant Kulok, and the clanleader's savvy sister Lea, Tal ultimately succeeds. David Churchill, writing in *School Librarian*, noted that *The Hunting of Shadroth* "is written with care and elegance," while *Times Literary Supplement* contributor Edward Blishen viewed the novel as a moralistic tale, "but without ever ceasing to be a story. There are satisfactory terrors . . . and the final struggle rises to one climax only to reveal another beyond it."

Battling Corruption of Adults

In the novel *Master of the Grove* a quest is again the task of the protagonist. Suffering from amnesia, Derin is encouraged to begin a journey he believes will reunite him with his father but is actually orchestrated by Derin's fellow townsmen as a way to break the power held by Krob, the land's evil ruler. Accompanied by Marna, an old woman whom Derin mistrusts and suspects is a witch, the boy ultimately helps remove the tyrannical Krob and restore representative government to the kingdom. While noting that the plot device of "a sorcerer's misuse of his knowledge may seem hackneyed, . . . it allows Kelleher to explore the theme of the responsibilities and temptations of power in a lively and well-fashioned narrative," according to *Times Educational Supplement* contributor Neil Philip. Other critics offered mixed reviews of the novel, some noting, with *School Librarian* contributor Dennis Hamley, that while *Master of the Grove* is a "worthy, well-crafted book," with its two-hundred pages of political intrigue, its "style is ponderous."

From the quasi-medieval settings of his early novels, Kelleher moved to the distant future in his award-winning 1986 novel *Taronga*. But in this future, life is absent the technology of the twentieth century, and heroism, a quick wit, and physical prowess are still key to one's survival. Kelleher's envisioning of a post-Armageddon Australia, where cities lie in rubble and rootless inhabitants wander the land in search of food and shelter, *Taronga* tells the story of fourteen- year-old Ben and his experiences at the gang-controlled Taronga Park Zoo. A gifted telepath, Ben is able to control the minds of the zoo animals. As knowledge of his ability becomes known, he is promoted by head gang leader Molly to the position of keeper of the big cats, and gains an assistant named Ellie, an Aboriginal teen. As cat-keeper, one of Ben's most challenging tasks is the nightly release of the tigers, which the gang orders as a way to frighten and repel hungry rival gangs who might find their way into the zoo compound. While allowed to roam in the dark, the cats must be collected and put back into their cages each morning. Ultimately, Ben regrets betraying the trust the animals have placed in him by sending them out on missions of violence, and he and Ellie decide to liberate all the zoo animals from their confines. It is a decision that results in violence. "The collapse of human integrity, the efforts of young people to prolong and organize life among ruins—these are powerful themes, worked out [in the novel] with honesty and force," according to *Growing Point* contributor Margery Fisher, who went on to praise Kelleher for his memorable descriptions of people and places. However, several reviewers were mixed in their opinion of the story. Expressing criticism of *Taronga* for what he characterizes as an implausible plot, Colin Greenland added in his *Times Literary Supplement* appraisal that "once again . . . Kelleher portrays the child's world as a miserable, shadowy place occupied by corrupt and violent adults."

Science-Fiction Themes Extend to Adult Novels

Other science-fiction novels by Kelleher include 1986's award-winning *The Makers*, which finds Jeth, a young warrior, questioning his loyalty to the god-like grotesques that tightly control the community known as the Keep, a desert society located on a post-Armageddon earth. *The Makers* was shortlisted for the Australian Children's Book of the Year Award in 1988. In Kelleher's trilogy of novels positing three possible sources of humankind on earth—*Parkland*, *Earthland*, and *Fire Dancer*—his setting is again the distant future of a planet whose environment has been destroyed by human misuse. In *Parkland* humans and quasi-human beings are engineered by otherworldly Keepers, cosmic gardeners who travel to other worlds to supervise the developing biological mix. Part of the current harvest of creatures cultivated in the enclosed area patrolled by the three Keepers and their bloodthirsty leopard-dog assistants, Cassie resents the Keepers' restrictions and decides to escape with the help of human-like friends Boxer and Ralph. A violent battle ensues, the consequence of which is that the formerly cared-for trio is forced to learn the true meaning of self-sufficiency. As *Magpies* contributor Carmel Ballinger noted, *Parkland* "is typical Kelleher, challenging the reader to rethink some of our most basic beliefs. What is freedom and what is the price?" In the second novel in the trilogy, *Earthsong*, two teens are in charge of developing the human embryos needed to repopulate an over-polluted Earth after their return from safety in a distant galaxy. *Fire Dancer*, Kelleher's concluding installment, finds Ivan and Josie transported from the twenty-first century to the distant past, where they must learn to combat their fear and draw on their instinct for survival in sharing their new home with neighboring Neanderthals.

Unlike the futuristic plots he devises for teen readers, most of Kelleher's adult fiction focuses on contemporary social ills. However, 1984's *The Beast of Heaven* closely mirrors his plots for younger readers. Set on an Earth decimated by the nuclear holocaust of the year 2027—now 100,000 years in the past—the book tells the tale of those descended from the survivors. A peaceful, nomadic people who subsist on "mustools," a mushroom/toadstool combo, their peace-filled existence is increasingly shattered by the predatory raids of a creature known as the Houdin, the "beast of Heaven." While the Houdin's aggressive tendencies increase, the land also appears to be slowly losing its ability to support life. Unbeknownst to the planet's nomadic inhabitants, two powerful supercomputers constructed before the nuclear catastrophe debate the continued value of the human race they have, up until now, allowed to continue. *The Beast of Heaven* "is an ingeniously constructed and often lyrically written novel which leads ineluctably to an apocalyptic ending of dreadful irony," according to essayist Laurie Clancy in *Contemporary Novelists,* while *Analog Science Fiction/Science Fact* columnist Tom Easton proclaimed Kelleher's work "a fable for our times, a warning, a chastisement, well equipped with portentous symbolism."

Adult Violence Takes Ghostly Form

As several reviewers have commented, Kelleher's fiction—in particular, his work for young adult readers—tends to focus on the darker, more shadowy aspects of human relationships and human nature. The majority of the adult characters that appear in his fiction—from brutal gang leader Molly in *Taronga* to the greedy Krob in *Master of the Grove*—are forbidding figures, forcing Kelleher's youthful protagonists to achieve heroic goals to order to preserve and protect both themselves and their society. Combining fast-paced, futuristic or fantastic plots with theauthor's personal philo-

If you enjoy the works of Victor Kelleher, you may also want to check out the following books and films:

Gary Crew, *Strange Objects,* 1993.
Margaret Mahy, *The Changeover,* 1984.
Robin McKinley, *Deerskin,* 1993.
The Sixth Sense, a film starring Bruce Willis, 1999.

sophical and social viewpoints is another characteristic of Kelleher's books. Indeed, he views the inclusion of a serious subtext involving challenging and socially pertinent issues to be among the central responsibilities of a young-adult novelist. But this responsibility does not detract from his ability to capture the imagination of his readers, even when his fictions stray into more imaginative genres, such as high fantasy and even the supernatural.

In 1988's *Baily's Bones,* Kelleher weaves ghosts, possession by evil spirits, and other unearthly mysteries into his characteristic fictional mix, while also delving into Australian history— particularly the violent relationship between native Aborigines and the early white settlers who inhabited the continent when it served as a penal colony. When the vengeful spirit of a dead convict named Frank Baily takes control over their mentally handicapped older brother, Kenny, siblings Alex and Dee Martin are forced to piece together the events leading up to Baily's death in an effort to put Baily's malevolent presence to rest. Jeanette Larson, writing in *School Library Journal,* declared *Baily's Bones* to be a "haunting tale . . . well told," and dubbed the work "an exciting story." *Voice of Youth Advocates* contributor Deborah L. Dubois agreed, commenting in her review's conclusion that Kelleher's "exciting suspense novel . . . will appeal to most young adults."

Kelleher combines fantasy with evil personified in *The Red King,* published in 1990. Medieval overtones and a classic combat between the forces of good and evil have caused some critics to compare the work with J. R. R. Tolkien's classic story *The Hobbit.* In Kelleher's novel, the lively Timkin, a skilled acrobat, is saved from the "red disease"—a plague unleashed by soldiers of the Red

King—by Petie, a magician and a thief. Petie plans to use Timkin's talents as an acrobat to help him steal the Red King's riches; Timkin accompanies the magician on his journey to the King's castle, hoping to gain her freedom. Noting that "excitement and suspense are maintained throughout," *School Library Journal* contributor Bruce Anne Shook wrote that "Fantasy lovers will find [*The Red King*] . . . intriguing" in that it "provides not only high adventure but also some challenging food for thought about the nature of good and evil." Laura Moss Gottlieb added in her *Voice of Youth Advocates* appraisal that the novel raises "thought-provoking questions" and awarded Kelleher's writing a grade of "excellent."

Lines between Good and Evil Drawn Darker

Hailed as "fantasy at its very best for young teens," by reviewer Gladys Hardcastle in *Voice of Youth Advocates*, Kelleher's *Brother Night* continues the medieval-tinged themes of *The Red King*. Bringing "a perilous quest through the shadowy realm of dark and light forces brilliantly to life," according to Hardcastle, *Brother Night* is the story of twin brothers—the handsome Ramon and the ill-favored, even grotesque giant Lal—who are the offspring of Jenna, a witch, and Solmak, the powerful Sun Lord. Separated at birth, the un-identical twins are eventually reunited, after Solmak visits their town to destroy the son he knows would compete for his power. The brothers begin a dangerous journey to the home of their uncle, the Night Lord Luan, angry Ramon to revenge himself against the father who put a price on his head and gentle Lal to bury their mother. Confronting Luan, who has been depicted as insane by the powerful Solmak, the young men learn about their own capacity for good and evil. Reviewing the novel for the *Bulletin of the Center for Children's Books*, Roger Sutton concluded that the work,"Darker-toned than much juvenile fantasy, . . . is an adept and satisfying blend of action and atmosphere." Lauding *Brother Night* as Kelleher's "best book for young people yet," *Australian Book Review* contributor Meg Sorensen noted that "With its thorough shaking up of pre- conceptions and uneasy resolutions, this book poses some worthy questions indeed."

Kelleher moves from the mythic worlds of *Brother Night* into the intricacies of modern horrors created by the human mind with *Del-Del*. The 1991 novel introduces readers to seven-year-old Sam, a brilliant boy who regresses into a persona he names "Del-Del" after the death of his oldest sister. Obnoxious and uncaring to the point of borderline evil, Del-Del/Sam terrorizes his family to the point that his parents resort to every form of help they can think of, even exorcism, to save their son. In reviewing Kelleher's novel of psychological evil, a reviewer in *Publishers Weekly* noted that the author "plots an unusual course for a sibling death theme, with confusing results," while Caroline S. McKinney claimed in *Voice of Youth Advocates* that readers will be unable to get "caught up in the horror, because it seems silly." However, other reviewers found much to praise in *Del-Del*; finding it a "tense, involving story," *School Library Journal* contributor Sara Miller summarized the work as "a psychological thriller that's guaranteed to hold readers' attention."

Branches out into the Horror Genre

Kelleher took his first step into the horror genre as early as 1984 with his novel *The Green Piper*, a story about a plant-like being determined to destroy all creatures of flesh. While he has continued to dabble in the genre by writing sometimes terror-tinged mainstream fiction for adults and interjecting slightly scary elements into his fantasy and science-fiction novels for younger readers, 1991's *Del-Del* marked a transition in Kelleher's focus that continued into the 1990s. Beginning in 1994 Kelleher began publishing out-and-out psychological horror novels under the pseudonym Veronica Hart. In *Double God*, published in 1994, a fifteen-year-old girl withdraws inside herself after an unsettling incident involving a dog occurs while she is caring for a small child. Taken by her family to a house in the country in the hopes that she will recover from her shock, the emotionally vulnerable young woman is instead drawn into the dark past of the house itself. *The House That Jack Built* again finds human protagonists battling the supernatural, as a seance performed at a late-night party summons forth the spirit of Jack the Ripper, and a spree of blood-letting terrorizes local residents. While noting that these books are are more commercial than Kelleher's other work, Paulsen and McMullen praise them as "slick and fast-paced, building their tension with a strong whodunit element combined with suspense and mounting terror." With the publication of his third entry in the horror genre, the

1996 work *Storyman,* Kelleher would drop the Hart pseudonym.

Having left his teaching position at the University of the New England in 1987, Kelleher continues to live in Australia, where he now devotes all his time to writing. Continuing to publish both teen and adult novels, he continues his exploration of the nature of good and evil through his adult fiction. Remarking on his career in *Twentieth-Century Children's Writers,* Kelleher once noted that, while he intentionally focuses attention on moral or philosophical issues, he begins his books for young readers without any specific "aim" in mind. "I try to write exciting, adventurous stories because those are the kinds of stories I appreciated as a child; and, like many writers, I enjoy recapturing the feelings and response of my childhood. . . . I suppose oneof the many advantages of writing for children is that in enables me to pursue certain ideas that the majority of adults simply don't take seriously. . . . Similarly, I'm free to express myself through the medium of story— an approach that is largely frowned on by critics of adult fiction." With novels like 1998's *Slow Burn,* which focuses on "green" politics and the ability of protest movements to affect change through nonviolent means, he also continues to introduce teens to timely and controversial topics through fast-moving and engaging stories.

■ Works Cited

Ballinger, Carmel, review of *Parkland,* in *Magpies,* November, 1994, p. 34.

Blishen, Edward, "Moral Beasts," in *Times Literary Supplement,* March 27, 1981.

Review of *Brother Night,* in *Bulletin of the Center for Children's Books,* June, 1991, p. 241.

Churchill, David, review of *The Hunting of Shadroth,* in *School Librarian,* June, 1981, p. 154.

Clancy, Laurie, "Victor Kelleher," in *Contemporary Novelists,* St. James Press, 1996, pp. 559-560.

Culpan, Norman, review of *Forbidden Paths of Thual,* in *School Librarian,* December, 1979.

Review of Del-Del, in *Publishers Weekly,* June 15, 1992.

Dubois, Deborah L., review of *Baily's Bones,* in *Voice of Youth Advocates,* April, 1990.

Easton, Tom, review of *The Beast of Heaven,* in *Analog Science Fiction/Science Fact,* April, 1987.

Fisher, Margery, review of *Taronga,* in *Growing Point,* March, 1988, pp. 4934-35.

Gottlieb, Laura Moss, review of *The Red King,* in *Voice of Youth Advocates,* June, 1990, p. 116.

Greenland, Colin, "Animal Liberation," in *Times Literary Supplement,* January 1, 1988, p. 21.

Hamely, Dennis, review of *Master of the Grove,* in *School Librarian,* June, 1982, p. 155.

Hardcastle, Gladys, review of *Brother Night,* in *Voice of Youth Advocates,* October, 1991, p. 244.

Kelleher, Victor, comment in *Twentieth-Century Children's Writers,* third edition, St. James Press, 1988, pp. 514-15.

Larson, Jeanette, review of *Baily's Bones,* in *School Library Journal,* November, 1989, p. 111.

Laski, Audrey, review of *Forbidden Paths of Thual,* in *Times Educational Supplement,* November 11, 1983.

McKinney, Caroline S., review of *Del-Del,* in *Voice of Youth Advocates,* June, 1992, p. 110.

Miller, Sara, review of *Del-Del,* in *School Library Journal,* June, 1992, p. 136.

Paulsen, Steven, and Sean McMullen, "Victor Kelleher," in *St. James Guide to Horror, Ghost, and Gothic Writers,* St. James Press, 1996, pp. 312-13.

Philip, Neil, "Action Men All," in *Times Educational Supplement,* April 23, 1982.

Shook, Bruce Anne, review of *The Red King,* in *School Library Journal,* July, 1990, p. 89.

Sorensen, Meg, review of *Brother Night,* in *Australian Book Review,* December, 1990, p. 47.

Tyle, Leonie, "Know the Author: Victor Kelleher," in *Magpies,* November, 1998, pp. 14-17.

■ For More Information See

BOOKS

Children's Literature Review, Volume 36, Gale, 1995.

PERIODICALS

Fantasy Review, September, 1984, p. 31.

Horn Book, March, 1990, p. 207.

Junior Bookshelf, August, 1995, p. 153; August, 1996.

Publishers Weekly, July 5, 1985, p. 58.

School Librarian, September, 1985, pp. 256, 259; September, 1996, p. 120.

School Library Journal, May, 1988; May, 1991, p. 111.

Science Fiction Review, May, 1986, p. 7.

Times Literary Supplement, March 26, 1982; April 12, 1985; January 1-7, 1988.

—Sketch by Lynn MacGregor

Paul Klee

Amsterdam; Tate Museum, London; Arte Moderna, Rome; and Museum of Modern Art, New York City. *Military service:* Was drafted into the German army, 1916-18.

■ Personal

Born December 18, 1879, in Muenchenbuchsee, near Berne, Switzerland; died June 29, 1940, in Muralto-Locarno, Switzerland; son of a music professor; married Lily Stumpf (a pianist), 1906; children: Felix. *Education:* Attended schools in Berne; attended Heinrich Knirr School of Art, Munich, 1989-90; studied privately with Wassily Kandinsky and with Franz Stuck at the Kunstakademie, Munich, 1900-01.

■ Career

Painter, writer, and musician. Berne Municipal Orchestra, violinist, 1903-05; full-time artist, 1906-40. Debschitz School, instructor, 1908; associated with the Sema Group, 1911, Der Blaue Reiter, 1912, and Der Neue Meunchen Sezession, 1914; the Bauhaus (Weimar, then Dessau, Germany), instructor, 1921-31; Der Blaue Vier, co-founder, 1924; Kunstakademie, Dusseldorf, Germany, professor, 1931. *Exhibitions:* Work included in permanent collections at museums, including Stedelijk Museum,

■ Writings

Paedagogische Skizzenbuch, [Dessau, Germany], 1925, translation published as *Pedagogical Sketchbook*, [New York City], 1944.
Klee Speaks in the Bauhaus, 1919-1928, [New York City], 1938.
Das Bildnerische Denken, edited by Jurg Spiller, Schwabe (Basel, Switzerland), 1956, translated by Ralph Manheim as *The Thinking Eye*, Overlook Press (Woodstock, NY), 1992.
Tagebucher, 1898-1918, edited by son, Felix Klee, DuMont (Cologne, Germany), 1957, edited by Wolfgang Kersten, G. Hatje (Stuttgart, Germany), 1988, translated as *The Diaries*, University of California Press (Berkeley), 1964.
Gedichte, edited by son, Felix Klee, Verlag der Arche (Zurich), 1960, portions translated as *Some Poems*, Scorpion Press (Lowestoft, England), 1962.
Uber die moderne Kunst (lecture), translated by Paul Findlay as *On Modern Art*, Faber (London), 1966.
Unendliche Naturgeschichte, edited by Jurg Spiller, Schwabe, 1970, translated by Heinz Norden as *The Nature of Nature: The Notebooks, Volume 2*, Overlook Press, 1992.
Die Ordung der Dinge: Bilder und Zitate, edited by Tilman Osterwold, Hatje, 1975.

Schriften: Rezensionen und Aufsatze, edited by Christian Geelhaar, Schwabe (Cologne, Germany), 1976.

Beitrage zur bildnerischen Formlehre, edited by Jurgen Glaesemer, DuMont, 1976.

Briefe an die Familie 1893-1940, two volumes, edited by son, Felix Klee, DuMont, 1979.

Die Zwitschermaschine und anderer Grotesken, edited by Lothar Lang, Eulenspiegel (Berlin), 1982.

Form—und Gestaltungslehre, edited by Jurg Spiller, translated by Ralph Manheim as *Paul Klee Notebooks*, Overlook Press, 1992.

Numerous exhibition catalogs of Klee's artworks have been published, and several of his musical scores are also in print.

Illustrator of works, including Curt Corinth, *Potsdamer Platz,* 1919, and Voltaire, *Candide,* 1920.

■ Sidelights

Despite the fact that his work is well known around the world, Swiss-born painter, violinist, essayist, poet, educator, and diarist Paul Klee remains difficult to classify as an artist. While his paintings have been labeled everything from cubist to surrealist, his small-scaled, highly intricate drawings and canvases exhibit a personal, highly fanciful world that remains unique. As Janice McCullagh noted in the *International Dictionary of Arts and Artists,* Klee's style could not be categorized within a defined "ism." "In spite of his prolific artistic production and his writings, something about this artist remains forever remote," McCullagh explained. "For Klee the artistic journey was focused on nature and nature's ways, but like a monk's his was essentially an inward examination." While his works were exhibited in museums and private collections around the world even during his lifetime, Klee was also a consummate violinist, and had a number of published books to his credit, including his groundbreaking *Pedagogical Sketchbooks* and *The Thinking Eye,* a collection of selections from his notebooks.

Born in the Swiss town of Muenchenbuchsee, near Berne, on December 18, 1879, Klee was raised in a musical family where personal creativity was encouraged, particularly by Klee's father, a professor of music. While his father's encouragement in musical endeavors caused the younger Klee to concentrate his time on mastering the violin, art remained a passion that he would later indulge. By the turn of the century Klee had decided to explore his aptitude in the visual arts, as opposed to music. He moved to Munich to study at that city's Academy under popular symbolist painter Franz von Stuck. A year later Klee went on a tour of Italy, where he discovered the works of Byzantine artists. Spanish painter Francisco de Goya would also serve as an inspiration to the budding artist.

Klee returned to Berne in 1903, when he was twenty-four, and resumed his musical associations by performing professionally with that city's municipal orchestra. However, his attention continued to be diverted toward the visual arts, and by 1905 he had committed to changing careers, laying down his violin in favor of etching, drawing with pen and ink, and painting with watercolor. Among Klee's most notable early works are "Virgin in a Tree" and "Two Men Meet, Each Believing the Other to Be of Higher Rank," both of which carry the unusual and imaginative titles characteristic of all of Klee's paintings.

Embraces Movement toward Abstraction

In 1906 Klee married Lily Stumpf, a pianist, with whom he would have one son, Felix Klee. The couple settled in Munich, which by then had gained a reputation as a center for avant garde artistic expression, and Klee exhibited his first collection of etchings. During his stay in Munich Klee became friends with artist August Macke and Russian-born French painter Wassily Kandinsky, the latter who encouraged Klee to become involved with a series of loosely associated artist movements—the Sema Group, der Blau Reiter, and der Neue Meunchen Sezession—the members of each of which were striving to create a truly modern art. Klee co-founded the expressionist Blau Reiter, or "Blue Rider," in 1911, along with Kandinsky, who would go on to front the Abstract movement.

1914 found Klee in Tunisia accompanying painters Macke and Louis Molliet and intent upon studying this new landscape. While in North

(Following page) The Greek goddess Aphrodite is the subject of this Cubist painting, *Aphrodite's Vases,* or *Ceramic/Erotic/Religious,* painted by Klee in 1921.

'921/97   Keramisch ·erotisch ·heiter

Africa he became fascinated by the intensity of the region's natural light, as well as by its many colorful mosaic installations. Upon his return Klee began to attempt to capture this radiance by painting canvases with square blocks of transparent watercolor, among them "Red and White Domes" (1914) and "Remembrance of a Garden" (1914). He also began incorporating numerals and letters into his colorful works, creating a new "language" of recognizable symbols that conveyed a visual meaning due to their unconventional placement. These symbol-laden canvases would soon become the artist's trademark, replacing Klee's works painted from nature.

By now a German citizen, Klee was drafted into the German army in 1916 and forced to serve his new country until Kaiser Wilhelm admitted defeat in the fall of 1918, marking the end of World War I. Under the terms of the Treaty of Versailles signed in November of that year, Germany underwent a period of social, political, and cultural transition under the leadership of the liberal government of the newly formed Weimar Republic. This period of flux was reflected in the Bauhaus, an arts and crafts school founded in 1919 by architect Walter Gropius. Gropius sought to provide artists, architects, and others with the opportunity to create a unified artistic expression for the new Germany. Klee began teaching at the Bauhaus in 1920, joining such innovative artists as Hungarian abstractionist Lazlo Moholy-Nagy, Feininger, van Doesburg, Kandinsky, and German architect/designer Ludwig Mies van der Rohe in their quest for functionalism. He followed the school to Dessau in 1925, the year his *Paedagogische Skizzenbuch* (*Pedagogical Sketchbooks*) was published.

Suffering from being labeled "Judeo-Bolshevist" by an increasingly vocal racist Nazi population, as well as from the internal conflict wrought by the confluence of artistic visions of its members, the Bauhaus remained in a state of constant instability. On the heels of his successful one-man show in New York's Museum of Modern Art—a rarity indeed for an artist still living—Klee finally left his teaching position there in 1931, two years before the school would be closed by German chancellor Adolph Hitler. Klee moved to Dusseldorf and taught at the Dusseldorf Academy until Nazi condemnation for threatening National Socialist *Kulturpolitik* caught up with him; his house was searched and he was dismissed. Klee and his family returned to Berne in 1933, leaving Germany shortly following Hitler's appointment as chancellor of that nation.

Work Censured by Nazi Reich

Klee's return to his native Switzerland was marked by both personal and professional setbacks. Although Switzerland had and would remain neutral throughout the escalating violence stretching from World War I through World War II, the Nazi movement had by now taken hold in Germany, where most of Klee's paintings and drawings remained. With many of his abstract art works perceived by the new government as "degenerate," his work was removed from galleries and museums and auctioned off with the work of other "degenerate" artists to earn money for the Nazi cause—much that was left in Nazi hands would later be destroyed. Meanwhile, the artist found himself isolated from the colleagues and friends who had encouraged and inspired him. Tragically, Klee soon contracted scleroderma, a rare, crippling collagen disease that forced him to curtail his artistic output and resulted in his death in June of 1940. The oppressive social and political setting of his final years can be seen in the larger canvases and thick, weighty black lines and images of war and death that characterized much of Klee's work of the late 1930s, including "Insula Dulcamara" (1938), "Captive" (1940), and "Death and Fire" (1940), the last which features a white skull marked by the German word for "death." Despite his failing health, the three years prior to his death were ones of incredible productivity for the artist, who produced over fifteen hundred line drawings during the period.

While he was an innovator rather than a follower of artistic trends—and therefore not easily classified in the artistic schools of his time—Klee, along with his contemporaries, believed the representational art characteristic of the Old Masters and the late nineteenth century was gradually declining in popularity and relevance with the arrival of abstraction. Abstraction, Klee felt, could provide man with a universal language, transcending language, public, and cultural differences.

Develops Abstract Style

Klee's earliest work, done circa 1905, consisted largely of etchings; book illustrations created be-

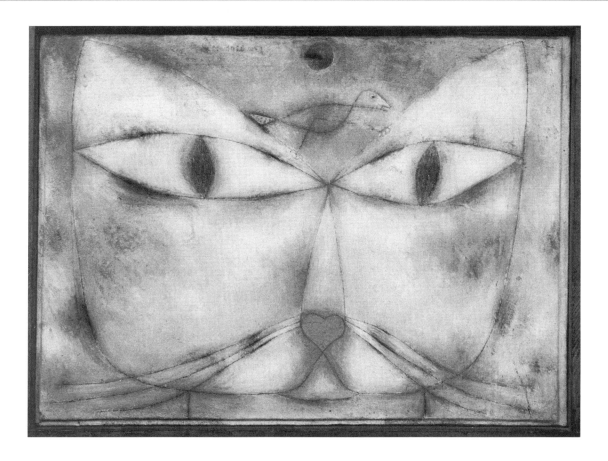

This 1928 painting, *Cat and Bird*, is the subject of various interpretations, including the theme of a hunter's intense fixation of its prey.

tween 1911 and 1912 for Voltaire's *Candide* and Curt Corinth's *Potsdamer Platz* also show him utilizing standard draftsman techniques. In later works he began to enhance these black-and-white drawings with bright watercolors. Inspired by the drawings of children and primitives, Klee developed a style that relied heavily on simplified lines and exquisite color. He preferred to work in small formats due to their intimacy, and the detail he used in his etchings in particular extended beyond the physical attributes of any object sketched, almost expressing its inner nature. Among his inspirations during this period was the work of Paul Cezanne that he discovered in 1909. The influences of cubism and his trip to Tunisia in 1914 would also become apparent as his personal style developed. As Klee wrote in a journal entry for April 16, 1914, that was later published in *The Diaries:* "Color has claimed me. I need no longer run after it. It has claimed me once and for all, that I

know. This is the meaning of the happiest hour; I and color are one. I am a painter."

After 1919 Klee switched to oils, producing paintings that demonstrate a great deal of technical skill. Noting that in the artist's canvases "images float in an atmosphere so dreamlike that it's hard to find a foothold," *Newsweek* contributor Cathleen McGuigan described Klee's technique: "His surfaces are often richly worked, built up of layers of paint and gesso, then etched all over in a tiny, fine hand."

Preferring a small, intimate canvas, Klee would often depict whimsical humans, animals, and fantastic creatures that somehow symbolize the folly of mankind. In other more abstract works, Klee reworked geometric planes and vectors, as well as such symbols as letters, arrows, musical notation, and stars and moons to represent new meanings, and he worked in a variety of media. Fresh inspirations continued to strike him, such as a trip to Egypt in the winter of 1928-28 that resulted in his depiction of a series of horizontal colorbands that recall archeological digs through the layers of earth of an Egyptian desert. One of his most well-known works, the fanciful and humorous "Twittering Machine" (1922), hangs in the Museum of Modern Art in New York City.

Most of Klee's written works focus on the development of his artistic vision. As aninstructor at the Bauhaus in Weimar and, later, Dessau, he was compelled to formalize the artistic impulses that found their way to his canvases, setting them down on paper for the benefit of his students. Klee's *Pedagogical Sketchbooks,* comprising a series of lectures, was his attempt to define and analyze the major visual elements of color and design, and suggest the various ways these elements could be combined. He was obsessed with the concept of art as an evolutionary process; "Follow the ways of natural creation, the becoming, the functioning of forms," he wrote in *Pedagogical Sketchbooks.* "This is the best school. Then, perhaps, starting from nature you will achieve formations of your own, and one day you may even become like nature yourself and start creating."

During his ten years at Bauhaus Klee became known as one of the greatest theorists of art history; his tenure as a teacher encouraged him to produce a large body of theoretical work that would eventually make its way into English translation in such works as *Klee Speaks in the Bauhaus, 1919-1928,* and the lecture *On Modern Art.* 1956's *The Thinking Eye,* released in English in 1961, presents the first collection of the artist's notebooks; others were transcribed and translated as *The Nature of Nature: The Notebooks,* and *Paul Klee Notebooks,* both published in 1992. 1920's *Creative Credo* includes a number of essays penned on the subject of modern art and its development. In addition to nonfiction, Klee also published poetry, some of which was included in *Gedichte,* portions of which were translated as *Some Poems* in 1962.

Journals Shed Light on Creative Insights

Students and others interested in Klee and his work would have to wait fifteen years after the

Although Klee contracted a crippling disease a few years prior to his death in 1941, the artist produced over 1,500 line drawings, including this one, *Insula Dulcamara,* **from 1938.**

artist's death in 1940 before the personal diaries he kept as an adult were made public. Edited by the artist's son, Felix Klee, the diaries first appeared in Germany in 1957 as *Tagebucher, 1898-1918*, and were translated as *The Diaries*, in 1964. Writing in the *New Statesman* about the 1964 translation of the *Diaries*, reviewer John Willett praised the appearance of the translation. "The appearance of an English . . . version of [Klee's] four early diaries is a great event, and not only for those who already know and love his work," remarked Willett. "For he himself couldn't help being a writer, as well as a violinist of professional standards and a small-scale but utterly beautiful and original painter, and the aids, reflections, verses, jokes, aphorisms with which he filled them are a repeated pleasure to read." Viewing the work from a literary perspective, Willett continued: "These four notebooks which he never showed anybody were written three times, and they show a combination of imagination and compression, of irony and trans-rational exploration, of observation and self-analysis, that can only be compared to Kafka's."

While praised by the art world as a key to the artist, the publication of Klee's diaries did not always receive positive reviews from the literary sphere. Commenting on Klee's *Diaries* in *Spectator*, Michael Podro faulted the work's translation as "uneven," going so far as to pronounce the work poorly edited. Nevertheless, Podro declared, the *Diaries* "are still a delight to read. They are made up of a strange combination of superbly written reflections, descriptions which are vivid and often very funny, prose poems, letters, and lists." While Willett likewise conceded that the "terse, slightly cryptic style sags a bit in translation," he added that within Klee's writing "there are succinct, original thoughts; there are quick, vivid snapshots; there is poetry."

More than half a century after his death, Klee remains an enigma within an era wherein artists were rigorously grouped according to a proliferation of politically and/or philosophically defined "schools." While difficult to fit within any single school due to his innovative approach, the wealth of writing he left behind upon his death—by its lucid examination of both modern art in general and his personal growth as an artist in particular—shows Klee's development nonetheless to have reflected the art world of the early twentieth century. Following a period of initial popular-

If you enjoy the works of Paul Klee, you may also want to check out the following:

The art of Russian-born painter Wassily Kandinsky.
The paintings of Spanish artist Joan Miró.
The works of American painter Jackson Pollack.

ity during the final two decades of his life, by mid-century Klee's work was dismissed by critics as insignificant due to its miniature canvases, and as clichéd in its use of line and symbol. However, a revival of interest in his paintings occurred in the 1980s, triggered by a major exhibit at New York City's Museum of Modern Art. "Klee's whimsy is only skin deep," maintained *New York* contributor Kay Larson. "Down in his heart and guts, he is a tougher, more sophisticated artist than popular prejudice would have it. . . . He played a role in virtually every major early twentieth-century art movement." Larson listed Mark Tobey, Jackson Pollock, and Adoph Gottlieb among those artists indebted to Klee's work.

Summarizing his place within the history of twentieth-century art, essayist McCullagh described Klee thusly in *International Dictionary of Art and Artists*: "His approach to art was a broad and encompassing one which attempted to penetrate the secret underlying rhythms of the creative forces of the universe. Klee's career exhibits a direct and deliberate development. His always personal approach remained consistent with his careful nature and reserved personality." From the viewpoint of his contemporaries he was much more; as early as 1917 artist Marcel Janco was quoted by Larson as stating that within Klee's "beautiful works we saw the reflection of all our efforts to interpret the soul of primitive man, to plunge into the unconscious and the instinctive power of creation."

■ Works Cited

Larson, Kay, "Signs and Symbols," in *New York*, March 2, 1987, pp. 96-97.
McCullagh, Janice, "Paul Klee," in *International Dictionary of Arts and Artists*, Volume 2: *Artists*, St. James Press, 1989, pp. 433-35.

McGuigan, Cathleen, "Whimsical Fun House," in *Newsweek*, February 16, 1987, pp. 70-71.

Podro, Michael, review of *The Diaries of Paul Klee*, in *Spectator*, June 18, 1985, p. 792.

Willett, John, review of *The Diaries of Paul Klee*, in *New Statesman*, July 16, 1965, p. 92.

■ For More Information See

BOOKS

Grohmann, Will, *Klee*, [Paris], 1929, translated, [New York City], 1954, new edition, 1987.

Klee, Paul, *Pedagogical Sketchbook*, [New York City], 1944.

PERIODICALS

Time, January 1, 1965, p. 70.

Times Literary Supplement, July 8, 1965, p. 577; November 5, 1971, p. 1378; April 19, 1974, p. 411; July 18, 1977, p. 298; March 8, 1994, p. 10.

Washington Post Book World, December 9, 1973, p. 4.

ON-LINE

WebMuseum, Paris, http://metalab.unc.edu/louvre/paint/auth/klee (February 9, 1999).*

—Sketch by Michael Wulftang

Dean R. Koontz

■ Personal

Born July 9, 1945, in Everett, PA; son of Ray and Florence Koontz; married Gerda Ann Cerra, October 15, 1966. *Education:* Shippensburg State College, B.A., 1966. *Religion:* Catholic.

■ Addresses

Home—Orange, CA. *Agent*—Robert Gottlieb, William Morris Agency Inc., 1325 Avenue of the Americas, New York, NY 10019.

■ Career

Writer. Teacher-counsellor with Appalachian Poverty Program, 1966-67; high school English teacher in Mechanicsburg, PA, 1967-69.

■ Awards, Honors

Atlantic Monthly creative writing award, 1966, for story "The Kittens"; Hugo Award nomination, World Science Fiction Convention, 1971, for novella *Beastchild*; Daedalus Award, 1988, for *Twilight Eyes*; Litt.D., Shippensburg State College, 1989. Several of Koontz's works have been Literary Guild selections.

■ Writings

NOVELS

Star Quest, Ace Books, 1968.
The Fall of the Dream Machine, Ace Books, 1969.
Fear That Man, Ace Books, 1969.
Anti-Man, Paperback Library, 1970.
Beastchild, Lancer Books, 1970.
Dark of the Woods, Ace Books, 1970.
The Dark Symphony, Lancer Books, 1970.
Hell's Gate, Lancer Books, 1970.
The Crimson Witch, Curtis Books, 1971.
A Darkness in My Soul, DAW Books, 1972.
The Flesh in the Furnace, Bantam, 1972.
Starblood, Lancer Books, 1972.
Time Thieves, Ace Books, 1972.
Warlock, Lancer Books, 1972.
A Werewolf among Us, Ballantine, 1973.
Hanging On, M. Evans, 1973.
The Haunted Earth, Lancer Books, 1973.
Demon Seed, Bantam, 1973.
(Under pseudonym Anthony North) *Strike Deep*, Dial, 1974.
After the Last Race, Atheneum, 1974.
Nightmare Journey, Putnam, 1975.
(Under pseudonym John Hill) *The Long Sleep*, Popular Library, 1975.

Night Chills, Atheneum, 1976.

(Under pseudonym David Axton) *Prison of Ice*, Lippincott, 1976, revised edition publishedunder name Dean R. Koontz as *Icebound*, Random House, 1995.

The Vision, Putnam, 1977.

Whispers, Putnam, 1980.

Phantoms, Putnam, 1983.

Darkfall, Berkley, 1984 (published in England as *Darkness Comes*, W. H. Allen, 1984).

Twilight Eyes, Land of Enchantment, 1985.

(Under pseudonym Richard Paige) *The Door to December*, New American Library, 1985.

Strangers, Putnam, 1986.

Watchers, Putnam, 1987.

Lightning, Putnam, 1988.

Midnight, Putnam, 1989.

The Bad Place, Putnam, 1990.

Cold Fire, Putnam, 1991.

Dean R. Koontz: Three Complete Novels, The Servants of Twilight, Darkfall, Phantoms, Outlet Book Company, 1991.

Dean R. Koontz: A New Collection, Wings Books, 1992.

Hideaway, Putnam, 1992.

Dragon Tears, Putnam, 1992.

Winter Moon, Ballantine Books, 1993.

Mr. Murder, Putnam, 1993.

Dark Rivers of the Heart, Knopf, 1994.

Strange Highways, Warner Books, 1995.

Intensity, Knopf, 1996.

Tick-Tock, Ballantine, 1996.

Beautiful Death, Viking, 1996.

Sole Survivor, Random House, 1996.

UNDER PSEUDONYM DEANNA DWYER

The Demon Child, Lancer, 1971.

Legacy of Terror, Lancer, 1971.

Children of the Storm, Lancer, 1972.

The Dark of Summer, Lancer, 1972.

Dance with the Devil, Lancer, 1973.

UNDER PSEUDONYM K. R. DWYER

Chase, Random House, 1972.

Shattered, Random House, 1973.

Dragonfly, Random House, 1975.

UNDER PSEUDONYM BRIAN COFFEY

Blood Risk, Bobbs-Merrill, 1973.

Surrounded, Bobbs-Merrill, 1974.

The Wall of Masks, Bobbs-Merrill, 1975.

The Face of Fear, Bobbs-Merrill, 1977.

The Voice of the Night, Doubleday, 1981.

Also author, under pseudonym Brian Coffey, of script for *CHIPs* television series, 1978.

UNDER PSEUDONYM LEIGH NICHOLS

The Key to Midnight, Pocket Books, 1979.

The Eyes of Darkness, Pocket Books, 1981, revised edition published under name Dean R. Koontz, Berkley, 1996.

The House of Thunder, Pocket Books, 1982.

Twilight, Pocket Books, 1984.

Shadowfires, Avon, 1987.

UNDER PSEUDONYM OWEN WEST

The Funhouse (novelization of screenplay), Jove, 1980.

The Mask, Jove, 1981.

FOR CHILDREN

Oddkins: A Fable for All Ages, illustrated by Phil Parks, Warner, 1988.

Santa's Twin, illustrated by Parks, HarperPrism, 1996.

OTHER

(With wife, Gerda Koontz) *The Pig Society* (nonfiction), Aware Press, 1970.

(With Gerda Koontz) *The Underground Lifestyles Handbook*, Aware Press, 1970.

Soft Come the Dragons (story collection), Ace Books, 1970.

Writing Popular Fiction, Writer's Digest, 1973.

How to Write Best-Selling Fiction, Writer's Digest, 1981.

Trapped (graphic novel), illustrated by Anthony Bilau, Eclipse Books, 1992.

Contributor to anthologies, including *Again, Dangerous Visions*, edited by Harlan Ellison, Doubleday, 1972; *Future City*, edited by Roger Elwood, Simon & Schuster, 1973; *Children of Infinity*, edited by Elwood, Putnam, 1974.

■ **Adaptations**

Demon Seed was filmed by Metro-Goldwyn-Mayer/Warner Bros. in 1977; *Shattered* was filmed by

Warner Bros. in 1977; and *Watchers* was adapted as a motion picture by Universal in 1988; *Hideaway* was produced as a motion picture in 1995; *Phantoms* was produced as a motion picture by Miramax/Dimension for 1997 release; *Intensity* was filmed by Mandalay Entertainment as a two-part miniseries for broadcast on Fox, 1997. CBS-TV has rights to *Dark Rivers of the Heart.*

■ Sidelights

Dean R. Koontz is an acknowledged master of a hybrid class of books that combine suspense, horror, romance, and science fiction. His more than seventy books have sold in the millions and have been adapted for such successful movies as *Demon Seed, Watchers,* and *Shattered.* Though often dubbed a horror novelist, Koontz himself rejects such labels. In an interview for a critical analysis of his work, *Sudden Fear: The Horror and Dark Suspense Fiction of Dean R. Koontz,* the author noted that "you can't find much hope, love, or optimism incurrent horror, but you can find all the nihilism you want, enough doom-saying and cynicism and pessimism." Koontz views his own work as basically optimistic, showing hard-fought battles between good and evil. A favorite Koontz theme is the conflict between emotion and reason, and the emotional level of his books—a step beyond the usual plot-heavy nature of much of the genre—has drawn in a wide variety of readers, including young adults. *Watchers* was chosen as one of the American Library Association's Best Books for Young Adults in 1987, and his novels *Lightning* and the juvenile *Oddkins* were both selected by the Enoch Pratt Free Library's Young Adult Advisory Board in its Youth-to-Youth reading list.

Koontz's own youth was one he was happy to escape. An only child, he grew up in Pennsylvania. As he once commented, "I began writing when I was a child, for both reading and writing provided much needed escape from the poverty in which we lived and from my father's frequent fits of alcohol-induced violence." While still in college, Koontz started selling his fiction and won an *Atlantic Monthly* fiction contest. Having married and graduated from college in the same year, Koontz took teaching positions for a while, writing in his spare time and selling stories and then novels. Finally he decided to make a try at full-time writing, using an assortment of pseudonyms in various genres, including science fiction, mys-

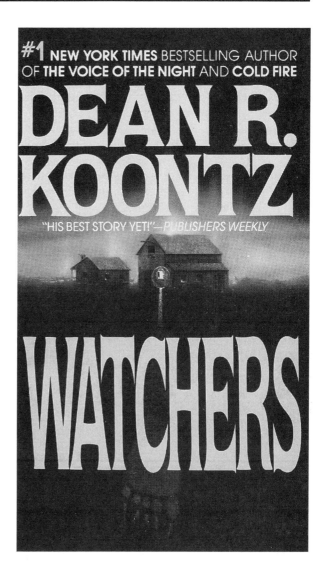

Two mutants created by failed DNA experiments roam the streets of Southern California in this 1987 novel.

tery, and thrillers. "The curse lies in the fact that much of the early work is of lower quality than what came after," Koontz remarked, "both because I was so young and unself-critical and because the low earnings from each book forced me to write a lot of them in order to keep financially afloat."

A *Real* Writer

Koontz marks *Chase,* a suspense novel written under the pseudonym K. R. Dwyer about the after-effects of Vietnam on a veteran, as "the beginning of my *real* career as a writer." He left science fiction behind with that book, and never looked back. Another early book that Koontz looks to as a watershed in terms of technique was the 1973 novel *Hanging On,* about a group of U.S. Army Engineers constructing a bridge in Nazi-held France. *Publishers Weekly* commented that "this book has suspense and, more important, some of the most hilarious scenes that have come along in a long time." Throughout the 1970s Koontz continued to produce several books per year under various pseudonyms, depending upon genre. However, as Koontz pointed out in an interview with Stanley Wiater in *Writer's Digest,* "I began to realize that all these books that were being well-reviewed under pen names were doing absolutely nothing to build my name." His first bestseller, *The Key to Midnight,* was written under the pseudonym Leigh Nichols, and the invisible Mr. Nichols has produced four further titles since then, though in the main Koontz now writes solely under his own name.

"I have attempted, book by book, to speak to the reader's intellect and emotions as well as to his desire for a 'good read'," Koontz once stated. "I believe the best fiction does three things well: tells an involving story, makes the reader think, and makes the reader feel." Koontz's early work in several genres was instrumental in his development of his own unique form of dark suspense, and his addition of humor, romance, and the occult to the brew has created a distinctive niche for him among other writers such as Stephen King and Peter Straub. "My real breakthrough came in 1980 with *Whispers,*" Koontz noted. A bestseller with over five million copies in print worldwide, Whispers is a dark and violent story of childhood cruelty, rape, and murder. Hilary Thomas is a survivor of abusive alcoholic parents who has become a successful screenwriter; sheis attacked by millionaire Bruno Frye, whom she subsequently stabs to death. Bruno, however, returns from the grave to stalk Hilary, and it is left to Hilary's police officer boyfriend to help her unravel the twisted tale of Bruno's childhood to reveal the powers at work in this "slick tale of horror," as Rex E. Klett described the book in *Library Journal.* A *Publishers Weekly* reviewer noted that the "psychological portrait of the sick, sick Bruno makes skin crawl."

THE SPELLBINDING **NEW YORK TIMES** BESTSELLER BY THE AUTHOR OF **WATCHERS** AND **MIDNIGHT**

DEAN R. KOONTZ

LIGHTNING

"A gripping novel... fast-paced and satisfying!" —*People*

In this work, popular novelist Laura Shane learns that an old friend is actually a time traveler now being pursued by killers from his own era.

Investigates the Supernatural

With *Phantoms* and *Darkfall,* Koontz made what he termed "sidesteps in my career," novels of horror and the supernatural which were long investigations of rational versus irrational belief, of technology versus emotion. The 1986 work *Strangers* forms a duo with *Whispers* that Koontz sees as benchmarks that he strives to maintain. "Without doubt, both novels have strong suspenseful plots, as well, and I intend that all of my future novels will be what are called 'page-turners'," Koontz once remarked. "However, the older I get the more I find that well-drawn characters and vivid backgrounds are just as important as plot to the success of a book."

When Frank Pollard, a sleepwalker, hires a husband-and-wife detective team to follow him at night, the two uncover more than their client's sleeping problem in this 1990 work.

The misuse of science is at the heart of the author's 1987 novel, *Watchers,* a book which also began to win Koontz a large audience among young adult readers. Recombinant DNA experiments go wrong at a government lab, and suddenly two mutants—one with human intelligence to be used for spying and the other a killer—are on the loose in Southern California. The intelligent mutant, a golden retriever, is pursued by the killer mutant, named Outsider, a blend of ape and dog. Soon two humans become involved in helping the dog, nicknamed Einstein, as well as themselves, escape the wrath of Outsider. Subplots

abound and a love interest figures between the two human protagonists, Travis and Nora. In short, Koontz had produced a blockbuster novel, and one which was chosen for the ALA Best Books for Young Adults list that year. As with all bestsellers, however, Koontz's books have their critics, including Audrey B. Eaglen, who described *Watchers* in *School Library Journal* as "about as horrifying as warm milk toast." Others disagreed, including *New York Times Book Review* contributor Katherine Weber, who had special praise for Einstein, calling the dog "the most richly drawn character in the book."

In *Lightning,* a tale somewhat reminiscent of *Whispers,* Koontz tells the story of Laura Shane, a successful novelist who has overcome a difficult childhood. A blind man who has helped Shane out at various difficult and dangerous times of her life reveals to her that he is a time traveller and is being pursued by killers from his own era. While some reviewers complained of over-plotting in this suspense novel, Dick Lochte noted in the *Los Angeles Times Book Review* that Koontz was "particularly skilled at setting up believable characters and situations." The novel was included on one list of recommended books for young adults. Christy Tyson, reviewing a later Koontz novel in *Voice of Youth Advocates,* analyzed the trend of Koontz's increasing YA popularity. She commented that YA horror readers looking for something beyond Stephen King were more and more turning to Koontz. "His stories are smoothly told, his premises well-developed, and his characters often more approachable. . . . In addition he often features characters and themes that strike home with young adult readers and adds touches of genuine warmth and humor."

One Koontz creation aimed specifically at the juvenile market, though called by the publishers "afable for all ages," is *Oddkins.* A fantastic setting is the venue for the author's usual theme of the battle between good and evil. Magical toys have been created for the children in *Oddkins,* toys which help kids when they need a special secret friend. These Oddkins are actually alive and have the power of speech, though they look and feel like simple stuffed toys. When the child is old and strong enough to be on his or her own, the Oddkins return once again to their inanimate state, and for the child they are simply a fond memory. But when evil toys created by another toymaker escape from the cellar of the toy factory, they must

First published in 1983, *Phantoms* was produced as a motion picture by Miramax/Dimension in 1997, featuring Peter O'Toole and Rose McGowan.

be stopped by the Oddkins. Once again, Koontz sends an optimistic message through his fiction, though painted in rather black and white terms. A *Publishers Weekly* commentator noted that *Oddkins* has "enough excitement and humor to hold a child's attention" although it might not appeal as much to adult readers. In 1996 Koontz again produced a picture book dealing with themes of good vs. evil; *Santa's Twin* presents the story of Father Christmas as he tries to save the holiday season from his evil double.

Throughout the 1990s, Koontz has maintained a string of bestsellers, from *The Bad Place*, which *Los Angeles Times Book Review* critic Don G. Campbell described as being "as close to actual physical terror as the printed word can deliver," to *Hideaway*, *Mr. Murder*, *Dragon Tears*, *Winter Moon*, *Dark Rivers of the Heart*, and *Intensity*. With all these titles Koontz continues to employ his blending of

genres. As Edward Bryant noted in *Locus*, "Koontz successfully does what most editors warn their writers not to do. He crosses genre boundaries with impunity. . . . He simply does pretty much what he wants, and the novels are then categorized as 'Dean R. Koontz books.'" In any genre, the critic added, Koontz "knows how to sink a narrative hook." Additionally, the author peppers his books with his own particular message. As he once remarked, he finds "the human species—and Western culture—to be primarily noble, honorable, and admirable. In an age when doomsayers are to be heard in every corner of the land, I find great hope in our species and in the future we will surely make for ourselves. . . . I think we live in a time of marvels, not a time of disaster, and I believe we can solve every problem that confronts us if we keep our perspectives and our freedom."

The Dark Side of Society

If the dangers of rampant technology is one of the major themes of his earlier works, a foreboding of social decay runs like a thread through later books. In *Dragon Tears,* two police officers have to battle a serial killer with mutant powers, a stand-in for modern rot. "Koontz gets a bit preachy about social decay," commented a *Kirkus Reviews* critic, "but his action never flags in this vise-tight tale." Evil stalks a family in *Mr. Murder,* in the guise of a monster killer. Similarly urban evil seems to follow a family as it resettles from Los Angeles to Montana in *Winter Moon,* as creatures from another dimension give this ex-urban family no peace. A *Publishers Weekly* reviewer called *Winter Moon* a "gripping parable about the real cost of 'getting away from it all.'"

A libertarian theme comes through in *Dark Rivers of the Heart,* in which a secret federal agency is trying to take over the country. The villain of the piece is not a right-wing extremist, but a liberal sociopath. And as in *Watchers* and *Dragon Tears,* there is a lovable dog to round out the human protagonists. "Expect this yarn to be denounced as right-wing alarmist trash by some," noted Ray Olson in *Booklist,* "hailed as a libertarian warning by others, and, like virtually everything Koontz writes, read by millions." *New York Times Book Review* contributor Jay E.Rosen observed that Koontz had succeeded in leaving the supernatural behind; "he has switched gears . . . and written a believable high-tech thriller."

From serial killers to out-of-control technology, Koontz has surveyed the darker regions of life. His novels not only address modern times but, in their depiction of violence, are mirrors of them as well. "I strongly believe that, in addition to entertaining, it is the function of fiction to explore the way we live, reinforce our noble traits, and suggest ways to improve the world where we can," Koontz once stated. Yet as reviewer Paul Wilner noted in the *Los Angeles Times Book Review,* the very popularity of Koontz's novels "indicates something disturbing about our fascination with military violence and violence in our own souls. . . . This broader fascination betokens problems that can't be resolved through wish-fulfillment fiction." Whether or not Koontz's novels are a reflection of today's social malaises, as some critics say, or are part of the solution, as Koontz contends, one thing is certain: Dean R. Koontz

If you enjoy the works of Dean R. Koontz, you may also want to check out the following books and films:

Michael Crichton, *Congo,* 1980.
Stephen King, *Firestarter*, 1980.
John Saul, *Creature*, 1989.
Jurassic Park, a film by Steven Spielberg, 1993.

keeps his readers turning pages and sitting on the edges of their seats.

■ Works Cited

Bryant, Edward, review of *The Bad Place, Locus,* March, 1990, pp. 67- 68.

Campbell, Don G., review of *The Bad Place, Los Angeles Times Book Review,* January 21, 1990, p. 12.

Review of *Dragon Tears, Kirkus Reviews,* November 1, 1992, p. 1327.

Eaglen, Audrey B., "Stunners to Stinkers: The '87 BBYA List," *School Library Journal,* April, 1988, p. 54.

Review of *Hanging On, Publishers Weekly,* September 10, 1973, p. 41.

Klett, Rex E., review of *Whispers, Library Journal,* May 15, 1980, p. 1187.

Koontz, Dean, interview in *Sudden Fear: The Horror and Dark Suspense Fiction of Dean R. Koontz,* edited by Bill Munster, Starmont House, 1988, p. 182.

Lochte, Dick, "The Perils of Little Laura," *Los Angeles Times Book Review,* January 31, 1988, p. 8.

Review of *Oddkins, Publishers Weekly,* September 2, 1988, pp. 87-88.

Olson, Ray, review of *Dark Rivers of the Heart, Booklist,* September 15, 1994, p. 84.

Rosen, Jay E., review of *Dark Rivers of the Heart, New York Times Book Review,* November 13, 1994, p. 58.

Tyson, Christy, review of *Dragon's Tears, Voice of Youth Advocates,* October, 1993, p. 230.

Weber, Katherine, review of *Watchers, New York Times Book Review,* March 15, 1987, p. 16.

Review of *Whispers, Publishers Weekly,* April 4, 1980, p. 61.

Wiater, Stanley, interview with Dean R. Koontz in *Writer's Digest,* November, 1989, pp. 34-38.

Wilner, Paul, review of *Watchers, Los Angeles Times Book Review,* March 8, 1987, p. 6.

Review of *Winter Moon, Publishers Weekly,* January 10, 1994, pp. 56-57.

■ For More Information See

BOOKS

Greenberg, Martin H., and Ed Gorman and Bill Munster, editors, *The Dean Koontz Companion,* Berkley Books, 1994.

Kotker, Joan G., *Dean Koontz: A Critical Companion,* Greenwood Press, 1996.

Munster, Bill, *Dean R. Koontz's Cold Terror,* Underwood-Miller, 1990.

Munster, Bill, editor, *Discovering Dean Koontz: Essays on America's Bestselling Writer of Suspense and Horror Fiction,* R. Reginald, 1995.

Twentieth-Century Young Adult Writers, St. James Press, 1994.

PERIODICALS

Kliatt, March, 1993, p. 8; May, 1993, p. 45; July, 1994, p. 50; November, 1994, p. 61; January, 1995, p. 9.

Library Journal, November 15, 1992, p. 120; March 1, 1993, p. 122; February 1, 1994, p. 128; May 1, 1994, p. 154; September 1, 1994, p. 215; August, 1995, p. 138; December, 1995, p. 156; March 1, 1996, p. 126.

New York Times Book Review, January 31, 1993, p. 20; October 31, 1993, p. 18.

Publishers Weekly, November 4, 1996, p. 20; December 14, 1998, pp. S1-S18.

Wilson Library Bulletin, October, 1992, p. 96; March, 1993, p. 71; May, 1993, p. 102.

—Sketch by J. Sydney Jones

Norman Mailer

44th Street, New York, NY 10036. *Agent*—Scott Meredith, Inc., 580 Fifth Ave., New York, NY 10022.

■ Personal

Born January 31, 1923, in Long Branch, NJ; son of Isaac Barnett (an accountant) and Fanny (owner of a small business; maiden name, Schneider) Mailer; married Beatrice Silverman, 1944 (divorced, 1952); married Adele Morales (an artist), 1954 (divorced, 1962); married Lady Jeanne Campbell, 1962 (divorced, 1963); married Beverly Rentz Bentley (an actress), 1963 (divorced, 1980); married Carol Stevens, 1980 (divorced, 1980); married Norris Church (an artist), 1980; children: (first marriage) Susan; (second marriage) Danielle, Elizabeth Anne; (third marriage) Kate; (fourth marriage) Michael Burks, Stephen McLeod; (fifth marriage) Maggie Alexandra; (sixth marriage) John Buffalo. *Education:* Harvard University, S.B. (cum laude), 1943; graduate studies at Sorbonne, Paris, France, 1947-48. *Politics:* "Left Conservative." *Hobbies and other interests:* Skiing, sailing, boxing, hiking.

■ Addresses

Home—142 Columbia Heights, Brooklyn, NY; Provincetown, MA. *Office*—c/o Rembar, 19 West

■ Career

Writer. Producer and director of and actor in films, including *Wild 90,* 1967, and *Maidstone: A Mystery,* 1968; producer of film *Beyond the Law,* 1967; actor in films, including *Ragtime,* 1981, *King Lear,* 1987, and *When We Were Kings,* 1996; director of films, including *Tough Guys Don't Dance,* 1987, and *Ringside,* 1999. Lecturer at colleges and universities, 1950-89; candidate for democratic nomination in mayoral race, New York City, 1960 and 1969. Co-founding editor of *Village Voice;* founder, Fifth Estate (merged with Committee for Action Research on the Intelligence Community), 1973. *Wartime service:* U.S. Army, 1944-46, field artillery observer; became infantry rifleman serving in the Philippines and Japan. *Member:* PEN (president of American Center, 1984-86), American Academy and Institute of Arts and Letters, National Institute of Arts and Letters.

■ Awards, Honors

Story magazine college fiction prize, 1941, for "The Greatest Thing in the World"; National Institute and American Academy grant in literature, 1960; elected to National Institute of Arts and Letters,

1967; National Book Award nomination, 1967, for *Why Are We in Vietnam?*; National Book Award for nonfiction, 1968, for *Miami and the Siege of Chicago;* National Book Award for nonfiction, Pulitzer Prize in letters-general nonfiction, and George Polk Award, all 1969, all for *Armies of the Night;* Edward MacDowell Medal, MacDowell Colony, 1973, for outstanding service to the arts; National Arts Club Gold Medal, 1976; National Book Critics Circle nomination, Notable Book citation from the American Library Association, and Pulitzer Prize in letters, all 1979, and American Book Award nomination, 1980, all for *The Executioner's Song;* Emmy nomination for best adaptation, for script for *The Executioner's Song;* University of Pennsylvania Pappas fellowship; Rose Award, Lord & Taylor, 1985, for public accomplishment; Emerson-Thoreau Medal for lifetime literary achievement, American Academy of Arts and Sciences, 1989.

■ Writings

NOVELS

The Naked and the Dead, Rinehart, 1948.

Barbary Shore, Rinehart, 1951.

The Deer Park (also see below), Putnam, 1955, with preface and notes by Mailer, Berkley, 1976.

An American Dream (originally serialized in *Esquire*, 1964), Dial, 1965.

Why Are We in Vietnam?, Putnam, 1967, with preface by Mailer, 1977.

A Transit to Narcissus: A Facsimile of the Original Typescript with an Introduction by the Author, Fertig, 1978.

The Executioner's Song (also see below), Little, Brown, 1979.

Ancient Evenings, Little, Brown, 1983.

Tough Guys Don't Dance (also see below), Random House, 1984.

Harlot's Ghost, Random House, 1991.

The Gospel according to the Son, Random House, 1997.

Also author of *No Percentage*, 1941.

NONFICTION NARRATIVES

The Armies of the Night: History as a Novel, the Novel as History, New American Library, 1968.

Miami and the Siege of Chicago, New American Library, 1968, published as *Miami and the Siege of Chicago: An Informal History of the American Political Conventions of 1968*, Weidenfeld & Nicolson (London), 1969.

Of a Fire on the Moon (originally published in *Life* magazine), Little, Brown, 1970, published as *A Fire on the Moon*, Weidenfeld & Nicolson, 1970.

King of the Hill: On the Fight of the Century (also see below), New American Library, 1971.

St. George and the Godfather, New American Library, 1972.

The Fight, Little, Brown, 1975.

How the Wimp Won the War, Lord John Press, 1991.

NONFICTION

The White Negro: Superficial Reflections on the Hipster (essays; includes "Communications: Reflections on Hipsterism"; "The White Negro" originally published in *Dissent*, 1957; also see below), City Lights, 1957.

The Bullfight: A Photographic Narrative with Text by Norman Mailer (with record of Mailer reading from text; also see below), CBS Legacy Collection/Macmillan, 1967.

The Prisoner of Sex (originally published in *Harper's*), Little, Brown, 1971.

Marilyn: A Biography, Grosset & Dunlap, 1973, expanded edition, Warner, 1975.

The Faith of Graffiti (also see below), photographs by Jon Naar, Praeger, 1974, published as *Watching My Name Go By*, Matthews Miller Dunbar (London), 1974.

(Editor and author of introductions) *Genius and Lust: A Journey through the Major Writings of Henry Miller*, Grove, 1976.

Of a Small and Modest Malignancy, Wicked and Bristling with Dots (essay; also see below), Lord John, 1980.

Huckleberry Finn: Alive at One Hundred (booklet; criticism), limited edition, Caliban Press, 1985.

Pablo and Fernande: Portrait of Picasso as a Young Man: An Interpretive Biography, Doubleday, 1994, published as *Portrait of Picasso as a Young Man: An Interpretive Biography*, Atlantic Monthly Press, 1995.

Oswald's Tale: An American Mystery, Random House, 1995.

The Time of Our Time, Random House, 1998.

PLAYS

The Deer Park: A Play (two-act; adaptation of novel *The Deer Park;* produced Off-Broadway, 1967),

Dell, 1967, adapted as *Wild 90* (screenplay), Supreme Mix, 1967.

Beyond the Law (screenplay), Supreme Mix/Evergreen Films, 1968.

Maidstone: A Mystery (film script; includes essay "A Course in Filmmaking"), New American Library, 1971.

The Executioner's Song (screenplay), Film Communication Inc. Productions, 1982.

Tough Guys Don't Dance (screenplay), Zoetrope, 1987.

Strawhead (play), produced at Actors Studio, 1985.

Also author of movie script for a modern version of *King Lear*.

COLLECTIONS

Advertisements for Myself (short stories, verse, articles, and essays), Putnam, 1959, with preface by Mailer, Berkley, 1976.

The Presidential Papers (also see below), Putnam, 1963, with preface by Mailer, 1976.

Cannibals and Christians (also see below), Dial, 1966, abridged edition, Panther, 1979.

The Short Fiction of Norman Mailer (also see below), Dell, 1967.

The Idol and the Octopus: Political Writings on the Kennedy and Johnson Administrations (includes selections from *The Presidential Papers* and *Cannibals and Christians*), Dell, 1968.

The Long Patrol: Twenty-five Years of Writing from the Work of Norman Mailer, edited by Robert F. Lucid, World, 1971.

Existential Errands (includes *The Bullfight: A Photographic Narrative*, "A Course in Filmmaking", and *King of the Hill*; also see below), Little, Brown, 1972.

Some Honorable Men: Political Conventions 1960-72 (narratives), Little, Brown, 1976.

The Essential Mailer (includes *The Short Fiction of Norman Mailer* and *Existential Errands*), New English Library, 1982.

Pieces and Pontifications (essays and interviews; includes *The Faith of Graffiti* and *Of a Small and Modest Malignancy, Wicked and Bristling with Dots*), edited by Michael Lennon, Little, Brown, 1982, published as *Pieces*, 1982, published as *Pontifications: Interviews*, 1982.

CONTRIBUTOR

Writers at Work, Third Series, Viking, 1967.

Running against the Machine: The Mailer-Breslin Campaign, edited by Peter Manso, Doubleday, 1969.

(Author of introduction and captions) *The 1974 Marilyn Monroe Datebook*, photographs by Eve Arnold and others, Simon & Schuster, 1973.

Writer's Choice, edited by Rust Hills, McKay, 1974.

(Author of preface) Hallie Burnett and Whit Burnett, *A Fiction Writer's Handbook*, Harper, 1975.

(Author of foreword) Eugene Kennedy, *St. Patrick's Day with Mayor Daley and Other Things Too Good to Miss*, Seabury, 1976.

(Author of introduction) Abbie Hoffman, *Soon to Be a Major Motion Picture*, Putnam, 1980.

Black Messiah, Vagabond, 1981.

(Author of introduction) Jack Henry Abbott, *In the Belly of the Beast: Letters from Prison*, Random House, 1981.

(Author of foreword) Harold Conrad, *Dear Muffo: Thirty-five Years in the Fast Lane*, Stein & Day, 1982.

(Bill Bronzini, editor) *Combat! Great Tales of World War II*, NAL/Dutton, 1992.

Also contributor to anthologies. Author of column "The Big Bite," *Esquire*, 1962-63; columnist for *Village Voice*, 1946, and for *Commentary*, 1962-63. Contributor to numerous periodicals, including *Harper's*, *Rolling Stone*, *New Republic*, *Playboy*, *New York Times Book Review*, and *Parade*. Contributing editor of *Dissent*, 1953-69; co-founding editor of *Village Voice*, 1955.

OTHER

Deaths for the Ladies and Other Disasters: Being a Run of Poems, Short Poems, Very Short Poems, and Turns of Prose, Putnam, 1962, with introduction by Mailer, New American Library, 1971.

Gargoyle, Guignol, False Closets (booklet; originally published in *Architectural Forum*, 1964), privately printed, 1964.

The Pulitzer Prize for Fiction, Little, Brown, 1967.

Of Women and Their Elegance (fictional interview), photographs by Milton H. Greene, Simon & Schuster, 1980.

The Last Night: A Story (originally published in Esquire, 1962), limited, signed edition, Targ Editions, 1984.

■ Adaptations

The Naked and the Dead was made into a film by Warner Bros. in 1958; *An American Dream* was adapted for film as *See You in Hell, Darling* produced by Warner Bros. in 1966.

■ Sidelights

Since the publication of his first novel, *The Naked and the Dead*, catapulted Norman Mailer to sudden fame in the late 1940s, he has been alternately praised and criticized due to his outspoken opinions regarding U.S. society and politics. With a body of work that includes both fiction and nonfiction and that is characterized by its author's flagrant disregard for literary tradition, Mailer—who *Dictionary of Literary Biography* contributor Andrew Gordon dubbed "the official Bad Boy of contemporary letters"—stands as one of the more controversial, albeit combative, figures within the arena of twentieth-century literature. Respected by some critics for his portrayal of modern culture and his efforts to confront readers' assumptions regarding the relationship between sex, violence, and power in postwar society, Mailer has been reviled by others for his radical political theories, his focus on murder, psychosis, suicide, and other acts of violence, and his invention of new means of expression that shatter the barriers between suchtime-honored classifications as fiction, journalism, and autobiography. Mailer's novels, particularly those written early in his career, often focus on individuals who challenge social or political restraints in their search for self-actualization. Among his nonfiction works are *The Armies of the Night*, published in 1968, 1979's *The Executioner's Song*, and 1991's *Harlot's Ghost*.

Mailer was born to Jewish parents on January 31, 1923, and spent his first three years in Long Branch, New Jersey. In 1927 he and his family moved to Brooklyn, where he attended Hebrew schools, studied the clarinet, and took up model airplane-building as a hobby. He also started writing at an early age, inspired by historical adventure novels such as those by Rafael Sabatini. Showing his versatility even at a young age, Mailer's first work of fiction was a science-fiction tale, while he made his publishing debut with a magazine article about model airplanes. His continued interest in aeronautics inspired Mailer to enroll at Harvard University, where he intended to study engineering; but within a year the precocious Mailer—who had entered Harvard at the age of sixteen—found his passion veering off course as he pursued a newfound interest in writing that was fueled by his exposure to the works of John Steinbeck, Ernest Hemingway, and John Dos Passos.

Literary Talent Transcends Social Hierarchy

Because of his Jewish background and an aggressive personality which had been honed on the streets of Brooklyn, Mailer's efforts to fit in with the predominately WASP student culture at Harvard greatly benefited from his obvious literary talents. Although still following his engineering studies, by his sophomore year he had also become associate editor of the university's literary magazine, the *Harvard Advocate*, and would publish several stories within the *Advocate*'s pages. His first published short story, "The Greatest Thing in the World," would go on to win first place in *Story* magazine's college fiction contest in 1941.

Encouraged by his teachers to continue his efforts at publication, Mailer had several other stories published while he completed his coursework at Harvard, from which he graduated with a B.S. in engineering in 1943. War still raged in theatres across Europe, and it was clear to Mailer that any career he might pursue should be put on hold. A year after graduation he joined the U.S. Army's 112th Cavalry as a rifleman and participated in the invasion of Luzon in the Philippines. Here, too, he found the need to mask his ethnicity, and quickly adopted a Texas accent and the appropriate accompanying mannerisms. Mailer's experiences in the Pacific theatre during World War II would provide much of the inspiration for his first novel, *The Naked and the Dead*.

The Naked and the Dead explores the conflict between individual will and established power through its focus on a U.S. infantry platoon leading an invasion of a Japanese-held island in the Philippines. The story unfolds through the viewpoint of Lieutenant Hearn, a Harvard graduate and a reasonable individual who contrasts his experiences under the leadership of an ambitious and fascist platoon commander named Sergeant Croft with Hearn's recollections of the imperious General Cummings and the general's administration of officers' camp. The fourteen men in Hearn's platoon are a varied crew; two are, like Mailer, Jewish, although one is assimilated and one is not, while a Texan, a Southerner, and other

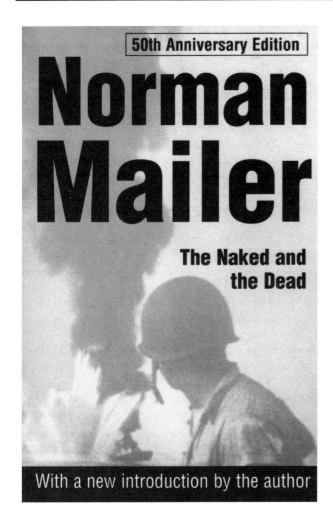

50th Anniversary Edition

Norman Mailer

The Naked and the Dead

With a new introduction by the author

In Mailer's first novel, the limits of each man belonging to a platoon of marines stationed on a Japanese-held island during World War II are tested as they patrol the island's mountainous regions.

men of European-immigrant ancestry round out the crew. A dangerous patrol into the island's mountain regions tests each man's limits, andnot all survive. By telling his story in a dispassionate voice, Mailer prevents the reader from identifying with any one character, but rather focuses attention on the quality of heroism attainable by the average individual, and the manner in which that natural nobility of character is often destroyed by society. As Richard Foster noted in his *Norman Mailer: "The Naked and the Dead* is much more than a 'war novel.'. . . Combat, for Mailer, is the chief means by which the higher laws of life become incarnate in human experience. War is his external subject matter . . . but his internal theme is

the 'crisis in human values'—identity, humanity, man, and the nature of their enemies in our time."

Fiction Debut Receives Instant Acclaim

When *The Naked and the Dead* was published in 1948, the novel was hailed by such critical luminaries as *New York Times Book Review* commentator Orville Prescott, who termed it "the most impressive novel about the Second World War that I have ever read." The massive novel stayed at the *New York Times* bestseller list's number-one spot for eleven weeks in a row, and the favorable criticism heaped on the book made it a literary event. The twenty-five-year-old Mailer suddenly found himself famous, but such early fame would cast a shadow over the rest of his career. As he would later write in his 1959 work *Advertisements for Myself,* "I had the freak of luck to start high on the mountain, and go down sharp while others were passing me."

Discharged in 1946, Mailer attended the Sorbonne in Paris under the G.I. Bill and did not return to the United States until the mid-1950s. During the years immediately following his initial publishing success, Mailer received what could almost be described as a critical backlash as book after book was berated by reviewers. His second novel, 1952's *The Barbary Shore,* which follows the activities of a group of social outcasts living in a Brooklyn rooming house, was characterized by Geoff Sadler in *Contemporary Popular Writers* as "a claustrophobic Cold War tale . . . [wherein the] tense action and violent finish make for disturbing reading." An examination of the individual's struggle against the dictates of art, sex, and money is the subject of Mailer's third novel, *The Deer Park.* The work takes place in a Southern California resort community, as a socially conscious film director attempts to resuscitate his career after being blacklisted by Hollywood producers for refusing to testify before a Congressional investigative committee. Like *The Barbary Shore* before it, *The Deer Park* received a somewhat less than enthusiastic critical reception, reviewer Alfred Kazin calling it "an extraordinarily uneven and somehow sick book with something peculiarly closed and airless about it" in an essay reprinted in his *Contemporaries.* And Brendan Gill asserted in a *New Yorker* review: "Only a writer of the greatest and most reckless talent could have flung [*The Deer Park*] between covers."

Public Life Mirrors Politically Incorrect Fiction

Contributing to Mailer's diminishing literary standing was his tarnished public image. While living in New York City, he hobnobbed with a number of prominent personalities whose acquaintance brought him into public view. As he would later admit in *Advertisements for Myself,* during the late 1950s and into the 1960s he attempted to live according to the values of what he called "the hipster" and set forth in his 1957 essay "The White Negro": "energy, life, sex, force, the Yoga's prana, the Reichian's orgone, Lawrence's blood, Hemingway's 'good,' the Shavian life-force; 'It'; God; not the God of the churches but the unachievable whisper of the mystery within the sex." His personal experimentation with sex, drugs, and alcohol, and his increasingly antisocial behavior resulted in the author's arrest when, after a party on November 19, 1960, he stabbed his wife, Adele, with a penknife. Fortunately for Mailer, Adele refused to press charges and he was able to walk away with a suspended sentence. Unfortunately, he chose not to alter his behavior; in the years following the stabbing his reputation for acts of public rebellion almost overshadowed his literary reputation. On one visit to Provincetown, Massachusetts, Mailer was arrested for fighting with police; later, after patronizing a trendy Manhattan night club, he again was ushered to the inside of a jail, the result of arguing with a bartender over his liquor tab.

Mailer's continued presence in the news continued into the 1970s, propelled by his failed bid for the Democratic nomination for mayor of New York City in 1969 on a platform supporting the Big Apple's secession from New York state. Several failed marriages and a number of offspring also contributed to his reputation as a self-styled "warrior, presumptive general, expolitical candidate, embattled enfant terrible of the literary world, wise father of six children, radical intellectual, existential philosopher, hard-working author,

Mailer wrote the screenplay for this 1982 version of *The Executioner's Song,* featuring Rosanna Arquette and Tommy Lee Jones.

champion of obscenity, husband of four battling sweet wives, amiable bar drinker, and much exaggerated street fighter, party giver, hostess insulter."

Writing as a Constructive Outlet

During the 1950s Mailer had co-founded the leftist Village Voice, thus providing himself with a constructive outlet for some of his aggression toward society, as well as for his vast ego. An outspoken public figure, Mailer continued to agitate the surface of contemporary culture, focusing his combative eye on everything from political campaigns and feminism to boxing, and his writing reflected this tendency. In 1965 he published *An American Dream*, the story of Stephen Rojack, a psychology professor who kills his wealthy but estranged wife and then disappears, exemplifying the Mailer ideal of the barbarian who sheds the confines of respectable society to emerge as a free, unencumbered individual. While a commercial success, the novel produced a mixed response from critics. In *Partisan Review* Elizabeth Hardwick had no second thoughts, describing it as "a very dirty book—dirty and extremely ugly," while *Life* contributor John Aldridge praised *An American Dream* as "a major creative breakthrough."

One of the unifying characteristics of Mailer's fiction during this time was his inclusion of characters that reflect the author himself, such as Lieutenant Hearn in *The Naked and the Dead*, Marion Faye in *The Deer Park*, and Stephen Rojack in *An American Dream*, Another such self-portrait appears in 1968's *The Armies of the Night*, a work that resuscitated its author's literary reputation by winning both the Pulitzer Prize and the National Book Award. Inspired by Mailer's own arrest for crossing the U.S. Federal Marshal's line during an anti-Vietnam march on the Pentagon in 1967, *Armies of the Night* comically inflates Mailer's role in the proceedings to create a sometimes comic portrait of individual orneriness personified by the novel's hero, a character named Norman Mailer, set against a backdrop of social injustice. In an appraisal of the journalistic work for *New Republic* Richard Gilman applauded "the central, rather wonderful achievement of the book, that in it history and personality confront each other with a new sense of liberation." In *Dictionary of Literary Biography*, Gordon called the novel "one of the most influential works of the New Journalism of

the 1960s, a movement in which reporters abandoned the pretense of objectivity toward their subjects and gave subjective responses or even participated in the events they reported."

Insights into Politics and Culture Gain Respect

In 1970 feminist Kate Millett's groundbreaking work *Sexual Politics* placed the ball squarely in Mailer's court. Painted by Millet as the archetypal male chauvinist pig, Mailer responded by participating in a debate on feminism at New York's Town Hall, and publishing *The Prisoner of Sex*, which, when serialized in *Harper's* magazine prior to its hardcover publication, resulted in the largest sales in the magazine's history. Mailer's political focus continued in the nonfiction work *Miami and the Siege of Chicago*, a fictional account of the 1972 national political conventions titled *St. George and the Godfather*, and the nonfiction novel *Why Are We in Vietnam?*, which details a disk jockey's crude impressions of an Alaskan bear hunt as an allegory of U.S. foreign policy during the Vietnam era. From these critiques of U.S. politics and society during the 1960s and 1970s Mailer gained a reputation as a leading commentator on national affairs.

Mailer would win his second Pulitzer Prize in 1979 for his nonfiction novel about the life and ultimate execution of death row inmate Gary Gilmore. Titled *The Executioner's Song*, the work is interesting due to its absence of Mailer's characteristically complex syntax, forceful tone, shocking references, political and philosophical asides, and the overbearing presence of its author throughout. In *The Executioner's Song* Mailer presents the true players in the unfolding drama, from lawyers and cops to friends, reporters, and even victims of Gilmore, allowing readers a view of the world as the murderer and those around him perceived it. Praised by critics, the work would draw comparisons to Truman Capote's seminal nonfiction novel *In Cold Blood*.

Clouded by Negative Press Despite Successes

Despite his status as an award-winning author and his redemption as a respected political analyst, Mailer again became the focus of public controversy after his persuasive and ultimately successful petition to Utah's prison parole board for

Actors Ryan O'Neal and Isabella Rossellini starred in 1987's *Tough Guys Don't Dance*, a film adapted and directed by Mailer from his own novel.

the release of convicted murderer Jack Henry Abbott backfired when Abbott killed again. Mailer had assisted Abbott in finding a publisher for Abbot's book, *In the Belly of the Beast*, after the two men became friends during Mailer's research for *The Executioner's Song*. Mailer was also dogged by financial problems resulting from demands by his numerous ex-wives and their offspring. In an effort to shoulder these monetary responsibilities, which had begun to strain the author's financial resources in the early 1970s, Mailer had begun work on an immense trilogy stretching from the age of antiquity through the present, and into the future. The first volume reached bookstore shelves in 1983. Weighing in at seven hundred pages, *Ancient Evenings* takes place during the nineteenth and twentieth dynasties of Egypt, and follows a royal courtier named Menenhetet through several reincarnations.

While well researched, *Ancient Evenings* suffered from by-now characteristic Mailerisms: a grandi-ose scheme, ornate but almost inscrutable stylistic elements, and the inclusion of excessive amounts of sex and violence. The work received mixed reviews. Panning Mailer's latest in the *New York Times Book Review,* contributor Benjamin DeMott called *Ancient Evenings* everything from "pitiably foolish in conception" to "a disaster." The ever-combative Mailer responded to such criticism by running a full-page advertisement for *Ancient Evenings* in which he juxtaposed scathing reviews of the work with similar attacks on classics by Herman Melville, Leo Tolstoy, and Walt Whitman. Viewed within the context of Mailer's career, *Ancient Evenings* "locates the historical genesis and implications of many of Mailer's ideas concerning sexuality, lineage, violence, public power, society, and religion," according to *Contemporary Novelists* essayist James Gindin. "Critically regarded as either the most probing or most pretentious of Mailer's fictions, *Ancient Evenings* manifests the enormous intellectual risks which the persona [of its author] confronts."

Adopts More Conservative Posture in 1980s

Foiled in his attempt to increase his income through his proposed trilogy, Mailer signed a $4 million contract with Random House to produce four novels within a nine-year period. He also got the publisher to release his mainstream murder mystery *Tough Guys Don't Dance,* which Mailer went on to adapt and direct as a motion picture. With financial backing from a major studio, *Tough Guys Don't Dance* was released in 1987 to good reviews and a positive response at that year's international film festival at Cannes.

While busy working on his film project, the aging Mailer was also seen to become more mellow in his public interactions. By now included among the nation's literary elder statesmen, Mailer became active in the writers' organization PEN (the International Association of Poets, Playwrights, Editors, Essayists, and Novelists), and was voted president of its American Center in 1984. But the organization's annual international PEN Congress, which convened in Manhattan in 1986, showed that Mailer had not lost his ability to create controversy. His decision to invite Secretary of State George Schultz to address the assembly of writers provoked fierce opposition, and this discontent was further fueled by women's factions who attacked Mailer for his male-focused program.

Continuing to delve into political topics, Mailer's more recent novels include *Harlot's Ghost,* which posits a scenario involving the Central Intelligence Agency (C.I.A.) and that agency's involvement in such events as the Cuban missile crisis and the Bay of Pigs during the 1960s. Planned as the first volume of a longer work and written over a seven-year period, the lengthy novel is narrated by Hedrick "Harry" Hubbard, a ghost writer working for the C.I.A. who discovers the agency's clandestine purpose from his mentor, a philosopher agent code-named Harlot. In the first of the novel's two parts, titled "Omega," the time is 1983, and Harlot's body has been discovered washed up on a beach in Chesapeake Bay. In "Alpha," which follows, readers are drawn back to the Cold War years between 1955 and 1963, the time period scrutinized by Harry in his attempts to discover the identity of Harlot's murderer.

Harlot's Ghost received, on balance, positive reviews, although complaints were voiced as to the novel's unwieldy 1,300-odd pages. In the opinion of *New Yorker* contributor Louis Menand, Mailer's ambition to include an entire century within his novel's scope ultimately suffocated the work. While praising the author's fearless examination of the Establishment during the 1960s and 1970s, Menand noted that Mailer "has never written a book so flaccid or so unwilling to challenge and provoke" as *Harlot's Ghost.*

Uncovering the Truth about the Kennedy Assassination

1995's *Oswald's Tale: An American Mystery* would reunite Mailer with his favorite theme: violence. A journalistic examination of the life of presidential assassin Lee Harvey Oswald, the book avoids interjecting fictional elements, instead reflecting Mailer's efforts to uncover the truth about Oswald, the assumed assassin of President John F. Kennedy and a man about whom history has recorded little due to his anonymity and quick death at the hands of a gunman. The book benefits from Mailer's exploration of Oswald's history in the Soviet Union and his activities as a communist. Contemplating Oswald's capacity for independent action in the Kennedy assassination, Mailer concludes that despite the plausibility that the shooting was the culmination of a Soviet-based conspiracy, Oswald had the wherewithal to act alone. Two years later Mailer would return to the distant past to write *The Gospel According to the Son,* a first-person narrative presented as the autobiography of Jesus Christ, which was published in 1997.

Once viewed as the literary successor to Ernest Hemingway, Mailer has instead produced a vast and inconsistent body of work, much of it quickly progressing to obsolescence due to its author's concentration on current events. While critics have acknowledged his energy, his intellect, and his originality, appraisals of Mailer's work are often overshadowed by the author's unflappable determination to interject his own multifaceted persona—political dissident, social critic, radical hipster—within his books. His innovative exploration of journalism, fiction, and nonfiction, while reaching its apex with such highly praised works as *The Armies of the Night* and *The Executioner's Song,* has been offset by works that are consistently cited for their excessive stylization and Mailer's overt political/philosophical badgering.

If you enjoy the works of Norman Mailer, you may also want to check out the following books and films:

Truman Capote, *In Cold Blood,* 1966.
Tom Wolfe, *The Right Stuff,* 1979.
The Thin Red Line, a film by Terence Malick, 1998.

However, Mailer's consistent attempts to break the static of literary tradition with a loud, if sometimes abrasive new voice and engage his critics in debate over controversial issues has been the backbone of his oeuvre. Equal praise has been given to his revealing portraits of U.S. culture, his superior prose style, and his willingness to risk criticism in experimenting with the chemistry of established literary formulas. In spite of himself, Mailer remains among the most important American writers of the twentieth century. Reflecting the opinion of several critics, Andrew O'Hagan praised the author for his courage and originality. "Norman Mailer has been as compulsive a literary character as we've had this half-century, but he has also been among the most compelling on the page," O'Hagan contended in the *London Review of Books.* "He has wasted much of his talent on money-spinning inelegance, and fruitless meanderings and quests into the mysteries of sex and destiny, but he has also risked and emboldened his talent by imagining himself at the core of things."

■ Works Cited

Aldridge, John, review of *An American Dream,* in *Life,* March 19, 1965, p. 12.

DeMott, Benjamin, review of *Ancient Evenings,* in *New York Times Book Review,* April 10, 1983.

Foster, Richard, *Norman Mailer,* University of Minnesota Press, 1968.

Gill, Brendan, review of *The Deer Park,* in *New Yorker,* October 22, 1955.

Gilman, Richard, review of *An American Dream,* in *New Republic,* April 17, 1965, p. 22.

Gindin, James, "Norman Mailer," in *Contemporary Novelists,* sixth edition, St. James Press, 1996.

Gordon, Andrew, "Norman Mailer," in *Dictionary of Literary Biography,* Volume 28: *Twentieth-Century American-Jewish Fiction Writers,* Gale, 1984.

Hardwick, Elizabeth, review of *An American Dream,* in *Partisan Review,* spring, 1965, p. 291.

Kazin, Alfred, "How Good Is Norman Mailer?," in *Contemporaries,* Little, Brown, 1962.

Mailer, Norman, *Advertisements for Myself,* Putnam, 1959.

Menand, Louis, review of *Harlot's Ghost,* in *New Yorker,* November 4, 1991, pp. 113-19.

O'Hagan, Andrew, review of *Oswald's Tale,* in *London Review of Books,* December 14, 1995, pp. 7-9.

Prescott, Orville, review of *The Naked and the Dead,* in *New York Times Book Review,* May 7, 1948.

Sadler, Geoff, "Norman Mailer," in *Contemporary Popular Writers,* St. James Press, 1995.

■ For More Information See

BOOKS

Adams, Laura, *Norman Mailer: A Comprehensive Bibliography,* Scarecrow Press, 1974.

Adams, Laura, editor, *Will the Real Norman Mailer Please Stand Up?,* Kennikat Press, 1974.

Adams, Laura, *Existential Battles: The Growth of Norman Mailer,* Ohio University Press, 1976.

Algeo, Ann M., *The Courtroom as Forum; Homicide Trials by Dreiser, Wright, Capote, and Mailer,* P. Lang, 1996.

Alter, Robert, *Motives for Fiction,* Harvard University Press, 1984.

Amis, Martin, *The Moronic Inferno and Other Visits to America,* J. Cape, 1986.

Anderson, Chris, *Style as Argument: Contemporary American Nonfiction,* Southern Illinois University Press, 1987.

Arlett, Robert, *Epic Voices: Inner and Global Impulse in the Contemporary American and British Novel,* Susquehanna University Press, 1996.

Bailey, Jennifer, *Norman Mailer: Quick-Change Artist,* Harper, 1979.

Begiebing, Robert J., *Acts of Regeneration: Allegory and Archetype in the Works of Norman Mailer,* University of Missouri Press, 1980.

Bloom, Harold, editor, *Norman Mailer,* Chelsea House, 1986.

Braudy, Leo Beal, editor, *Norman Mailer: A Collection of Critical Essays,* Prentice-Hall, 1972.

Bufithis, Philip H., *Norman Mailer,* Ungar, 1978.

Concise Dictionary of American Literary Biography: Broadening Views, 1968-1988, Gale, 1989.

Contemporary Authors Bibliographical Series, Volume 1: *American Novelists,* Gale, 1986.

Contemporary Literary Criticism, Gale, Volume 1, 1979, Volume 2, 1974, Volume 3, 1975, Volume 4, 1975, Volume 5, 1976, Volume 8, 1978, Volume 11, 1979, Volume 14, 1980, Volume 28, 1984, Volume 39, 1986, Volume 74, 1993.

Dictionary of Literary Biography, Gale, Volume 2: *American Novelists since World War II,* 1978, Volume 16: *The Beats: Literary Bohemians in Postwar America,* 1983.

Dictionary of Literary Biography Documentary Series, Gale, Volume 3, 1983.

Dictionary of Literary Biography Yearbook, Gale, *1980,* 1981, *1983,* 1984.

Ehrlich, Robert, *Norman Mailer: The Radical as Hipster,* Scarecrow Press, 1978.

Girgus, Sam B., *The New Covenant: Jewish Writers and the American Idea,* University of North Carolina Press, 1984.

Glenday, Michael K., *Norman Mailer,* St. Martin's Press, 1995.

Gordon, Andrew, *An American Dreamer: A Psychoanalytic Study of the Fiction of Norman Mailer,* Farleigh Dickinson University Press, 1980.

Guest, David, *Sentenced to Death: The American Novel and Capital Punishment,* University Press of Mississippi (Jackson), 1997.

Gutman, Stanley T., *Mankind in Barbary: The Individual and Society in the Novels of Norman Mailer,* University Press of New England, 1975.

Jackson, Richard, *Norman Mailer,* University of Minnesota Press, 1968.

Kazin, Alfred, *Bright Book of Life: American Novelists and Storytellers from Hemingway to Mailer,* Little, Brown, 1973.

Kellman, Steven, G., *Loving Reading: Erotics of the Text,* Archon, 1985.

Kernan, Alvin B., *The Imaginary Library: An essay on Literature and Society,* Princeton University Press, 1982.

Leeds, Barry H., *The Structured Vision of Norman Mailer,* New York University Press, 1969.

Leigh, Nigel, *Radical Fictions and the Novels of Norman Mailer,* St, Martin's Press, 1990.

Lennon, J. Michael, editor, *Critical Essays on Norman Mailer,* G. K. Hall, 1986.

Lennon, J. Michael, editor, *Conversations with Norman Mailer,* University Press of Mississippi, 1988.

Lounsberry, Barbara, *The Art of Fact: Contemporary Artists of Nonfiction,* Greenwood Press, 1990.

Lucid, Robert F., editor, *Norman Mailer: The Man and His Work,* Little, Brown, 1971.

Mailer, Adele, *The Last Party: Scenes from My Life with Norman Mailer,* Barricade Books, 1997.

Manso, Peter, *Mailer: His Life and Times,* Simon & Schuster, 1985.

Merrill, Robert, *Norman Mailer,* G. K. Hall, 1978.

Middlebrook, Jonathan, *Mailer and the Times of His Time,* Bay Books (San Francisco), 1976.

Millett, Kate, *Sexual Politics,* Doubleday, 1970.

Mills, Hilary, *Mailer: A Biography,* Empire, 1982.

Poirier, Richard, *Norman Mailer,* Viking, 1972.

Radford, Jean, *Norman Mailer: A Critical Study,* Harper, 1975.

Rollyson, Carl, *The Lives of Norman Mailer: A Biography,* Paragon House, 1991.

Sokoloff, B. A., *A Biography of Norman Mailer,* Darby Books, 1969.

Solotaroff, Robert, *Down Mailer's Way,* University of Illinois Press, 1974.

Sorkin Adam J., editor, *Politics and the Muse: Studies in the Politics of Recent American Literature,* Bowling Green State University Popular Press, 1989.

Weatherby, William J., *Squaring Off: Mailer vs. Baldwin,* Mason/Charter, 1977.

Wenke, Joseph, *Mailer's America,* University Press of New England, 1987.

PERIODICALS

American Spectator, April, 1992, p. 78.

Atlantic, July, 1971; September, 1984; May, 1995, pp. 120-25.

Canadian Review of American Studies, fall, 1986.

Chicago Tribune, December 20, 1982; September 21, 1987.

Contemporary Literature, winter, 1990.

Criticism, spring, 1987.

Esquire, June, 1966; December, 1968; June, 1986; May, 1995, p. 142.

Film Comment, August, 1987.

Journal of American Studies, December, 1987; December, 1990.

Life, September 24, 1965; February 24, 1967; September 15, 1967.

London Review of Books, November 7, 1991.

Los Angeles Times, September 23, 1984.

Los Angeles Times Book Review, December 14, 1980; July 11, 1982; April 24, 1983; August 19, 1984; October 15, 1995, pp. 2, 15.

Maclean's, December 2, 1991, p. 90; June 5, 1995, p. 69.

Michigan Quarterly Review, summer, 1989.

Modern Fiction Studies, spring, 1987.

Nation, May 27, 1968; June 25, 1983; September 15, 1984; November 6, 1995, p. 543.

National Review, April 20, 1965; November 4, 1991, p. 54; August 28, 1995, p. 42; February 12, 1996, p. 50.

New Criterion, January, 1992.

New Republic, February 9, 1959; February 8, 1964; June 8, 1968; January 23, 1971; May 2, 1983; August 27, 1984; November 25, 1991, p. 42; July 17, 1995, p. 46.

New Statesman, September 29, 1961.

Newsweek, December 9, 1968; April 18, 1983; August 6, 1984; April 24, 1995, p. 60.

New York, September 28, 1987; September 11, 1995, p. 80; October 16, 1995, p. 28.

New Yorker, October 23, 1948; April 10, 1995, p. 56; December 11, 1995, p. 42.

New York Review of Books, May 6, 1971; June 15, 1972; December 5, 1991, pp. 41-48; May 11, 1995, p. 52; June 22, 1995, p. 7; January 11, 1996, pp. 4-8.

New York Times, October 27, 1968; April 28, 1983; December 23, 1985; September 22, 1991, p. 28.

New York Times Book Review, September 17, 1967; May 5, 1968; October 27, 1968; January 10, 1971; February 18, 1972; October 7, 1979; September 20, 1980; December 7, 1980; June 6, 1982; January 30, 1983; April 10, 1983; July 20, 1984; July 29, 1984; April 11, 1985; September 29, 1991; April 30, 1995, pp. 1, 32; October 15, 1995, p. 16.

New York Times Sunday Magazine, September, 1979.

Partisan Review, fall, 1965; summer, 1967; July, 1980.

People, May 30, 1983; October 5, 1987.

Publishers Weekly, March 22, 1965; October 8, 1979; March 20, 1995, p. 48; June 5, 1995, p. 34; September 11, 1995, p. 69.

Saturday Review, January, 1981.

Sight and Sound, spring, 1987.

Texas Studies in Literature and Language, summer, 1986.

Time, May 28, 1951; June 28, 1982; April 18, 1983; January 27, 1986; September 30, 1991, p. 70; May 1, 1995, p. 94.

Times (London), June 10, 1983.

Times Literary Supplement, October 3, 1968; January 11, 1980; March 6, 1981; December 10, 1982; June 10, 1983; October 19, 1984.

Tribune Books (Chicago), October 7, 1979; November 30, 1980; June 13, 1982; April 10, 1983; August 5, 1984; July 14, 1985.

Village Voice, February 18, 1965; January 21, 1971.

Washington Post, August 22, 1989.

Washington Post Book World, July 11, 1970; October 14, 1979; November 30, 1980; July 11, 1982; April 10, 1983; August 12, 1984; November 24, 1985; November 5, 1995, pp. 1, 10.

Yale Review, February, 1986.

—Sketch by Nancy Rae Tarcher

Richard Matheson

■ Personal

Born February 20, 1926, in Allendale, NJ; son of Bertolf (a tile floor installer) and Fanny (Mathieson) Matheson; married Ruth Ann Woodson, July 1, 1952; children: Richard, Alison, Chris, Bettina. *Education:* University of Missouri, B.A., 1949. *Hobbies and other interests:* Musical composition, theatre, amateur acting.

■ Addresses

Office—P.O. Box 81, Woodland Hills, CA 91365. *Agent*—Don Congdon Associates, 156 Fifth Ave., New York, NY 10010.

■ Career

Television and screenwriter, novelist, short story writer, and playwright. *Member:* Writers Guild, Dramatists Guild.

■ Awards, Honors

Hugo Award for best motion picture, World Science Fiction Convention, 1958, for *The Incredible Shrinking Man;* guest of honor at World Science Fiction Convention, 1958, 1976; Writers Guild award, 1973, for best anthology adapted from another medium; World Fantasy award for best novel, 1976, for *Bid Time Return.*

■ Writings

Born of Man and Woman (short stories), Chamberlain Press, 1954, abridged edition published as *Third from the Sun,* Bantam, 1970.
Fury on Sunday (novel), Lion Books, 1954.
I Am Legend (novel), Fawcett, 1954, reprinted as *The Omega Man: I Am Legend,* Berkley Publishing, 1971.
Someone Is Bleeding (novel), Lion Books, 1954.
The Shrinking Man (novel; also see below), Fawcett, 1956.
The Shores of Space (short stories), Bantam, 1957.
A Stir of Echoes (novel), Lippincott, 1958.
Ride the Nightmare (novel), Ballantine, 1959.
The Beardless Warriors (novel; also see below), Little, Brown, 1960.
Shock: Thirteen Tales to Thrill and Terrify, Dell, 1961, reprinted as *Shock I,* Berkley Publishing, 1979.
Shock II (short stories), Dell, 1964.
Shock III (short stories), Dell, 1966.
Shock Waves (short stories), Dell, 1970.
Hell House (novel; also see below), Viking, 1971.
Bid Time Return (novel; also see below), Viking, 1975, published as *Somewhere in Time,* Tor, 1980.
What Dreams May Come (novel), Putnam, 1978.

(As Logan Swanson) *Earthbound,* Playboy (New York City), 1982, under name Richard Matheson, Tor (New York City), 1994.

(With others) *The Twilight Zone: The Original Stories,* Avon (New York City), 1985.

Journal of the Gun Years: Being Choice Selections from the Authentic Never-before-printed Diary of the Famous Gunfighter-lawman Clay Halser! Whose Deeds of Daring Made His Name a By-word of Terror in the Southwest between the Years of 1866 and 1876, M. Evans (New York City), 1991.

By the Gun: Six from Richard Matheson, M. Evans, 1993.

The Path: Metaphysics for the '90s (nonfiction), Capra Press (Santa Barbara, CA), 1993.

Seven Steps to Midnight, Forge (New York City), 1993.

The Gun Fight, M. Evans, 1993.

Shadow on the Sun, M. Evans, 1994.

Now You See It. . ., Tor, 1995.

Robert Bloch: Appreciations of the Master, Tor, 1995.

The Memoirs of Wild Bill Hickock, Jove (New York City), 1995.

SCREENPLAYS

The Incredible Shrinking Man (adapted from Matheson's novel, *The Shrinking Man*), Universal, 1957.

(With Lewis Meltzer) *The Beat Generation,* Metro-Goldwyn-Mayer, 1959.

The House of Usher (adapted from the novel *The Fall of the House of Usher* by Edgar Allan Poe), American International, 1960.

The Pit and the Pendulum (adapted from the short story by Poe), American International, 1961.

Master of the World (adapted from two novels by Jules Verne, *Master of the World* and *Robur, the Conqueror*), American International, 1961.

Tales of Terror (adapted from four short stories by Poe: "Facts in the Case of M. Valdemar," "Morella," "The Black Cat," and "Cask of Amontillado"), American International, 1962.

(With Charles Beaumont) *Burn, Witch, Burn* (adapted from the novel *Conjure Wife* by Fritz Lieber), American International, 1962.

The Raven (adapted from the poem by Poe), American International, 1963.

The Comedy of Terrors, American International, 1964.

Die! Die! My Darling! (adapted from the novel *Nightmare* by Anne Blaisdell), Columbia, 1965.

The Young Warriors (adapted from Matheson's own novel, *The Beardless Warriors*), Universal, 1967.

The Devil's Bride (adapted from the novel *The Devil Rides Out* by Dennis Wheatley), Twentieth Century-Fox, 1968.

De Sade, American International, 1969.

Legend of Hell House (adapted Matheson's own novel, *Hell House*), Twentieth Century-Fox, 1973.

Somewhere in Time (adapted from own novel, *Bid Time Return*), Universal, 1980.

(With George Clayton Johnson and Mellisa Mathison [writing as Josh Rogan]) *Twilight Zone—The Movie,* Warner Bros., 1983.

(With Carl Gottlieb) *Jaws 3D,* Universal, 1983.

(With Richard Christian Matheson) *Loose Cannons,* Tristar, 1990.

TELEPLAYS

Duel (adapted from Matheson's short story), American Broadcast Corp. (ABC-TV), 1971.

Ghost Story, National Broadcast Corp. (NBC-TV), 1972.

The Night Stalker, ABC-TV, 1972.

The Night Strangler, ABC-TV, 1973.

Dying Room Only, ABC-TV, 1973.

Scream of the Wolf, ABC-TV, 1973.

Dracula, Columbia Broadcast System (CBS-TV), 1974.

Trilogy of Terror, ABC-TV, 1974.

The Stranger Within, ABC-TV, 1974.

The Morning After, ABC-TV, 1974.

Dead of Night, ABC-TV, 1975.

The Strange Possession of Mrs. Oliver, NBC-TV, 1977.

The Martian Chronicles (mini-series; adapted from the novel by Ray Bradbury), NBC-TV, 1980.

Also author of teleplays for *The Dreamer of Oz,* 1990; *Twilight Zone: Rod Serling's Lost Classics,* 1994; and *Trilogy of Terror II,* 1996. Author of numerous other scripts for television programs, including *Lawman, Twilight Zone, Star Trek, Girl from U.N.C.L.E.,* and *Chrysler Playhouse.*

■ Sidelights

Richard Matheson has enjoyed a long career as a writer of films, television scripts, novels, and short stories. His work is characterized by ordinary characters who suddenly find themselves in bizarre, often threatening circumstances. As Gary K. Wolfe notes in *Twentieth- Century Science-Fiction Writers,* Matheson has "a gift for imagining almost archetypal situations of paranoia and loss of con-

I AM LEGEND

"The most clever and riveting vampire novel since *Dracula*."
– Dean Koontz

RICHARD MATHESON

Originally published in 1954, this novel about one man's struggle against a world of vampires is considered one of the top novels of vampirism.

trol. . . . Matheson's technique is to assume a single fantastic premise and explore it with a rigor and logic that belies the sensational aspects of the initial premise." Stefan Dziemianowicz explains in the *St. James Guide to Horror, Ghost, and Gothic Writers* that "the key to Matheson's fiction and its unsettling effect is his style, which is as plain and simple as the ordinary objects he imbues with malice. His prose is straightforward, and devoid of the portentous descriptions many horror writers use to create atmosphere. The almost clinical quality of his writing actually adds gravity to his horrors by giving them a solid and seemingly irrefutable basis in reality, no matter how outlandish they seem at first." Among the most popular films based on Matheson's screenplays are *The Incredible Shrinking Man, The House of Usher, Duel,*

The Legend of Hell House, Somewhere in Time and *Twilight Zone—The Movie*. He also has written classic episodes of *The Twilight Zone* television program, nearly a hundred short stories, and many popular novels.

Matheson was born in Allendale, New Jersey, and raised in Brooklyn, New York. He served in the U.S. Army during World War II, then attended the University of Missouri to study journalism. While in college, Matheson first became a "published" writer when his music reviews appeared in the campus magazine *Columbian Missourian*. After college, he took a job as a linotype operator and wrote short stories at night. When his stories began selling regularly to magazines in the late 1940s, Matheson made the commitment to became a freelance writer. He lives with his wife, Ruth, in Woodland Hills, California; the couple has four grown children.

In 1961 Matheson drew on his military background to write *The Beardless Warriors*, a novel set during World War II and focusing on young, inexperienced U.S. soldiers engaged in an attack ona German town. The story revolves around the strong bond formed during the prolonged battle between the squadron leader and a young recruit. Daniel Talbot in *Saturday Review* calls the novel "well told, unpretentious, and continually absorbing." Reviewing the work for the *New York Times Book Review,* William Wise finds that *The Beardless Warriors* "proceeds to paint an individual and memorable picture of battle. It does so with almost none of the interminable flashbacks, the grandiose philosophizing or the bogus love stories that have marred many over- long and highly praised war novels of the past decade."

Matheson's first screenplay was the basis for the 1957 Universal film *The Incredible Shrinking Man*. Based on his own novel, *The Shrinking Man*, the story tells of Scott Carey who, while boating with his wife, passes through a strange, glowing cloud of gas. Following the odd incident, Scott soon notices that he is losing weight and even body height, his clothes hanging on him grotesquely. A medical examination shows that Scott is shrinking for some unknown reason and no way can be found to reverse the process. Scott is eventually forced to live in a doll's house set up in the living room of his own home, the tiny toy furniture being just the right size for his six-inch-tall frame. Because of his small size, Scott finds himself in desperate battles with the family cat and, when he has grown even smaller, with a hungry spider. Lack of food and drinking water also threaten his existence. At story's end, still shrinking, Scott leaves behind his familiar world entirely to enter a microscopic universe in which the very atoms of existence are to him as planetary systems. Although dead to the world of his birth, Scott believes that he is destined to continue living in this strange new universe that fate has given to him. Roberta Sharp, commenting on the film in the *Dictionary of Literary Biography,* finds that it "bespeaks Matheson's interest in the questions of man's place in the universe and man's fate after death." *The Incredible Shrinking Man* won Matheson the Hugo Award for best science-fiction picture of 1958, and it is still ranked among the more inventive films of the 1950s. Commenting in *Entertainment Weekly,* Matheson remarked that "for its time, [*The Incredible Shrinking Man*] was quite unique."

Matheson-Corman Partnership

In the early 1960s Matheson teamed with famed low-budget film director Roger Corman to write several movies based on the stories of Edgar Allan Poe: *The House of Usher* (1960), *The Pit and the Pendulum* (1961), *Tales of Terror* (1962), and *The Raven* (1963). Starring horror film veterans Vincent Price, Basil Rathbone, Peter Lorre, and Boris Karloff, Matheson's Poe films helped to revive the careers of these actors in stories which introduced them to a new audience too young to remember the classic horror films of the 1930s.

Matheson's adaptation of *The House of Usher* starred Price as Roderick Usher, whose apparently dead sister has really been buried prematurely in the family crypt. The story ends with the now-mad sister strangling Usher as the family mansion is consumed in flames. Although Matheson changed Poe's original story somewhat for the

Grant Williams starrred in the 1957 sci-fi classic *The Incredible Shrinking Man,* for which Matheson received the 1958 Hugo Award for best motion picture.

screen, *The House of Usher* was popular at the box office and spurred a spate of other film adaptations of Poe's works.

Price lent his acting talents to another Matheson screenplay adaptation, this time Poe's *The Pit and the Pendulum.* Enlarging greatly on the original story, *The Pit and the Pendulum* is set during the Spanish Inquisition. Again playing a careless spouse, Price again fears that he hasprematurely buried his wife; however, this time he finds that she and her lover have staged her death in an effort to drive him mad. The lovers' plotting proves effective, but also backfires. Price does go mad, and, insane with jealousy, he tortures his rival in the dungeon of the castle with the great bladed pendulum of Poe's story.

In *Tales of Terror* Matheson took four Poe stories—"Ligeia," "The Cask of Amontillado," "The Black Cat," and "The Facts in the Case of M. Valdemar"—and adapted them as a trilogy of stories. Starring Price in each story, *Tales of Terror* also includes Lorre as the maniacal killer who entombs Price behind a cellar wall in "The Cask of Amontillado," and Rathbone as a mesmerist murdered by the dying man he has hypnotized.

Pens Horror with a Twist

The Raven is perhaps the most enjoyable of Matheson's Poe adaptations. A parody of Poe's horror poem, the film allows Price, Lorre, and Karloff to play off their forbidding screen characters in a spoof of the horror film genre. The story climaxes with a rollicking magical battle between competing wizards. In 1964 Matheson wrote *The Comedy of Terrors,* a witty horror film in which Price and Lorre are undertakers who decide to drum up some business by murdering wealthy residents in their town. Their attempts to kill Rathbone, who is prone to death-like comas, provides a mixture of laughs and chills.

Matheson's 1954 novel *I Am Legend* is the story of a plague that turns humanity into a race of vampires. The sole surviving human, Robert Neville, must fight off the vampires who are bent on killing him. Candace R. Benefiel in the *Wilson Library Bulletin* ranks *I Am Legend* among the "group of classics every vampirologist should read." Speaking of *The Shrinking Man* and *I Am Legend,* Wolfe notes that both novels are "haunt-

> "*. . . the key to Matheson's fiction and its unsettling effect is his style, which is as plain and simple as the ordinary objects he imbues with malice. . . . The almost clinical quality of his writing actually adds gravity to his horrors by giving them a solid and seemingly irrefutable basis in reality, no matter how outlandish they seem at first.*"
>
> —Stefan Dziemianowicz

ing portraits of sensitive individuals losing control over their worlds, and both are unusual for their time in their open discussions of frustrated sexual longings." Adapted for the screen in 1963 by Matheson and William Leicester, *I Am Legend* was filmed in Italy with Price and released as *The Last Man on Earth.* Unfortunately, Matheson so disliked the film that he used the pseudonym Logan Swanson in the screen credits. A later adaptation, 1971's *The Omega Man,* starred Charleton Heston as a struggling survivor in a ravaged New York City.

In addition to his film writing, Matheson also wrote extensively for television during the 1960s. He wrote episodes for such popular series as *The Chrysler Playhouse, The Alfred Hitchcock Theatre, Star Trek, Cheyenne, Have Gun—Will Travel,* and *Night Gallery.* He is perhaps best known for the fourteen episodes he wrote for Rod Serling's *Twilight Zone,* episodes that helped establish the series as the premiere television showcase for tales of the horrific and surreal. Among his most popular episodes are "Nightmare at 20,000 Feet," in which William Shatner plays an airline passenger on a night flight who thinks he sees a gremlin dismantling the wing of the plane and cannot convince anyone else it is happening, and "Night Call," in which an elderly widow is plagued by phone calls from beyond the grave.

From Screenplays to Short Fiction

While the 1960s proved a productive time for Matheson in film and television, he alsofound time to write some fifty short stories that were published as the "Shock" series: *Shock!* (1961), *Shock II* (1964), *Shock III* (1966), and *Shock Waves* (1970).

Matheson wrote the screenplay for this 1973 film *The Legend of Hell House*, which is based on his novel *Hell House* and features Roddy McDowell (left) Gayle Hunnicutt, and Clive Revill.

As Dziemianowicz notes, "To read the fiction of Richard Matheson is to enter a world in which the ordinary unexpectedly shows its dark side and the familiar objects of daily life suddenly develop teeth and claws." Matheson's horror stories, written in straight-forward prose and dealing with contemporary situations, were enormously influential in turning the horror genre away from the ornate and deliberately mythic horror of such writers as H. P. Lovecraft and Clark Ashton Smith. Matheson showed that ordinary life could also be a fertile setting for the fearful and unnerving.

Matheson explains in the introduction to his *Collected Stories* that he aimed to write about "the individual isolated in a threatening world, attempting to survive." This theme recurs in many

of his best stories. In "First Anniversary" a young husband learns that his lovely wife is in reality a monster who has been deceiving him with a fraudulent appearance. "Legion of Plotters" finds a man discovering—or paranoid enough to believe—that the everyday irritations involved in going to work are in fact the machinations of a conspiracy meant to drive him mad. And in "Trespass" a pregnant woman comes to believe that her odd food cravings are a sign that the baby she is carrying must not be human.

Finds Success with Horror Fans

In 1971 Matheson wrote the novel *Hell House*, which tells of a group of people investigating the haunted goings-on at an old country estate. One of the group, a physicist, believes that he can "de-magnetize" the psychic energy with which the house is bedeviled by using a special device he has invented. Such poltergeist phenomena as doors closing and opening on their own, an attempted possession, and household objects floating in the air provide the chills as the team of investigators work to dispel the malevolent force operating in the house. Critical reaction to the novel was generally positive. Newgate Callendar of the *New York Times Book Review,* for example, calls *Hell House* "a fine horror story" and "a walloping good book of its kind." Similarly, Benjamin Paul John Przekop in *Best Sellers* labels the novel "an artfully written piece of fiction, containing just enough gore, perversity, and terror to delight the most demand-

ing and most seasoned of 'horror story' readers." In 1973 Matheson adapted *Hell House* for the screen. Released as *The Legend of Hell House,* the film echoed the eerie atmosphere of the novelist/ screenwriter's earlier Poe adaptations.

Matheson has also written original television movies. In 1971 he scripted *Duel,* based on a novelette he had previously published in *Playboy* magazine. The story of a motorist who finds himself in a senseless, deadly chase with the unseen driver of a diesel truck, the movie starred actor Dennis Weaver and marked twenty-four-year-old Steven Spielberg's directorial debut. Speaking of Spielberg's work on the film, Matheson told *Entertainment Weekly:* "It's such a simple idea—but done with extraordinary skill, and it works." Duel earned Matheson a Writer's Guild of America nomination for best film of the year.

In 1972 Matheson adapted Jeff Price's story "The Kolchak Papers" as the television movie *The Night Stalker.* Set in Las Vegas, the story follows an eccentric newspaper reporter as he tracks down what he believes is a modern-day vampire preying upon young women. At the time of its initial broadcast *The Night Stalker* was the most-watched television movie in history, drawing an estimated audience of 75 million viewers. Matheson also won a Writer's Guild Award for the film. Following up on the success of *The Night Stalker,* Matheson penned *The Night Strangler* in 1973. The two films led to the popular *Night Stalker* television series of the 1970s starring Darren McGavin as Kolchak, the reporter who specializes in investigating occult phenomena. The series has been credited as a forerunner of the popular *The X-Files* series of the 1990s.

In 1983 Matheson revisited his earlier success with *The Twilight Zone* with his screenplay for *Twilight Zone—The Movie,* based on four episodes of the classic television program. Three of the four episodes were scripted by Matheson, who updated them for the film. In "Kick the Can," directed by Spielberg, the elderly residents of a rest home find a second childhood when they begin playing traditional children's games. In "It's a Good Life," a young boy with strange powers dominates his terrified family. The last episode, "Nightmare at 20,000 Feet," is a remake of Matheson's classic episode. The same year saw Matheson involved in another big-budget movie: *Jaws 3-D.* A sequel to the popular shark movie of 1975, *Jaws 3-D*

In this work, a man's obsession with a nineteenth-century actress is so strong that it sends him back in time to meet her.

Robin Williams (left) and Cuba Gooding, Jr. star in Matheson's screenplay adaptation of his own 1978 novel, *What Dreams May Come,* a story about the afterlife.

takes place at a Florida amusement park. Not well received by the critics, the film was nonetheless popular with audiences seeking aquatic thrills.

Time Travel and the Afterlife

Additional novels by Matheson include 1975's *Bid Time Return.* In this story Richard Collier, while visiting a luxury hotel, becomes infatuated with a seventy-five-year-old photograph of a beautiful woman. Then he finds his name signed in the old hotel's register for November 20, 1896. Soon Collier is obsessed with the belief that he and the dead woman, a stage actress named Elise Mc-Kenna, have somehow known each other before. When Collier begins to dress and act like an 1890s gentleman, he finds Elise there to greet him. Martin Levin, reviewing the novel for the *New York Times Book Review,* calls it "a fine atmospheric

trip." In 1980 Matheson scripted a film version of the novel that was released as *Somewhere in Time,* starring Christopher Reeve and Jane Seymour. Matheson remarks to *Entertainment Weekly* that "the critics lambasted it, but now everybody tells me, 'I love that film.' There's a fan club dedicated to it."

Matheson created a tale of the afterlife with 1978's novel *What Dreams May Come.* In it, a writer named Chris Nielson is killed in an automobile accident. Unable to accept his death, Chris's spirit lingers on the Earth until a deceased relative takes on the role of spirit guide in the afterworld. Matheson borrows from a number of mystical traditions to create an entire fictional world where dead spirits live among an odd geography of thought-forms. When Chris's wife Ann, overcome by grief over his death, commits suicide, Chris is charged with helping her rise from the hellish afterworld reserved for suicides. While a *Kirkus Reviews* critic notes that "more plot and less metageography would have made a stronger book," *What Dreams May Come* has enjoyed cult status among many readers in the New Age market. In 1998, the novel was adapted as a $100 million film starring Robin Williams. Producer Stephen Simon was moved to film the story by his own feelings about its visionary quality. He had also known persons near death who had read the book and found solace in its hopeful story.

Twisting Plots Characterize Novels

The Great Delacorte, once a great stage magician but now bed-ridden by a stroke, is the focus of Matheson's *Now You See It. . .,* published in 1995. When the Great Delacorte invites friends and relatives to his estate, the event becomes a chance to wreak a dreadful revenge. Rigged up with magical stage props from Delacorte's performing days, the mansion is the scene of disappearances, mutilations, and inexplicable phenomena of every type. Plot twists mount until, Dennis Winters remarks in *Booklist,* "the reader doesn't know, any more than the characters, exactly what to believe." The critic for *Publishers Weekly* calls *Now You See It. . .* a "dazzler that offers top-flight fun," while Tim Sullivan in the *Washington Post Book World* finds it "absorbing" and believes that the narrative "whips the action along as in a lively stage play." Winters concludes that in *Now You See It. . .* "Matheson has created a luminous tour de force of terror."

A long-married couple—David and Ellen—hope to save their troubled marriage in Matheson's novel *Earthbound,* another tale of the supernatural that was originally published under a pseudonym in 1982. Renting a seaside cottage, the couple begin a second honeymoon. But soon a strange woman begins visiting David whenever Ellen is away. Her odd nature intrigues him and, against his wishes, David finds that he is drawn to her romantically. With this initial attraction, through, comes possession and it is only too late that he realizes that this strange, attractive woman is an evil spirit intent on taking him over. David's efforts to free himself only puts Ellen in danger as well. The two must flee the cottage in order to save themselves from possession. "While the first half of this book is not entirely convincing," writes Marylaine Block in *Library Journal,* "the second half is incredibly powerful."

If you enjoy the works of Richard Matheson, you may also want to check out the following books and films:

Allen Appel, *Time after Time,* 1985.
Lois Duncan, *The Third Eye,* 1984.
Stephen King, *The Tommyknockers,* 1987.
Anne Rice, *Interview with the Vampire,* 1976.
The Haunting, a film based on Shirley Jackson's story "The Haunting of Hill House," 1963.

In 1993's *Seven Steps to Midnight* Matheson presents Chris Barton, who picks up a mysterious hitchhiker on a country road. The stranger bets Chris that he doesn't know what reality is, and Chris accepts the odd wager. While thinking this eccentric bet is easily won, Chris soon finds that reality is a more unstable concept than he had imagined. Returning home, he finds another man named Chris Barton living at his house. Worse, strange men begin chasing him and Chris must flee across Europe in a desperate bid to escape. A critic for *Publishers Weekly* praises the lead character: "Chris is a likable everyman whose wry humor draws parallels between his predicament and the stuff of fiction, thus providing a clever touch of irony while poking fun at the literary traditions Matheson helped pioneer."

Tales of Old West Are Change of Pace

In addition to his writing in the horror and science fiction genres, Matheson has also written a number of works in the Western genre. His collection *By the Gun* gathers together stories first written for magazines in the 1950s. In most of these stories, Matheson presents an Old West where civilization and its orderly personal values comes into conflict with the more chaotic frontier way of life. In one story, a man is reluctantly pushed into a gunfight, which he wins by killing his opponent. Relieved that the unwanted violence is over, the man then discovers that he is now considered a "fast gun" who will be challenged by every young gunfighter around. A reviewer for *Publishers Weekly* believes that the stories in *By the Gun* display "spare prose and restrained use of action."

In 1993 Matheson wrote a new Western novel, *Gunfight*, in which a retired Texas Ranger is the subject of malicious personal gossip. When a young girl confesses she has romantic fantasies about the gunman, her jealous boyfriend becomes violent. Carol P. Clark in *School Library Journal* calls Gunfight "an action-packed suspenseful tale." The critic for *Publishers Weekly* describes it as "an absorbing parable about the terrible effects of gossip and the tragedy of a peaceable man driven to violence."

While he has been a successful, much published author for much of his decades-long career, by the 1990s Matheson's work seemed to be undergoing what *Entertainment Weekly* contributor calls "a renaissance." His early sci-fi novel *I Am Legend* was slated for a feature film adaptation, while another work from the 1950s, *A Stir of Echoes*, was also slated for release to expectant cinemagoers. With many of his films from the 1960s and 1970s now available on videocassette, and the recent publication of critically praised novels in the Western genre drawing new readers to his thoughtful, speculative approach, Matheson's well-written and entertaining fiction continues to find new fans.

■ **Works Cited**

Benefiel, Candace R., "Fangs for the Memories: Vampires in the Nineties," *Wilson Library Bulletin*, May, 1995, p. 36.

Block, Marylaine, review of *Earthbound*, *Library Journal*, June 15, 1994, p. 96.

Callendar, Newgate, review of *Hell House*, *New York Times Book Review*, August 29, 1971, p. 27.

Clark, Carol P., review of *Gunfight*, *School Library Journal*, June, 1994, p. 160.

Dziemianowicz, Stefan, "Richard Matheson," *St. James Guide to Horror, Ghost and Gothic Writers*, St. James Press, 1998, pp. 393-395.

"Grand Illusionist," *Entertainment Weekly*, October 23, 1998, p. 8.

Levin, Martin, review of *Bid Time Return*, *New York Times Book Review*, March 30, 1975, p. 21.

Przekop, Benjamin Paul John, review of *Hell House*, *Best Sellers*, August 15, 1971, p. 220.

Review of *By the Gun*, *Publishers Weekly*, January 24, 1994, p. 51.

Review of *Gunfight*, *Publishers Weekly*, March 15, 1993, p. 70.

Review of *Now You See It. . .*, *Publishers Weekly*, December 12, 1994, p. 49.

Review of *Seven Steps to Midnight*, *Publishers Weekly*, August 23, 1993, p. 60.

Review of *What Dreams May Come*, *Kirkus Reviews*, July 15, 1978, p. 769.

Sharp, Roberta, "Richard Matheson," *Dictionary of Literary Biography*, Volume 44: *American Screenwriters*, Gale (Detroit), 1986, pp. 237-244.

Sullivan, Tim, review of *Now You See It. . .*, *Washington Post Book World*, April 30, 1995, p. 8.

Talbot, Daniel, review of *The Beardless Warriors*, *Saturday Review*, August 20, 1960, p. 22.

Winters, Dennis, review of *Now You See It. . .*, *Booklist*, February 15, 1995, p. 1060.

Wise, William, review of *The Beardless Warriors*, *New York Times Book Review*, August 28, 1960.

Wolfe, Gary K., "Richard Matheson," *Twentieth-Century Science-Fiction Writers*, 3rd edition, St. James Press (Detroit), 1991, pp. 533-534.

■ **For More Information See**

BOOKS

Contemporary Literary Criticism, Volume 37, Gale, 1986.

Dictionary of Literary Biography, Gale, Volume 8: *Twentieth-Century American Science-FictionWriters*, 1981, Volume 44: *American Screenwriters, Second Series*, Gale, 1986.

Science Fiction and Fantasy Literature: A Checklist (two volumes), Gale, 1979.

PERIODICALS

Best Sellers, August 15, 1971.

Booklist, February 15, 1995, p. 1060; October 15, 1995, p. 386.

Chicago Sunday Tribune, August 21, 1960.

Entertainment Weekly, May 20, 1994, pp. 49-50.

Library Journal, April 15, 1994, p. 116; June 15, 1994, p. 96.

Locus, February, 1995, p. 57.

New York Herald Tribune Book Review, September 4, 1960.

New York Times, March 2, 1958.

New York Times Book Review, August 28, 1960, August 29, 1971, March 30, 1975.

Publishers Weekly, January 24, 1994, p. 51; April 25, 1994, p. 59; June 20, 1994, p. 95; December 12, 1994, p. 49.

Saturday Review, August 20, 1960.

School Library Journal, June, 1994, p. 160.

Science Fiction Chronicle, February, 1995, p. 37.

Variety, November 17, 1971; May 16, 1994, p. 34.
Washington Post, August 19, 1971.
West Coast Review of Books, November, 1978.
Wilson Library Bulletin, May, 1995, p. 36.*

—Sketch by Chas. M. Lowdith

Jean Davies Okimoto

■ Personal

Born December 14, 1942, in Cleveland, OH; daughter of Norman Hugh (in business) and Edith (Williams) Davies; married Peter C. Kirkman (an Air Force officer), August 26, 1961 (divorced, 1971); married Joseph T. Okimoto (a psychiatrist), May 19, 1973; children: (first marriage) Katherine, Amy; stepchildren: Stephen Okimoto, Dylan Okimoto. *Education:* Attended DePauw University, 1960-63, and University of Washington, Seattle, 1971-72; Antioch College, M.A., 1976. *Hobbies and other interests:* Swimming, sailing, painting, spectator sports, especially soccer.

■ Addresses

Office—2700 East Madison St., Seattle, WA 98112.

■ Career

Writer, 1968—. High school tutor of remedial reading in Seattle, WA, 1972-73; University of Washington, Seattle, editorial project consultant in child

psychiatry, 1973-74; Mount Baker Youth Service Bureau, Seattle, assistant to director, 1974-75; in private practice of psychotherapy, Seattle, 1975—. Mount Baker Community Club, vice president, 1968; Seattle Public Schools, volunteer tutor, 1969; Franklin Area School Council, chairman. 1970; Mount Baker Youth Service Bureau, chairman, 1973. Also founder and co-chairperson of Seattle Reading Awards (formerly the Mayor's Reading Awards), 1986—. *Member:* American Personnel and Guidance Association, PEN, Authors Guild, Authors League of America, Dramatists Guild, Pacific Northwest Writers' Conference.

■ Awards, Honors

Washington State Governor's Award, 1982, for *It's Just Too Much*; Best Book for Young Adults citation, American Library Association, and Choice Book designation, International Reading Association, both 1987, both for *Jason's Women*; International Reading Association-Children's Book Council Young Adult Choice Award, 1990, for *Molly by Any Other Name*; Junior Literary Guild selection, Lone Star Reading List selection, Mark Twain Award nomination, and Pacific Northwest Booksellers Association Award nominee, all 1990, all for *Take a Chance, Gramps!*; Maxwell Medallion for Best Children's Book of the Year, and Smithsonian notable book citation, both 1993, both for *A Place for Grace*; Parent's Choice Award, 1995, for *Talent Night*; Smithsonian notable book citation, 1995, for *No Dear, Not Here*; Best Book for Young Adults citation, American Library Association, 1998, for *The Eclipse of Moonbeam Dawson.*

■ Writings

YOUNG ADULT NOVELS

My Mother Is Not Married to My Father, Putnam, 1979.
It's Just Too Much, Putnam, 1980.
Norman Schnurman, Average Person, Putnam, 1982.
Who Did It, Jenny Lake?, Putnam, 1983.
Jason's Women, Atlantic Monthly Press, 1986.
Molly by Any Other Name, Scholastic, Inc., 1990.
Take a Chance, Gramps!, Little, Brown, 1990.
Talent Night, Scholastic, Inc., 1995.
The Eclipse of Moonbeam Dawson, Tor, 1997.
To Jaykae—Life Stinx, Tor, 1999.

PICTURE BOOKS

Blumpoe the Grumpoe Meets Arnold the Cat, illustrated by Howie Schneider, Little, Brown, 1990.
A Place for Grace, illustrated by Doug Keith, Sasquatch, 1993.
No Dear, Not Here: The Marbled Murrelets' Quest for a Nest in the Pacific Northwest, illustrated by Celeste Henriquez, Sasquatch, 1995.

OTHER

(With Phyllis Jackson Stegall) *Boomerang Kids: How to Live with Adult Children Who Return Home,* Little, Brown, 1987.
Uncle Hideki, Rain City Projects, 1995.

Contributor of short stories to anthologies, including *Visions,* Delacorte, 1988, and *Connections,* Delacorte, 1989; contributor of one-act play *Hum It Again, Jeremy,* published in *Center Stage,* Harper, 1990.

■ Adaptations

Blumpoe the Grumpoe Meets Arnold the Cat was adapted for television with narration by John Candy and appeared on Showtime and HBO as part of *Shelly Duvall's Bedtime Stories.*

■ Sidelights

Balancing her career as a young-adult novelist with her work as a practicing psychotherapist,

Jean Davies Okimoto draws on her own memories as well as the experiences of her children in writing "problem" novels—stories that depict average teens dealing with realistic situations within their families and school. "Okimoto brings a light, easy style to her books," commented *Twentieth-Century Young Adult Writers* contributor Bill Buchanan, adding that her novels "should be high on anyone's list who is counseling middle schoolers through adjustment problems related to relationships in the home or school setting." While Okimoto's fiction contains the happy endings that are not always guaranteed in real life, critics have praised many of her books, which include the

"[A] well-paced, amusing slice-of-life novel."
—*The Horn Book*

JEAN DAVIES OKIMOTO

In this 1990 work, seventh grader Janie Higgins must listen to some of her own advice about taking chances after her best friend moves away.

award-winning *Jason's Women, Molly by Any Other Name,* and *The Eclipse of Moonbeam Dawson.* "In writing for young people, I attempt to entertain, to write as honestly as I can, and to say something which I believe to be true about the human condition," Okimoto once revealed. "In my novels I want my readers to be able to find themselves in my characters and, through compassion for the characters, have compassion for themselves. I want to give my readers two things: a fun time and the realization that they are not alone in what they feel."

Born in Cleveland, Ohio, in 1942, Okimoto first began to take her writing seriously when she reached middle school. "I had a newspaper on my block with my next-door neighbor and best friend, Lola Ham," the novelist once recalled. "This newspaper was written in pencil, duplicatedon carbon paper, and stapled together. It cost two cents a copy and lasted for one issue as it was censored by an adult. This person shall remain nameless; however, revenge is one of my motives for writing." While continuing to write, Okimoto also focused her intellectual curiosity in another area, earning her master's degree at Antioch College and beginning a career as a psychotherapist.

Publishes Debut Novel

Begun during the mid-1970s—at the same time that she was beginning her private practice in psychotherapy in Seattle, Washington—Okimoto's first novel for young adults, *My Mother Is Not Married to My Father,* was turned down by seventeen publishers before Putnam Publishing released it in 1979. "I almost gave up trying to get the book published," the author recalled, "but I kept on because of my youngest daughter, Amy. She was ten years old at the time and seemed to have an unshakable faith in the book and insisted I keep submitting it."

My Mother Is Not Married to My Father introduces readers to a personable sixth-grader named Cynthia Browne, as she deals with her parents' divorce and her mother's pending second marriage to someone new. Shuttling between the family home and her father's new apartment, parental dating, and her own feeling that she might be to blame for the breakdown of her parents' marriage are just some of the adjustments eleven-year-old Cynthia must face in a book that *Horn Book*

If you enjoy the works of Jean Davies Okimoto, you may also want to check out the following books and films:

Judy Blume, *Then Again, Maybe I Won't,* 1971.
Jackie French Koller, *A Place to Call Home,* 1995.
Slums of Beverly Hills, a film starring Natasha Lyonne and Marisa Tomei, 1998.

contributor Karen M. Klockner described as "a humane and funny look at a situation increasingly common in family life today." While noting that the story line is "fairly routine," *Bulletin of the Center for Children's Books* reviewer Zena Sutherland praised Okimoto's writing for its "vitality and humor," and the novel's young protagonist for her resiliency and ability to stay focused on her own life during her family's upheaval.

Cynthia Browne returns in Okimoto's second young adult novel, 1980's *It's Just Too Much,* and readers follow her narrative as she copes with new step-siblings, as well as the embarrassment wrought by the physical changes of her own adolescence—braces, pimples, and the humiliation of being the last of the "no bra" girls in her class. While the book contains a great deal of humor, a *Booklist* contributor commented that Okimoto does resist poking fun at her ungainly protagonist; "universal tribulations of puberty are given a measure of dignity."

The problems of old age are compared with those confronted by teens in Okimoto's *Take a Chance, Gramps!* Janie Higgins suddenly finds herself on her own after her best friend moves away at the start of seventh grade. While she attempts to create a new social life for herself, she also begins to understand the loneliness experienced by her recently widowed grandfather. Being firm and encouraging the somewhat resistant Gramps to attend his community's weekly seniors dance, Janie gains the self-confidence needed to take a chance on meeting friends her own age. *Take a Chance, Gramps!* "illuminate[s] the stumbling efforts of a very likeable adolescent" and depicts two people "who prod each other along with affection and good advice and share the ups and downs of making a new start," in the opinion of *Horn Book* reviewer Margaret A. Bush. And *Booklist* contributor Leone McDermott praised the novel for its ability to "provide entertaining encouragement for the many [teens] facing similar trials."

Finds Humor Important

"Basically, I feel that there is so much suffering and sadness in the world that we should treasure a good laugh whenever we find one," Okimoto once stated. "I guess that's why my books have been described as 'sad and funny.'" The book often praised by critics for its down-to-earth humor is Okimoto's 1982 novel, *Norman Schnurman, Average Person*. Living under the shadow of his father, well-known former collegiate football hero "Mad Dog" Schnurman, puts a lot of stress on sixth-grader Norman, who is not the least bit interested in following in his father's footsteps. While he joins the football team to try to please his dad, the teen's real passion is flea markets, where he finds all sorts of tacky but fascinating stuff. He also meets new friends when he runs into neighbors Carrie Koski and her grandfather. When Carrie makes it clear that she likes Norman for who he is rather than for whose son he is, the young man gains the confidence to assert his independence and quit the football team. *Booklist* contributor Ilene Cooper described the novel as "rowdy and ribald as sixth-grade boys themselves," and a reviewer in *School Library Journal* praised Okimoto's ability to introduce teen readers—particularly boys—to "a positive character who has good potential for growth."

Another book of special interest to teen boys is Okimoto's 1986 novel, *Jason's Women*. Lonely due to his parents' preoccupation with their disintegrating marriage, and frustrated by the fact that he turns into a total bumbling idiot every time he tries to talk to a girl, sixteen-year-old Jason Kovak decides to do his homework where women are concerned. Copiously studying such key texts as *The Sensuous Male* and *How to Fascinate Women*, he starts answering personal ads and winds up landing a job with wealthy, eccentric octogenarian Bertha Jane Filmore and assisting her in her offbeat bid for mayor of Seattle. Noting that *Jason's Women* "convincingly captures the adolescent voice" in "moving moments" as well as in "hilarious, if sometimes slightly ribald, snatches of text," *Horn Book* contributor Karen Jameyson

"A must read for all ages!" —*Explorations*

Moonbeam Dawson's values conflict with his mother's traditional ones until he moves out on his own in Okimoto's 1997 novel.

praised Okimoto's novel as "sparkl[ing] with wit and life from beginning to end." While noting that the novel's ending is somewhat weak, *Booklist* reviewer Hazel Rochman contended that Jason's story is told with "humor and sensitivity, and teens will enjoy his bumbling attempts to set up a smoldering sexual encounter."

Examines Racial Issues

In her more recent teen novels, Okimoto has begun to focus on the unique problems faced by Asian American and biracial children. In *Molly by Any Other Name*, she introduces Molly Jane

Fletcher, an all-American high school senior, except for the fact that she's adopted and is of Asian heritage. Curious about her heritage—is she Chinese, Japanese, Korean, Filipino, Thai?—Molly learns about an organization that can help her track down her birth mother. With the support of her parents as well as her best friend Roland Hirada, Molly pursues her search with ever-growing maturity, ultimately connecting with her Japanese Canadian mother and her half-brother. "With considerable candor, Okimoto writes about the elemental search for roots, the fear as well as the great happiness it can bring," commented Rochman. Praising the author for balancing Molly's search for her roots with relationships with friends and a blossoming romance with Roland, *Voice of Youth Advocates* contributor Florence H. Munat called *Molly by Any Other Name* "a book about an important subject, skillfully written, that can make you laugh and cry at a single sitting."

Other issues of relevance to Asian American teens are dealt with in *Talent Night*, which Okimoto published in 1995. Not deterred by cultural stereotypes, seventeen-year-old Rodney Suyama is determined to become the first Japanese American rap star. He is also determined to win the heart of Ivy Ramos, the most popular girl in his high school and the current steady of star football player Lavell Tyler. Rodney banks on his performance at his high-school's talent night to accomplish both his goals, in a novel buoyed by "Rodney's wit, determination, and sunny outlook," in the opinion of a *Publishers Weekly* reviewer. The theme of identity for biracial teens is also explored in *The Eclipse of Moonbeam Dawson,* about the attempts of Moonbeam Dawson, who is half-Native American, to have a "normal" life after living in a commune with his mother. After rebelling and taking his own apartment, testing out a new name, and trying to fit in with local kids, Moonbeam comes to realize that the values his mother taught him are ones that he truly believes in as well. "Teens will find themselves cheering him on," Connie Tyrrell Burns noted in *School Library Journal,* "suffering with him in his oh-so-embarrassing moments, and figuring out with him the meaning of family, first love, and friendship."

■ Works Cited

Buchanan, Bill, *Twentieth-Century Young Adult Writers*, St. James Press, 1994, pp. 502-3.

Burns, Connie Tyrrell, review of *The Eclipse of Moonbeam Dawson, School Library Journal*, November, 1997, p. 122.

Bush, Margaret A., review of *Take a Chance, Gramps!, Horn Book,* November/December, 1990, pp. 744-45.

Cooper, Ilene, review of *Norman Schnurman, Average Person, Booklist,* September 1, 1982, p. 46.

Review of *It's Just Too Much, Booklist,* September 1, 1980, p. 46.

Jameyson, Karen, review of *Jason's Women, Horn Book,* May-June, 1986, pp. 332-33.

Klockner, Karen M., review of *My Mother Is Not Married to My Father, Horn Book,* June, 1979, pp. 301-03.

McDermott, Leone, review of *Take a Chance, Gramps!, Booklist,* January 15, 1991, p. 1059.

Moesch, Christine A., review of *A Place for Grace, School Library Journal,* August, 1993, p. 149.

Munat, Florence H., review of *Molly by Any Other Name, Voice of Youth Advocates,* December, 1990, p. 287.

Review of *Norman Schnurman, Average Person, School Library Journal,* December, 1982, p. 84.

Rochman, Hazel, review of *Jason's Women, Booklist,* May 1, 1986, p. 1304.

Rochman, Hazel, review of *Molly by Any Other Name, Booklist,* January 15, 1991, pp. 1053-54.

Sutherland, Zena, review of *My Mother Is Not Married to My Father, Bulletin of the Center for Children's Books,* September, 1979, p. 15.

Review of *Talent Night, Publishers Weekly,* January 30, 1995, p. 101.

■ For More Information See

PERIODICALS

Booklist, May 15, 1979, p. 1142; October 15, 1983, p. 362.

Bulletin of the Center for Children's Books, January, 1981, p. 99; February, 1983, pp. 114-15; January, 1984, p. 93; November, 1986, p. 55.

Five Owls, August, 1990, p. 106.

Horn Book, July-August, 1990, p. 447.

Journal of Youth Services in Libraries, winter, 1993, pp. 119-20.

Publishers Weekly, November 9, 1990, p. 58; April 19, 1993, p. 61.

School Library Journal, November, 1980, p. 78; August, 1986, p. 105; December, 1990, pp. 106, 122; May, 1995, p. 122.

Katherine Paterson

United States, Board of World Missions, Nashville, TN, missionary in Japan, 1957-62; Pennington School for Boys, Pennington, NJ, master of sacred studies and English, 1963-65. *Member:* Authors Guild, Authors League of America, PEN, Children's Book Guild of Washington.

■ Personal

Born October 31, 1932, in Qing Jiang, China; daughter of George Raymond (a clergyman) and Mary (Goetchius) Womeldorf; married John Barstow Paterson (a clergyman), July 14, 1962; children: Elizabeth Po Lin, John Barstow, Jr., David Lord, Mary Katherine. *Education:* King College, A.B. (summa cum laude), 1954; Presbyterian School of Christian Education, M.A., 1957; postgraduate study at Kobe School of Japanese Language, 1957-60; Union Theological Seminary, New York City, M.R.E., 1962. *Politics:* Democrat. *Religion:* "Presbyterian Church in the United States." *Hobbies and other interests:* Reading, swimming, tennis, sailing.

■ Addresses

Home—Barre, VT. *Office*—c/o E. P. Dutton, 2 Park Ave., New York, NY 10016.

■ Career

Writer, 1966—. Public school teacher in Lovettsville, VA, 1954-55; Presbyterian Church in the

■ Awards, Honors

American Library Association (ALA) Notable Children's Book, 1974, and Phoenix Award, Children's Literature Association, 1994, for *Of Nightingales That Weep*; ALA Notable Children's Book, 1976, National Book Award for Children's Literature, 1977, runner-up for Edgar Allan Poe Award (juvenile division), Mystery Writers of America, 1977, and American Book Award nomination (children's fiction paperback), 1982, all for *The Master Puppeteer*; ALA Notable Children's Book, 1977, John Newbery Medal, 1978, Lewis Carroll Shelf Award, 1978, and Michigan Young Reader's Award Division II runner-up, 1980, all for *Bridge to Terabithia*; ALA Notable Children's Book, 1978, National Book Award for Children's Literature, 1979, Christopher Award (ages 9-12), 1979, Newbery Honor Book, 1979, CRABbery (Children Raving About Books) Honor Book, 1979, American Book Award nominee (children's paperback), 1980, William Allen White Children's Book Award, 1981, Garden State Children's Book Award (younger division), New Jersey Library Association, 1981, Georgia Children's Book Award, 1981,

Iowa Children's Choice Award, 1981, Massachusetts Children's Book Award (elementary), 1981, all for *The Great Gilly Hopkins*; Hans Christian Andersen Award U.S. nominee, 1980, *New York Times* Outstanding Book List, 1980, Newbery Medal, 1981, CRABbery Honor Book, 1981, American Book Award nominee (children's hardcover), 1981, children's paperback, 1982, all for *Jacob Have I Loved*; Outstanding Books and Best Illustrated Books selection, *New York Times*, 1981, for *The Crane Wife*, illustrated by Suekichi Akaba and translated by Paterson from a retelling by Sumiko Yagawea; Parent's Choice Award, Parent's Choice Foundation, 1983, for *Rebels of the Heavenly Kingdom*; Irvin Kerlan Award "in recognition of singular attainments in the creation of children's literature," 1983; University of Southern Mississippi School of Library Service Silver Medallion, 1983, for outstanding contributions to the field of children's literature; Parent's Choice Award, Parent's ChoiceFoundation, and Notable Books list, *New York Times*, both 1985, both for *Come Sing, Jimmy Jo*; Laura Ingalls Wilder Award nominee, 1986; ALAN Award, 1987; Keene State College Award, 1987; Regina Medal Award, Catholic Library Association, 1988, for demonstrating "the timeless standards and ideals for the writing of good literature for children"; Best Illustrated list, *New York Times*, 1990, and Best Picture Books selection, *Boston Globe-Horn Book*, 1991, both for *The Tale of the Mandarin Ducks*; Irma S. and James H. Black Award, 1992, for *The King's Equal*; Scott O'Dell Award for Historical Fiction, Scott O'Dell Foundation, 1997, for *Jip: His Story*. Litt.D., King College, 1978; D.H.L., Otterbein College (Westerville, OH), 1980; Litt. D., St. Mary's of the Woods, 1981; Litt. D., University of Maryland, 1982; Litt. D., Shenandoah College, 1982; D.H.L., Washington and Lee University, 1982; D.H.L., Norwich University and Mount St. Vincent University, both 1990.

■ Writings

The Sign of the Chrysanthemum, illustrated by Peter Landa, Crowell Junior Books, 1973.
Of Nightingales That Weep, illustrated by Haru Wells, Crowell Junior Books, 1974.
The Master Puppeteer, illustrated by Haru Wells, Crowell Junior Books, 1976.
Bridge to Terabithia, illustrated by Donna Diamond, Crowell Junior Books, 1977.
The Great Gilly Hopkins, Crowell Junior Books, 1978.

Angels and Other Strangers: Family Christmas Stories, Crowell Junior Books, 1979 (published in England as *Star of Night: Stories for Christmas*, Gollancz, 1980).
Jacob Have I Loved, Crowell Junior Books, 1980.
Rebels of the Heavenly Kingdom, Lodestar, 1983.
Come Sing, Jimmy Jo, Lodestar, 1985.
Park's Quest, Lodestar, 1988.
The Smallest Cow in the World, illustrated by Jane Clark Brown, Vermont Migrant Education Program, 1988.
The Tale of the Mandarin Ducks, illustrated by Leo and Diane Dillon, Lodestar, 1990.
Lyddie, Lodestar, 1991.
The King's Equal, illustrated by Vladimir Vagin, HarperCollins, 1992.
Flip-Flop Girl, Lodestar, 1994.
A Midnight Clear: Stories for the Christmas Season, Lodestar, 1995.
The Angel and the Donkey (retelling), illustrated by Alexander Koshkin, Clarion Books, 1996.
Jip: His Story, Lodestar, 1996.
Marvin's Best Christmas Present Ever, illustrated by Jane Clark Brown, HarperCollins, 1997.
Celia and the Sweet, Sweet Water, illustrated by Vladimir Vagin, Lodestar, 1998.
(With John Paterson) *Images of God*, illustrated by Alexander Koshkin, Clarion Books, 1998.
(Reteller) *Parzival: The Quest of the Grail Knight*, Lodestar, 1998.
Preacher's Boy, Clarion Books, 1999.

Contributor of articles and reviews to periodicals; co-editor of *The Big Book of Our Planet* and *The World in 1492*. Reviewer, *Washington Post Book World*, 1975—; member of editorial board, Writer, 1987—.

NONFICTION

Who Am I? (curriculum unit), CLC Press, 1966.
To Make Men Free (curriculum unit; includes books, records, pamphlets, and filmstrip), John Knox, 1973.
Justice for All People, Friendship, 1973.
Gates of Excellence: On Reading and Writing Books for Children, Lodestar, 1981.
(With husband, John Paterson) *Consider the Lilies: Flowers of the Bible*, Crowell Junior Books, 1986.
The Spying Heart: More Thoughts on Reading and Writing Books for Children, Lodestar, 1989.
A Sense of Wonder: On Reading and Writing Books for Children (includes *Gates of Excellence* and *The Spying Heart*), Plume, 1995.

TRANSLATOR

Sumiko Yagawa, *The Crane Wife*, Morrow, 1981.
Momoko Ishii, *Tongue-Cut Sparrow*, Lodestar, 1987.

Also translator of Hans Christian Andersen's *The Tongue Cut Sparrow*, for Lodestar.

■ **Adaptations**

The Great Gilly Hopkins was filmed by Hanna-Barbera, 1980; *Bridge to Terabithia* was filmed for PBS television, 1985, and adapted as a play with music, libretto by Paterson and Stephanie Tolan and music by Steve Liebman, French, 1992; *Jacob Have I Loved* was filmed for PBS, 1990. Several of Paterson's books, including *Bridge to Terabithia*, *The Great Gilly Hopkins*, *Angels and Other Strangers*, and *Jacob Have I Loved*, have also been adapted for audio cassette by Random House.

■ **Sidelights**

Two-time Newbery Medal winner Katherine Paterson writes of children in crisis, at the crossroads of major decisions in their lives. Her youthful protagonists turn "tragedy to triumph by bravely choosing a way that is not selfishly determined," according to M. Sarah Smedman in *Dictionary of Literary Biography.* "They embody the theme of redemption through sacrifice of oneself and one's ambitions," Smedman noted, "a theme that resounds convincingly, never cliched, never preached, always with the force of fresh discovery." Paterson's delicate touch with emotionally heavy topics such as death and familial jealousy sets her apart from other problem book authors. "The distinctive quality of Paterson's art," commented Smedman, "is her colorful concision. Whether she is narrating or describing, her mode is understatement, her style pithy. She dramatizes, never exhorts. . . . [She is] a major artist, skilled, discerning, and compassionate."

Smedman might also have added humorous. Paterson's wry understatement saves her work from sentimentality. In books such as *Bridge to Terabithia* and *Jacob Have I Loved*, she tackles serious themes head on, but always with compassion and strong storytelling skills. In others, such as *The Great Gilly Hopkins*, her humor and wit are showcased. Paterson establishes a powerful iden-

tification with the reader because she so strongly believes what she writes. "Why do I keep writing stories about children and young people who are orphaned or otherwise isolated or estranged?" Paterson asked in *Theory into Practice.* "It's because I have within myself a lonely, frightened child who keeps demanding my comfort. I have a rejected child, a jealous and jilted adolescent inside who demands, if not revenge, a certain degree of satisfaction. I am sure it isshe, or should I say they, who keep demanding that I write for them."

Paterson often writes about children who are orphaned or estranged from their parents, teens who isolate themselves or who associate only with one or two close friends. These recurring situations reflect the instability of the author's childhood. "If I tell you that I was born in China of Southern Presbyterian missionary parents, I have already given away three chief clues to my tribal memory," Paterson once wrote in *Horn Book.* The third of five children, Paterson spent her early years in China, repatriating to the United States by the onset of World War II. Chinese being her first language, Paterson learned English with a distinct British accent, and dressed in missionary hand-me-downs—a sure recipe for ridicule from her classmates in North Carolina where the family resettled. Paterson, bereft of friends, found consolation in the school library and in books. Perennially the new kid in school—the family moved fifteen times in thirteen years— Paterson learned survival skills on the playground and delved even further into her private world of books and began writing her own stories. She was a self-confessed outsider and "weird" kid. "I'm sure there are plenty of fine writers who have overcome the disadvantage of a normal childhood and gone on to do great things," Paterson wrote in *Gates of Excellence: On Reading and Writing Books for Children.* "It's just that we weird little kids do seem to have a head start."

After high school, Paterson attended King College in Bristol, Tennessee, majoring in English literature. A year of teaching in a rural Virginia school followed, then a master's degree in education, and finally missionary work in Japan. Until that time her only contact with the Japanese had been with conquering soldiers when she was a child in war-torn China. But the four years she spent in Japan were a revelation for her, and she grew to love the country and its people. Paterson's experiences in Japan figured prominently in her first books,

Set in twelfth-century Japan, Paterson's second novel tells the story of a deceased samurai's daughter, Takiko, who eventually learns the meaning of samurai honor.

written several years later. In 1961 she returned to the United States, married, and began raising a family of four children, two of whom were adopted. Slowly she turned to writing as a private solace at the end of long and hectic days. Her literary career officially began with works for church school curricula. When finished with the project, she turned her hand to fiction, her first love. Seven years later, she had what she considered publishable material.

First Works Set in Japan

Paterson's first three books are historical fiction, set in Japan. The twelfth century and its civil wars

are the setting for *The Sign of the Chrysanthemum* and *Of Nightingales That Weep*, while her third novel, *The Master Puppeteer*, is a mystery set in eighteenth-century Osaka during a great famine. All three books deal with teenagers who are either orphaned or have lost one parent and who must make it on their own in exceptionally difficult times. In *The Sign of the Chrysanthemum*, young Muna experiences the loss of his mother and tries without success to find his samurai father, whom he would know by the tatoo of a chrysanthemum on his shoulder. Although he does not find his father, in searching for him Muna travels a road of self-discovery that is not without its own rewards. Reviewing this first novel in *Horn Book*, Virginia Haviland noted that "the storytelling holds the reader by the quick pace of the lively episodes, the colorful detail, and the superb development of three important characters." Graham Hammond, writing in *Times Literary Supplement*, commented that "the book is about pain, wisdom, choosing, and growing up, but it is far from didactic." *Of Nightingales That Weep*, Paterson's second novel, deals with the fortunes of a young girl during the same period in Japan, and could, according to Margery Fisher of *Growing Point*, "satisfy adolescents and adults alike with its exotic flavour and mature handling of characters." Marcus Crouch, writing in *Junior Bookshelf*, noted his own initial reluctance to read a book dealing with twelfth-century Japan, but concluded that once started, the book was "hypnotically dominating."

Paterson's third novel, *The Master Puppeteer*, was her break-out book for which she won a National Book Award in 1977. Using the world of traditional Japanese puppet drama as a backdrop, Paterson wove a mystery around young Jiro and his best friend Kinshi, the son of a puppet master. Both boys are alienated from their fathers and find stability in their relationship with one another. Diana L. Spirt in her *Introducing More Books: A Guide for the Middle Grades*, described the book as "engrossing," and noted that "the author has blended a literate mix of adventure and Japanese history with a subtle knowledge of young people." Zena Sutherland, reviewing the novel in *Bulletin of the Center for Children's Books*, compared *The Master Puppeteer* to "intricate embroidery," and concluded with a terse, telling description: "good style, good story." The interplay of technique and content was also noted by Dora Jean Young in *School Library Journal*. "This novel . . . should be very popular for its combination of excellent writing and irresistible intrigue," Young declared.

Newbery Winners

Paterson turned to a contemporary rural American setting for her fourth novel, inspired by the death of her son David's favorite friend, who was struck by lightning. In *Bridge to Terabithia*, Jess and Leslie are fifth-graders whose loneliness brings them together as fast friends. They build a secret hideout and call it the magical kingdom of Terabithia. Heavy rains make it impossible to go there for a time, but after returning from a trip, Jess learns that Leslie has drowned trying to get to their hideout. Thereafter, he builds his own monument to the young girl. A Newbery Award

Paterson received her first Newbery Medal in 1978 for this moving story about friendship and courage.

winning novel, *Bridge to Terabithia* is "an unromantic, realistic, and moving reaction to personal tragedy," according to Jack Forman in *School Library Journal*. Jill Paton Walsh, reviewing the work in the *Christian Science Monitor*, commends it as "tender and poetic without ever being sentimental, written in simple language which never fails to carry the emotional charge." A novel with a lighter touch is *The Great Gilly Hopkins*, a somewhat comic view of a spunky foster child and the foster mother who ultimately wins the girl's affection. The novel was the result of Paterson's own experiences as a foster mother for two months. "This is quite a book!" proclaimed Ellen M. Davidson in *Children's Book Review Service*. "It confronts racism, sexism, ageism, I.Q.ism and just about all the other prejudices of our society." However, Bryna J. Fireside in *New York Times Book Review* took Paterson to task for this very plenitude of issues. Fireside commented that the novel would have been better "without mixing up race relations, learning disabilities, the important relationships between young and old, and a terrific young girl who gamely comes to terms with her status as a foster child." Yet most reviewers—and awards committees—responded more favorably. Natalie Babbitt, reviewing the book in *Washington Post Book World*, concluded that *The Great Gilly Hopkins* "is a finely written story. Its characters linger long in the reader's thoughts after it is finished."

Smedman, writing in *Dictionary of Literary Biography*, described Paterson's next novel, *Jacob Have I Loved*, as the author's "most complex." A second Newbery Award winner, this novel examines the feelings of a twin for her tremendously talented sibling. Set on a Chesapeake islandat the outset of World War II, the story is about Sara Louise—known as Wheeze—and her delicate and musically talented sister Caroline, as related from the adult Wheeze's retrospective point of view. Paul Heins, writing in *Horn Book*, commented that Paterson had again "written a story that courageously sounds emotional depths." *Christian Science Monitor* contributor Betty Levin dubbed the book "a breathtaking novel for older children and adults . . . a book full of humor and compassion and sharpness."

Paterson returned to Far Eastern settings for *Rebels of the Heavenly Kingdom*, set in nineteenth-century China. The story of a young peasant boy, Wang Lee, kidnapped by bandits, and his friendship with and growing love for Mei Lin, who helps to rescue him, the book is "on the epic scale" and is "skillfully crafted," according to *Publishers Weekly*. Mary Hobbs, writing in *Junior Bookshelf*, noted that the story "is beautifully told," and painlessly teaches the reader about details of "the traditional Chinese ways of life and thought."

Lessons to be Learned

Biblical and universal themes are at the heart of Paterson's books. Never preachy in tone, her stories nonetheless teach lessons—of humility, responsibility, and hope. As the author once wrote in *Horn Book*, "I have learned, for all my failings and limitations, that when I am willing to give myself away in a book, readers will respond by giving themselves away as well, and the book I labored over so long becomes in our mutual giving something far richer and more powerful than I could have ever imagined." Paterson elaborated on her artistic philosophy in an article for *The Writer*, where she explains: "I keep learning that if I am willing to go deep into my own heart, I am able miraculously to touch other people at the core. But that is because I do have a reader I must try to satisfy—that is the reader I am and the reader I was as a child. I know this reader in a way that I can never know a generic target out there somewhere. This reader demands honesty and emotional depth. She yearns for clear, rhythmically pleasing language. . . . And above all she wants characters who will make her laugh and cry and bind her to themselves in a fierce friendship."

Come Sing, Jimmy Jo and *Park's Quest* are two of Paterson's works that have been praised for the honesty, emotional depth, and character recognition that the author seeks to impart. The former relates the story of eleven-year-old James Johnson, a small, timid child taken from his grandmother and their quiet Appalachian mountain home to join his musician family on stage and on television. The family's agent, who has recognized the child's gifted voice, changes James's name to Jimmy Jo and propels him toward stardom—while James must learn to deal with all that fame offers, including difficulties among jealous family members and with schoolmates. "Paterson captures the subtleties of childhood friendships in James's relationships with his classmates and records family interaction with a sensitive ear," noted *School Library Journal* contributor Cathryn A. Camper. A *Bulletin of the Center for Children's Books* reviewer similarly maintained that "Paterson creates strong characters and convincing dialogue, so that her story is effective even to those to whom the heavy emphasis on country music strikes no sympathetic chord." Denise M. Wilms of *Booklist* concluded that *Come Sing, Jimmy Jo* is "a rich, sensitive portrayal of growing up." *Park's Quest* is Paterson's tale of a boy's efforts to learn more about his father, who was killed in the Vietnam War. "In a multilayered novel filled with themes of reconciliation and renewal," wrote a *Kirkus Reviews* commentator, "[Paterson] draws parallelsbetween a boy's quest for the family of his father, killed in Vietnam, and the Arthurian legends. . . . Park's quest is a fine journey of discovery, and the characters he meets are uniquely memorable." Many

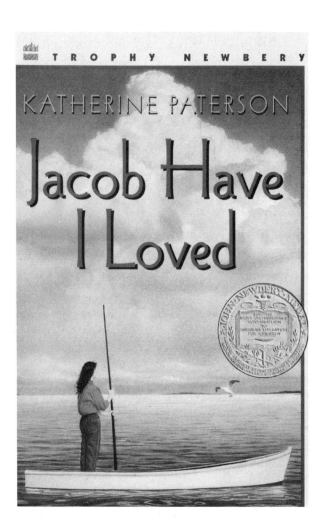

Sara Louise, a.k.a. Wheeze, shares her most intimate feelings about her twin sister Caroline in Paterson's second Newbery Medal-winning story.

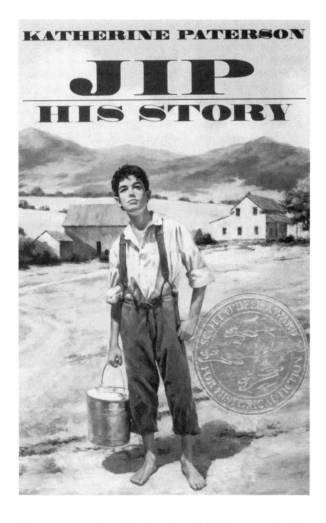

KATHERINE PATERSON
JIP
HIS STORY

After a young boy is abandoned in Vermont by his runaway slave father in 1855, he lives on a small, poor farm until his teacher, Lyddie, and friend Luke help him escape to Canada.

critics commented favorably on the author's skillful interweaving of Park's favorite reading matter—tales of Arthur and his knights—with the boy's own determination to solve the "mystery" of his father's life. The story is "a quest," according to Ethel L. Heins of *Horn Book,* "that will ultimately be fraught with emotional peril and stunning revelations." Heins added that *Park's Quest* "realistically presents a heroic response to a contemporary condition."

Pens Challenging Short Works

In addition to her longer juvenile and young adult novels, Paterson has written short stories for

Christmas, gathered in *Angels and Other Strangers* and *A Midnight Clear,* and picture books, including the award winning *Tale of the Mandarin Ducks* along with *The Smallest Cow in the World, The King's Equal,* and *The Angel and the Donkey.* Two companion novels written in the 1990s are *Lyddie* and *Jip: His Story,* both set in New England in the middle to late nineteenth century. In the first of the novels, thirteen- year-old Lyddie is hired out as a servant after the failure of the family farm. She soon flees this situation for the mills of Lowell, Massachusetts, only to discover an even more grueling life in this new labor. She finds refuge in books and determines to get a college degree and pull herself out of her degrading existence.

Voice of Youth Advocates contributor Mary L. Adams commented: "While the setting is interesting and authentic, the story and characterizations are Paterson at her best. Readers will carry the image of Lyddie with them for many years." Zena Sutherland, writing in *Bulletin of the Center for Children's Books,* noted that Paterson maintained her "usual fine job" in blending narrative with history in this book of "industrial oppression, workers' and women's rights, and prejudice." Elizabeth S. Watson of *Horn Book* concluded that this was "a superb story of grit, determination, and personal growth." Lyddie makes another appearance in *Jip: His Story,* when as a teacher she helps young Jip, the son of a runaway slave, to escape his impoverished life and the miserable conditions of a poor farm for a new start in Canada. *School Library Journal* contributor Ellen Fader noted that readers of *Jip* would be rewarded "with memorable characters and a gripping plot," adding that "Paterson's story resonates with respect for the Vermont landscape and its mid-19th-century residents, with the drama of life during a dark period in our nation's history, and with the human quest for freedom." Mary M. Burns of *Horn Book* praised Paterson's work as "an intense, third-person novel that maintains its riveting pace from the opening chapter to the final moment when the protagonist triumphs over adversity."

A tale with a more contemporary setting, *Flip-Flop Girl* is Paterson's story of distraught nine-year-old Vinnie, grieving for the death of her father. Forced to move to her grandmother's house, Vinnie is an outsider at school, her only friend the mysterious "Flip-Flop Girl" Lupe, whose own father is in jail

If you enjoy the works of Katherine Paterson, you may also want to check out the following books:

Clara Gillow Clark, *Annie's Choice*, 1993.
Leon Garfield, *The Empty Sleeve*, 1988.
Lensey Namioka, *Island of Ogres*, 1989.
Marilyn Sachs, *Call Me Ruth*, 1982.

for having killed her mother. The positive attention of Vinnie's male teacher helps matters for a time, though his simultaneous concern for Lupe and his later engagement to be married both come as a betrayal to Vinnie. A *Publishers Weekly* commentator noted that Paterson is "a master of rendering the intensity of childhood emotions," adding that in *Flip-Flop Girl* she explores "the impact of grief and the slow process of healing." Similarly, *Junior Bookshelf* reviewer Marcus Crouch maintained that "Paterson is always particularly good at exploring relationships and probing the minds of troubled children," noting that *Flip-Flop Girl* "is a beautifully planned and developed narrative which treats the minor pains and embarrassments of childhood with due seriousness." Ellen Fader, in *Horn Book*, concluded that "all children will discover parts of themselves in Vinnie, and, like Vinnie, will know more about themselves when they get to the conclusion of this powerful story."

For all the prizes and critical acclaim she has received, Paterson remains typically understated about her achievements. As she once commented in *Theory into Practice*, her aim, "like that of most writers of fiction, is to tell a story. My gift seems to be that I am one of those fortunate people who can, if she works hard at it, uncover a story that children will enjoy."

■ Works Cited

Adams, Mary L., review of *Lyddie*, *Voice of Youth Advocates*, April, 1991, p. 34.

Babbitt, Natalie, "A Home for Nobody's Child," *Washington Post Book World*, May 14, 1978, pp. 1-2.

Burns, Mary M., review of *Jip: His Story*, *Horn Book*, November-December, 1996, pp. 739-40.

Camper, Cathryn A., review of *Come Sing, Jimmy Jo, School Library Journal*, April, 1985, p. 91.

Review of *Come Sing, Jimmy Jo, Bulletin of the Center for Children's Books*, June, 1985, pp. 191-92.

Crouch, Marcus, review of *Of Nightingales That Weep, Junior Bookshelf*, August, 1977, pp. 239-40.

Crouch, Marcus, review of *Flip-Flop Girl, Junior Bookshelf*, August, 1994, pp. 146-47.

Davidson, Ellen M., review of *The Great Gilly Hopkins, Children's Book Review Service*, April, 1978, p. 89.

Fader, Ellen, review of *Flip-Flop Girl, Horn Book*, March-April, 1994, pp. 200-201.

Fader, Ellen, review of *Jip: His Story, School Library Journal*, October, 1996, p. 124.

Fireside, Bryna J., "Two Orphans without Mothers," *New York Times Book Review*, April 30, 1978, p. 54.

Fisher, Margery, review of *Of Nightingales That Weep, Growing Point*, March, 1977, p. 3060.

Review of *Flip-Flop Girl, Publishers Weekly*, November 22, 1993, p. 64.

Forman, Jack, review of *Bridge to Terabithia, School Library Journal*, November, 1977, p. 61.

Hammond, Graham, "Feminine Insight," *Times Literary Supplement*, September 19, 1975, p. 1056.

Haviland, Virginia, review of *The Sign of the Chrysanthemum, Horn Book*, October, 1975, p. 468.

Heins, Ethel L., review of *Park's Quest, Horn Book*, July-August, 1988, pp. 496-97.

Heins, Paul, review of *Jacob Have I Loved, Horn Book*, September, 1980, pp. 622-23.

Hobbs, Mary, review of *Rebels of the Heavenly Kingdom, Junior Bookshelf*, December, 1983, pp. 254-55.

Levin, Betty, "A Funny, Sad, Sharp Look Back at Growing Up," *Christian Science Monitor*, January 21, 1981, p. 17.

Review of *Park's Quest, Kirkus Reviews*, March 1, 1988, p. 358.

Paterson, Katherine, "Newbery Medal Acceptance," *Horn Book*, August, 1981.

Paterson, Katherine, "Sounds in the Heart," *Horn Book*, December, 1981.

Paterson, Katherine, *Gates of Excellence: On Reading and Writing Books for Children*, Elsevier/Nelson, 1981.

Paterson, Katherine, "The Aim of the Writer Who Writes for Children," *Theory into Practice*, Autumn, 1982, pp. 325-31.

Paterson, Katherine, "What Writing Has Taught Me: Three Lessons," *The Writer*, August, 1990.

Review of *Rebels of the Heavenly Kingdom, Publishers Weekly*, May 6, 1983, p. 98.

Smedman, M. Sarah, "Katherine Paterson," *Dictionary of Literary Biography*, Volume 52: *American Writers for Children Since 1960*, Gale, 1986, pp. 296-314.

Spirt, Diana L., "Forming a View of the World: 'The Master Puppeteer'," *Introducing More Books: A Guide for the Middle Grades*, R. R. Bowker, 1977, pp. 114-17.

Sutherland, Zena, review of *The Master Puppeteer*, *Bulletin of the Center for Children's Books*, July-August, 1976, p. 181.

Sutherland, Zena, review of *Lyddie*, *Bulletin of the Center for Children's Books*, February, 1991, p. 151.

Walsh, Jill Paton, "Novels for Teens: Delicate Themes of Friendship, Fantasy," *Christian Science Monitor*, May 3, 1978, p. B2.

Watson, Elizabeth S., review of *Lyddie*, *Horn Book*, May-June, 1991, pp. 338-39.

Wilms, Denise M., review of *Come Sing, Jimmy Jo*, *Booklist*, May 1, 1985, p. 1257.

Young, Dora Jean, review of *The Master Puppeteer*, *School Library Journal*, March, 1976, p. 117.

■ **For More Information See**

BOOKS

Children's Literature Review, Volume 7, Gale, 1984.

Cullinan, Mary, with Mary K. Karrer and Arlene M. Pillar, *Literature and the Child*, Harcourt, 1981.

Peterson, Linda, and Marilyn Solt, *Newbery and Caldecott Medal and Honor Books: An Annotated Bibliography*, Twayne, 1982.

Schmidt, Gary D., *Katherine Paterson*, Twayne, 1994.

Twentieth-Century Children's Writers, 4th edition, St. James Press, 1995.

PERIODICALS

Booklist, September 1, 1990, p. 59; September 15, 1991, p. 169; December 15, 1993, p. 755; September 15, 1995, p. 171; March 1, 1996, p. 1189.

Books for Keeps, November, 1996, p. 11.

Bulletin of the Center for Children's Books, April, 1988, pp. 164-65; September, 1990, pp. 14-15; November, 1995, pp. 102-103; December, 1996, p. 147.

Horn Book, July-August, 1985, p. 456; November-December, 1990, pp. 753-54; November-December, 1995, pp. 729-30.

Junior Bookshelf, October, 1996, p. 205.

Kirkus Reviews, May 15, 1985, p. J53; July 15, 1991, p. 933; December 15, 1993, p. 1596; October 1, 1995, p. 1435; January 1, 1996, p. 72.

New Advocate, fall, 1997, pp. 5-14.

Publishers Weekly, July 27, 1990, p. 233; July 12, 1991, p. 65; February 12, 1996, p. 71.

School Library Journal, May, 1988, p. 111; October, 1990, p. 111; January, 1992, p. 96; May, 1994, p. 117; March, 1996, p. 213; August, 1999, p. 160.

—*Sketch by J. Sydney Jones*

Ellis Peters

■ Personal

Born Edith Mary Pargeter, September 28, 1913, in Horsehay, Shropshire, England; died October 14, 1995; daughter of Edmund Valentine and Edith (Hordley) Pargeter. *Education:* Attended schools in England. *Hobbies and other interests:* Music (especially opera and folk), reading, theatre, art.

■ Career

Pharmacist's assistant and dispenser in Dawley, Shropshire, England, 1933-40; full-time novelist and translator of prose and poetry from the Czech and Slovak. *Wartime service:* Women's Royal Naval Service, 1940-45; became petty officer; received British Empire Medal. *Member:* International Institute of Arts and Letters, Society of Authors, Authors League of America, Authors Guild, Crime Writers Association.

■ Awards, Honors

Edgar Allan Poe Award for best mystery novel, Mystery Writers of America, 1961, for *Death and the Joyful Woman;* Gold medal, Czechoslovak Society for International Relations, 1968; Silver Dagger, Crime Writers Association, 1981, for *Monk's-Hood.*

■ Writings

NOVELS

Hortensius, Friend of Nero, Dickson, 1936, Greystone Press, 1937.

Iron-Bound, Dickson, 1936.

(Under pseudonym Peter Benedict) *Day Star,* Dickson, 1937.

(Under pseudonym Jolyon Carr) *Murder in the Dispensary,* Jenkins, 1938.

(Under pseudonym Jolyon Carr) *Freedom for Two,* Jenkins, 1939.

The City Lies Foursquare, Reynal, 1939.

(Under pseudonym Jolyon Carr) *Death Comes by Post,* Jenkins, 1940.

(Under pseudonym Jolyon Carr) *Masters of the Parachute Mail,* Jenkins, 1940.

(Under pseudonym John Redfern) *The Victim Need a Nurse,* Jarrolds, 1940.

Ordinary People, Heinemann, 1941, published as *People of My Own,* Reynal, 1942.

She Goes to War, Heinemann, 1942.

The Eighth Champion of Christendom, Heinemann, 1945.

Reluctant Odyssey (sequel to *The Eighth Champion of Christendom*), Heinemann, 1946.

Warfare Accomplished (sequel to *Reluctant Odyssey*), Heinemann, 1947.

The Fair Young Phoenix, Heinemann, 1948.

By Firelight, Heinemann, 1948, published as *By This Strange Fire,* Reynal, 1948.

Lost Children, Heinemann, 1950.

Fallen into the Pit, Heinemann, 1951.
Holiday with Violence, Heinemann, 1952.
This Rough Magic, Heinemann, 1953.
Most Loving Mere Folly, Heinemann, 1953.
The Soldier at the Door, Heinemann, 1954.
A Means of Grace, Heinemann, 1956.
The Heaven Tree (also see below), Doubleday, 1960.
The Green Branch (also see below), Heinemann, 1962.
The Scarlet Seed (also see below), Heinemann, 1963.
A Bloody Field by Shrewsbury, Macmillan, 1972, published as *The Bloody Field,* Viking, 1973.
The Marriage of Megotta, Viking, 1979.
The Heaven Tree Trilogy (contains *The Heaven Tree, The Green Branch,* and *The Scarlet Seed*), Warner Books, 1993.

NOVELS; "BROTHERS OF GWYNEDD" SERIES

Sunrise in the West, Macmillan (London), 1974.
The Dragon at Noonday, Macmillan (London), 1975.
The Hounds of Sunset, Macmillan (London), 1976.
Afterglow and Nightfall, Macmillan (London), 1977.

NOVELS; UNDER PSEUDONYM ELLIS PETERS

Death Mask, Collins, 1959, Doubleday, 1960.
Where There's a Will, Doubleday, 1960, published as *The Will and the Deed,* Collins, 1960, Avon, 1966.
Funeral of Figaro, Collins, 1962, Morrow, 1964.
The Horn of Roland, Morrow, 1974.
Never Pick up Hitch-Hikers!, Morrow, 1976.

"FELSE FAMILY" DETECTIVE NOVELS; UNDER PSEUDONYM ELLIS PETERS

Death and the Joyful Woman, Collins, 1961, Doubleday, 1962.
Flight of a Witch, Collins, 1964.
Who Lies Here?, Morrow, 1965, published as *A Nice Derangement of Epitaphs,* Collins, 1965.
The Piper on the Mountain, Morrow, 1966.
Black Is the Colour of My True-Love's Heart, Morrow, 1967.
The Grass-Widow's Tale, Morrow, 1968.
The House of Green Turf, Morrow, 1969.
Mourning Raga, Macmillan, 1969, Morrow, 1970.
The Knocker on Death's Door, Macmillan, 1970, Morrow, 1971.
Death to the Landlords!, Morrow, 1972.
City of Gold and Shadows, Macmillan, 1973, Morrow, 1974.
Rainbow's End, Macmillan, 1978, Morrow, 1979.

"CHRONICLES OF BROTHER CADFAEL" MYSTERIES; UNDER PSEUDONYM ELLIS PETERS

A Morbid Taste for Bones (also see below), Macmillan, 1977, Morrow, 1978.
One Corpse Too Many (also see below), Macmillan, 1979, Morrow, 1980.
Monk's-Hood, Macmillan, 1980, Morrow, 1981.
Saint Peter's Fair, Morrow, 1981.
The Leper of St. Giles, Macmillan, 1981, Morrow, 1982.
The Virgin in the Ice, Macmillan, 1982, Morrow, 1983.
The Sanctuary Sparrow, Morrow, 1983.
The Devil's Novice, Macmillan, 1983, Morrow, 1984.
Dead Man's Ransom, Morrow, 1984.
The Pilgrim of Hate, Macmillan, 1984, Morrow, 1985.
An Excellent Mystery, Morrow, 1985.
The Raven in the Foregate, Morrow, 1986.
The Rose Rent, Morrow, 1986.
The Hermit of Eyton Forest, Headline, 1987, Mysterious Press, 1988.
The Confession of Brother Haluin, Headline, 1988, Mysterious Press, 1989.
A Rare Benedictine (short stories), Headline, 1988, Mysterious Press, 1989.
The Heretic's Apprentice, Headline, 1989, Mysterious Press, 1990.
The Potter's Field, Headline, 1990, Mysterious Press, 1990.
(With Roy Morgan) *The Summer of the Danes,* Mysterious Press, 1991.
The Benediction of Brother Cadfael (contains *A Morbid Taste for Bones, One Corpse Too Many,* and *Cadfael Country: Shropshire and the Welsh Border*), Mysterious Press, 1992.
The Holy Thief, Mysterious Press, 1993.
Brother Cadfael's Penance, Mysterious Press, 1994.

SHORT FICTION

The Assize of the Dying: Two Novelletes (contains "The Assize of the Dying" and "Aunt Helen"), Doubleday, 1958, published with "The Seven Days of Monte Cervio," as *The Assize of the Dying: Three Stories,* Heinemann, 1958.
The Lily Hand and Other Stories, Heinemann, 1965.

TRANSLATIONS FROM THE CZECH

Jan Neruda, *Tales of the Little Quarter* (short stories), Heinemann, 1957, Greenwood Press, 1977.

Frantisek Kosik, *The Sorrowful and Heroic Life of John Amos Comenius,* State Educational Publishing House (Prague), 1958.

A Handful of Linden Leaves: An Anthology of Czech Poetry, Artia (Prague), 1958.

Joseph Toman, *Don Juan,* Knopf, 1958.

Valja Styblova, *The Abortionists,* Secker & Warburg, 1961.

(With others) Mojmir Otruba and Zdenek Pesat, editors, *The Linden Tree: An Anthology of Czech and Slovak Literature, 1890-1960,* Artia (Prague), 1962.

Bozena Nemcova, *Granny: Scenes from Country Life,* Artia (Prague), 1962, Greenwood Press, 1977.

Joseph Bor, *The Terezin Requiem,* Knopf, 1963.

Alois Jirasek, *Legends of Old Bohemia,* Hamlyn, 1963.

Karel Hynek Macha, *May,* Artia (Prague), 1965.

Vladislav Vancura, *The End of the Old Times,* Artia (Prague), 1965.

Bhumil Hrabel, *A Close Watch on the Trains,* J. Cape, 1968, as *Closely Watched Trains,* Northwestern University Press, 1995.

Josefa Slanska, *Report on My Husband,* Macmillan, 1969.

Ivan Klima, *A Ship Named Hope: Two Novels,* Gollancz, 1970.

Jaroslav Seifert, *Mozart in Prague,* Artia (Prague), 1970.

CONTRIBUTOR

Alfred Hitchcock Presents: Stories Not for the Nervous, Random House, 1965.

Alfred Hitchcock Presents: Stories That Scared Even Me, Random House, 1967.

George Hardinge, editor, *Winter's Crimes 1,* St. Martin's Press, 1969.

A. S. Burack, editor, *Techniques of Novel Writing,* The Writer, 1973.

Hilary Watson, editor, *Winter's Crimes 8,* St. Martin's Press, 1976.

Hardinge, editor, *Winter's Crimes 11,* St. Martin's Press, 1979.

Hardinge, editor, *Winter's Crimes 13,* St. Martin's Press, 1981.

OTHER

The Coast of Bohemia (travel), Heinemann, 1950.

(Under pseudonym Ellis Peters, with Roy Morgan) *Shropshire,* Mysterious Press, 1992.

(Under pseudonym Ellis Peters, with Morgan) *Strongholds and Sanctuaries: The Borderland of England and Wales,* A. Sutton, 1993.

Also author of *The Horn of Roland,* bound with *Danger Money* by Mignon G. Eberhart and *The Romanov Succession* by Brian Garfield, for the Detective Book Club by W. J. Black. Contributor of short stories to magazines, including *Argosy, Good Housekeeping, The Saint,* and *This Week.*

■ **Adaptations**

The Assize of the Dying was filmed under the title *The Spaniard's Curse; Death and the Joyful Woman* was presented on *The Alfred Hitchcock Hour; Mourning Raga* and *The Heaven Tree* were adapted for radio in 1971 and 1975, respectively; the short story "The Purple Children" was produced on television in Canada and Australia. Several of the "Brother Cadfael" books were adapted as television programs starring Derek Jacobi, beginning in 1994.

■ **Sidelights**

Ellis Peters, the chosen nom de plume of British novelist Edith Pargeter, is best remembered for bringing to life the world of the middle ages in her popular chronicle of the later life of the likeable Brother Cadfael. A crusader-turned-monk and herbalist, Brother Cadfael appears in a series of novels and short stories that combines historical facts, a touch of romance, and a healthy dollop of detection into a popular mix. Setting her novels on the Welsh border near the abbey town of Shrewsbury where she herself made her home, Peters positions her characters back in time during the tumultuous reign of Stephen of England, when skirmishes between the man who claimed the throne and his cousin the Empress Maud waged continuously throughout the realm.

Prior to writing the "Brother Cadfael" novels that would occupy her until her death in 1995, Peters wrote a series of thrillers that focus on innocent but savvy teens grappling with murder and assorted mayhem while finding their own place in the adult world. Despite the fact that her plots usually hinged on murder most foul, Peters was consistently able to create likeable protagonists who reflected their creator's resolute belief that the best of human nature would prevail over evil.

Born in Shropshire in 1913, Peters spent her early childhood in the shadow of war. World War I

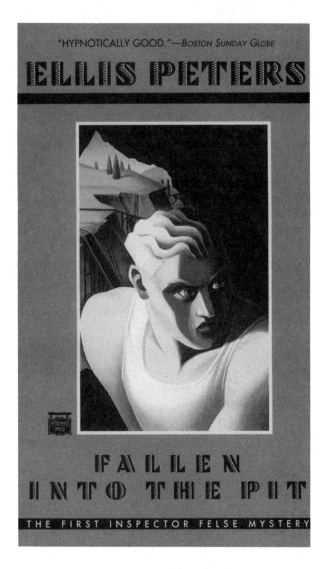

"HYPNOTICALLY GOOD."—*Boston Sunday Globe*

ELLIS PETERS

FALLEN INTO THE PIT

THE FIRST INSPECTOR FELSE MYSTERY

Peters broke into the mystery genre in 1951 with this novel about a student determined to clear his teacher from murder charges.

ended in 1918, when Peters was six, and her teens were spent relatively uneventfully, attending elementary school and then the Coalbrookdale High School for Girls. Beginning in 1933, whenshe was twenty, Peters began work as a pharmacist's assistant, dispensing medications to customers in a shop in the Shropshire town of Dawley. Her spare time was spent writing, and her first novel, *Hortensius, Friend of Nero,* was published in 1936, when Peters was twenty-three. That same year saw her first short story, "The Face of Wax," published in *Good Housekeeping;* Peters would continue to sporadically publish short fiction throughout her career, some of which would later be anthologized

in *The Assize of the Dying* and *The Lily Hand and Other Stories.*

By 1939 war again raged in Europe, and in 1940, at the age of twenty-seven, Peters followed her country's call and joined the war effort. Serving with the Women's Royal Navy Service until World War II ended in 1945, she earned the rank of petty officer and was awarded the British Empire Medal. Peters' experiences would be recounted through the eyes of her young protagonist Catherine Saxon in the 1942 novel *She Goes to War,* which introduces readers to an impulsive young woman on her way to Devonport to join the Women's Royal Navy Service, unsure of her reasons for joining up and about to encounter totally unforeseen consequences of her spur-of-the-moment decision.

Among Peters' favorite authors were Rudyard Kipling and Thomas Mallory, but she also loved to tell her own stories. She would later describe herself as "essentially a storyteller," adding that "in my view no one who can't make that statement can possibly be a novelist, the novel being by definition and extended narrative reflecting the human condition, with the accent on the word 'narrative.'" In the 1950s and 1960s Peters would draw on yet another talent, using the Czech she learned from Czechoslovakian attaches she befriended during her wartime service with the Royal Navy to translate a number of works from such Czech writers as Ivan Klima, Valja Styblova, and Bhumil Hrabel into English for several major British publishers.

Peters began her full-time fiction-writing career penning romance novels during World War II. As Sue Feder commented in *Twentieth-Century Crime and Mystery Writers,* it would take Peters "nearly three decades before she found a way to meld her love of puzzles with her love of history" through the Brother Cadfael novels and other historical fiction. Her early works focus on the war then raging in Europe and the effects their author saw taking place around her. Peters' novel trilogy composed of *The Eighth Champion of Christendom, Reluctant Odyssey,* and *Warfare Accomplished* feature protagonist Jim Benson as he departs from the quiet of his small English village and comes of age amid the destruction of World War II. In the first novel of the series, Benson bids his sweetheart farewell when he goes to fight in the French countryside. Experiencing the horrors of modern warfare, he is also inspired by his growing friendship with a Jewish refugee named Miriam, and Benson returns home a changed man. As Patricia Altner noted of Peters' early work in *Twentieth-Century Romance and Historical Writers,* such novels as *Reluctant Odyssey* and *She Goes to War* "give a vivid account of attitudes of the period since they were written and published during war years." Other novels influenced by Peters' war experiences include 1956's *A Means of Grace,* which finds a young woman named Emmy about to return to her native Germany after the Iron Curtain of communism has divided East from West following World War II. While the friends she made while enjoying refuge in England during the war years think Emmy is crazy to return, the German teen resolves to rebuild her shattered life, while also maintaining relationships with friends despite political differences.

Mystery Novels Warrant New Name

As Peters once commented in *Twentieth-Century Crime and Mystery Writers,* she became a mystery writer "having . . . approached the detective story almost inadvertently" through her 1951 novel *Fallen into the Pit.* The story, which turns on the events following World War II, features protagonist Dominic Felse, a young protege of a former soldier-turned-teacher who would prefigure many of the characteristics of a future Peters protagonist, crusader-turned-monk Brother Cadfael. While other Peters novels feature assorted members of the Felse family, *Fallen into the Pit* finds poor Dominic left on his own to solve a murder and deal with a particularly unpleasant villain.

As Peters quickly found out following *Fallen's* publication, "the reading public likes to know just what to expect from an author, and resents being disconcerted." After receiving letters complaining that *Fallen into the Pit* was not like the other novels published under her real name of Edith Pargeter, Peters "acknowledged, reluctantly, that a pseudonym might after all be more, not less, honest, and that those who wanted only one side of me had a right to some guidance as to where to find it." "Ellis Peters" was born, Ellis being the name of the novelist's brother.

It would be several years before Peters published her second mystery novel, but finally, in 1959, *Death Mask* appeared. Dominic Felse, the hero of Peters' first mystery, is again the focal point. In *Death Mask* he finds himself in trouble when his guardian is killed in a mysterious accident. Dominic is then taken abruptly from his home by his estranged mother, all the while feeling that something threatening lurks around the next corner.

Dominic reaches age sixteen in *Death and the Joyful Woman,* published in 1961. Honored by the Mystery Writers of America with their Edgar Allan Poe Award, the novel finds the usually resilient teen smitten by a young woman who winds up

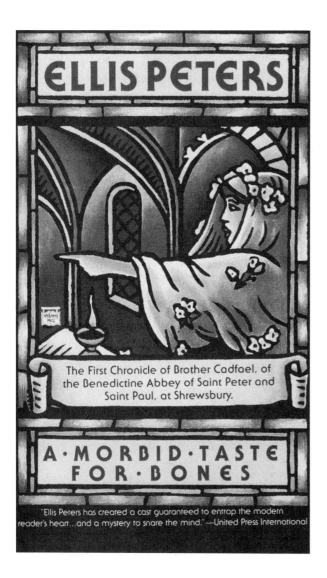

ELLIS PETERS

The First Chronicle of Brother Cadfael, of the Benedictine Abbey of Saint Peter and Saint Paul, at Shrewsbury.

A·MORBID·TASTE FOR·BONES

"Ellis Peters has created a cast guaranteed to entrap the modern reader's heart...and a mystery to snare the mind."—United Press International

Sent to Gwytherin to obtain the bones of St. Winifred, Brother Cadfael instead finds a town divided on handing over the saint in this mystery.

"Streams of consciousness and probings of the solitary, and usually uninteresting, human-soul-at-the-end-of-its-tether are not for me. Nor do I find vice and evil more interesting than virtue, and I hope my books go some way to defy and disprove that too-easily accepted judgment. It gives me great satisfaction that many times people have written to me to tell me, in varying terms, that I have made them feel better, not worse, about being human. That's all the acknowledgment I need."

—Ellis Peters

mobilizes toinvade the tiny Welsh nation. Other novels in the series include *The Dragon at Noonday, The Hounds of Sunset,* and *Afterglow and Nightfall.* The equally popular *The Bloody Field* is also set in Shrewsbury's historical past, this time in the early fifteenth century, as Welsh leader Owen Glendower leads a rebellion against Henry IV, who had seized the English throne from Richard II.

In her "Heaven Tree" trilogy, published again under her actual name of Edith Pargeter, Peters returns to the thirteenth century: in *The Heaven*

suspect number one in a murder investigation. Fortunately, with the help of George Felse, all is right in the end. Peters places her characters far from their ancestral British home in *Mourning Raga,* as twenty-something Dominic and his girlfriend travel to India as escort for a young girl returning home to her father after an extended stay in Shrewsbury. When it is discovered that her father has been missing for over a year, Dominic attempts to track him down in an unfamiliar country.

Born and raised in Shropshire, a region in western England that borders on the tiny country of Wales, Peters grew up fascinated with the history of the region she called home. As she stated in the introduction to *The Benediction of Brother Cadfael,* she "never . . . found any sound reason for leaving it, except perhaps for the pleasure of coming back to it again, after forays into regions otherwise delightful in themselves but no substitute for home." Shropshire and the nearby "Marches of Wales", especially Shrewsbury, were central to much of the author's work. Her "Brothers of Gwynedd" novels, published between 1974 and 1977 under the name Edith Pargeter, take place in this border region of Wales during the thirteenth-century reign of Llewelyn ap Griffith, the first Prince of Wales, as Griffith unites the people of his small nation against marauding Englishmen led by Henry III and Henry's successor, Edward. In the first Gwynedd novel, 1974's *Sunrise in the West,* Prince David and his illegitimate brother Griffith squabble over their inheritance, sowing the seeds of future factionalism as England

ONE OF THE ACCLAIMED BROTHER CADFAEL NOVELS THAT INSPIRED THE PBS-TV SERIES *CADFAEL* STARRING DEREK JACOBI.

ELLIS PETERS

The Ninth Chronicle of Brother Cadfael, of the Benedictine Abbey of Saint Peter and Saint Paul, at Shrewsbury.

D E A D · M A N' S · R A N S O M ·

"Each addition to the series is a joy. Long may the Chronicles continue." —*USA Today*

Brother Cadfael is called upon to help solve the murder of a sheriff, a man believed to have been killed by his daughter's lover.

Tree to depict the cruelty of King John in ordering the death of the foster son of the Welsh prince; in *The Green Branch* to follow a young man's efforts to avenge the death of his father and foil the machinations of the English king; and in *The Scarlet Seed* to show how one man's treachery against his native Wales is thwarted by his own hubris and the threat of civil war in England. Focusing on Harry Talvace, a young stone carver of noble lineage who is the artistic genius behind a lovely stone cathedral known as "the heaven tree," the series follows Harry and his son as they attempt to remain true to their artistic vision within an oppressive feudal society. Peters focuses particularly on the "creative genius of the artist and the complex bonds of loyalty that linked medieval men and women," according to *Library Journal* contributor Dean James. Harry Sr. is subject to the increasingly demanding whims of his wealthy Welsh benefactor Lord Ralf Isambard, whose naked ambition had caused the Heaven Tree cathedral to be built in his honor. When Harry Sr. is murdered after he wins the affection of his patron's beautiful mistress, Madonna Benedetta, artisan son Harry Jr. returns to Wales to avenge his father's death, only to find himself trapped in the villainous Isambard's castle.

Peters "Vividly represent[s] . . . all of the strata of feudal society and its political intrigue, warmaking, nobility of character, cruelty, love, and devotion," according to *Contemporary Novelists* essayist Alan Shucard. *Booklist* reviewer Emily Melton also had praise for the "carefully researched" trilogy, noting that Peters' "charismatic writing and near-magical storytelling skill transport her readers across the centuries to medieval Britain and keep them engaged for the more than 900 pages of this magnificent chronicle. The "Heaven Tree" novels, originally published separately in the early 1960s, were re-released as a trilogy in 1993.

Enter Cadfael, Middle-aged Sleuth

When *The Heaven Tree Trilogy* was re-published in the early 1990s, it caused a *Publishers Weekly* critic to note that, while the work was "well plotted and proficiently detailed," it "may disappoint some Cadfael fans, for [the three "Heaven Tree" novels] lack the crisp, canny characterization and punchy action of Pargeter/Peters's craft at its most maturely honed." Indeed, fans of Peters' histori-

Brother Cadfael's sleuthing skills are put to the test in this 1990 installment of Peters' twelfth-century whodunit series.

cal novels had by now been treated to numerous installments in the growing history of Brother Cadfael, a chronicle that had its beginning in chance.

In the mid-1970s Peters' lifelong fascination with the history of Shrewsbury and surrounding environs caused her to ponder an historical incident involving the relocation of the bones of St. Winnifred to an abbey in the city of Shrewsbury. What a perfect opportunity to hide another body, the mystery writer thought to herself, and the seed was planted for another in her series of historical novels following such works as *The Heaven Tree*. But this time, the stuff of history would be spiced with a dash of murder, as Peters combined her historical fiction with techniques drawn from the pages of her modern thrillers. 1977 saw the first appearance of Brother Cadfael in *A Morbid Taste for Bones.*

"All of [Ellis Peter's] fictions are, in some way, morality dramas in which the villains are . . . redeemed, or come to rue the evil they have wrought, or seem to simply pale into insignificance against the triumph of good, often in the form of love."

—Alan Shucard

Cadfael, a product of the Welsh borders, "sprang to life suddenly and unexpectedly when he was already approaching sixty, mature, experienced, fully armed and seventeen years tonsured," his creator explained in her introduction to *A Rare Benedictine.* Born in Wales slightly more than a decade after William of Normandy seized the crown of England, Cadfael joined the First Crusade as a teen and served under Godfrey de Bouillon in the sieges of Antioch, Ascalon, and Jerusalem. Learning the healing arts of the herbalist on the battlefield, Cadfael gains a respect for the life force and a growing curiosity about all that he encounters in his travels. Returning to England just as King Henry I's legitimate son and heir drowns, Cadfael first makes readers' acquaintance in *A Morbid Taste for Bones,* which takes place a decade later, in 1137. Now a monk, he has joined a small Benedictine company sent into Wales by a covetous English prior with the task of securing the supposedly miracle-producing remains of St. Winnifred from the village of Gwytherin. Once arrived in this tiny Welsh village, Cadfael becomes less than convinced that the spirit of the sainted lady really wishes to be moved, or that the townspeople wish to relinquish her. A pair of murders follow shortly after the monks' arrival, causing Cadfael to play detective, keep the sainted Winnifred in Wales, and act as matchmaker into the bargain.

When she wrote *A Morbid Taste for Bones,* Peters never envisioned Cadfael as an ongoing character in a novel series. However, the indomitable world traveler refused to go quietly, and she was compelled to bring him forth to sleuth again in *One Corpse Too Many.* Again based on an actual historic occurrence, this second Cadfael novel is set shortly after King Stephen's 1138 siege and capture of Shrewsbury from cousin Maud. While preparing the corpses of 94 captured soldiers—executed as a result of their loyalty to Empress Maud—for a proper Christian burial, Cadfael realizes that the body count is actually 95. "To Cadfael," noted *Washington Post Book World* contributor Jean M. White, "it is an individual soul to be avenged," and the monk's efforts to do just that are relayed in a tale of action and suspense that culminates as "a surprise villain is unmasked and compelled to face his accuser in a bloody duel to the death with sword and dagger."

Peters' vivid evocation of Shropshire in the Brother Cadfael chronicles allows her readers to understand both the region and its history. Her ability to depict the "daily hardships suffered by the common people," as well as the ever present political machinations of the era's well-to-do, drew praise from *Twentieth-Century Romance and Historical Writers* contributor Patricia Altner, who commended Peters for her "thorough research. She writes in the melodic prose often associated with medieval historical fiction," added Altner, "and carries it off well. . . . [She] manages also to create in each character a distinct personality and a unique voice."

Unusual Perspective for a Cleric

As with *A Morbid Taste for Bones* and *One Corpse Too Many,* most of Cadfael's adventures reflect the violence and political unrest of the turbulent middle years of twelfth- century England. Although choosing to live his elder years as a monk, Cadfael's past makes his understanding of human nature less one based on a sheltered life devoted to the contemplation of men's souls than one gleaned from his years as a crusader, warrior, and sailor. Reflecting Cadfael's worldly views, Sue Feder described Peters' fictional sleuth in *Twentieth-Century Crime and Mystery Writers* as "a medieval renaissance man who can give Mr. Holmes a run for the money in a contest of the keenest and cleverest eyes. . . . soldier, sailor, Crusader and lover, [Cadfael] come[s] to the cloistered life late and of his own volition."

If you enjoy the works of Ellis Peters, you may also want to check out the following books and films:

Karen Cushman, *Catherine, Called Birdy*, 1994, and *The Midwife's Apprentice*, 1995.
Sharon Kay Penman, *When Christ and His Saints Slept*, 1995.
The Name of the Rose, a film starring Sean Connery, 1986.

In *Monk's-Hood*, published in 1980, Cadfael's ability as a sleuth on par with the legendary Sherlock Holmes is put to the test when he recognizes the signs of monks'-hood—or wolfsbane—poisoning in the death Gervase Bonel, a wealthy landowner who was on the verge of making a large bequest to Shrewsbury Abbey when he was murdered. Three suspects quickly make themselves known, and one of them, the widow Bonel, is a woman who the monk had loved before leaving to join the Crusades. While solving the crime, Cadfael manages to deal tactfully with his former lover's ego; "he is content to allow Mistress Bonel to believe her romantic notion that he entered the monastery because of thwarted love when she tired of waiting for him and married another," noted White. Praising Peters for imbuing her story with "humor and compassion," a *Publishers Weekly* contributor praised *Monks'-Hood* as "perfect escapism and a corking good mystery."

Additional Cadfael novels complete the saga of twelfth-century borderland life. 1982's *The Leper of St. Giles* finds the amiable sleuth aiding a frantic young man named Joscelin and his girlfriend after their efforts to elope and escape an arranged marriage are foiled by accusations that Joscelin killed his girlfriend's elderly intended. "Once again Ellis Peters has combined a proper, carefully plotted detective story with a carefully detailed, convincing evocation of medieval life, and once again the combination is . . . successful and gripping," in the opinion of *Times Literary Supplement* contributor T. J. Binyon. In *The Virgin in the Ice*, the sixth Cadfael offering, the monk must deal with aspects of his own warrior past as he attempts to solve the murder of a young nun discovered in a frozen brook as well as weather the political factions between King Stephen and the Empress Maud that now threaten members of his Benedictine order. A wandering minstrel is saved from an angry mob in *The Sanctuary Sparrow*, while in Peters' 1986 work *The Raven in the Foregate*, gardener Cadfael and his new horticultural assistant are required to do more than yardwork when a newly appointed priest winds up doing a dead man's float in the Abbey's mill pond. Praising Peters' work, *Los Angeles Times Book Review* contributor Nick B. Williams noted: "It's a delight now and then to roll back the centuries and breathe the chilling air of medieval England. None does this better than Ellis Peters."

While many of the early Cadfael novels provide a portrait of everyday life in twelfth-century England, more recent novels have built upon Cadfael's character, as well as a series of romantic entanglements left over from his former life. Also, as Feder noted, in the "more recent chronicles . . . the medieval mindset is put to its fullest use." Feder cited 1989's *The Heretic's Apprentice* and the following year's *The Potter's Field* as examples of Peters' "powerful and evocative" writing and her ability to reflect how sharply modern attitudes and sensibilities differ from those of her historic characters. In addition to novels, Cadfael also appears in the short-story collection *A Rare Benedictine*, which includes "A Light on the Road to Woodstock," which answers readers' questions about why the former adventurer opted for a more cloistered life.

Triumph of Good over Evil

While holding character development as one of the prime challenges of novel-writing, Peters also maintained one "sacred rule" with regard to her craft. The thriller novel must be "a morality, she commented in *Twentieth-Century Crime and Mystery Writers*. "If it strays from the side of the angels, provokes total despair, wilfully destroys . . . the innocent and the good, takes pleasure in evil, that is unforgivable sin." "Streams of consciousness and probings of the solitary, and usually uninteresting, human-soul-at-the-end-of-its-tether are not for me," the novelist later noted. "Nor do I find vice and evil more interesting than virtue, and I hope my books go some way to defy and disprove that too-easily accepted judgment. It gives me great satisfaction that many times people have written to me to tell me, in varying terms, that I have made them feel better, not worse, about being human. That's all the acknowledgment I need."

The thriller novel must be "a morality. If it strays from the side of the angels, provokes total despair, wilfully destroys . . . the innocent and the good, takes pleasure in evil, that is unforgivable sin."

—Ellis Peters

Critics have been quick to agree with Peters' assessment of her fictional underpinnings. "A strong thread running through all of [her] work . . . is her deep sense of morality," Alan Shucard noted in *Contemporary Novelists.* "All of her fictions are, in some way, morality dramas in which the villains are . . . redeemed, or come to rue the evil they have wrought, or seem to simply pale into insignificance against the triumph of good, often in the form of love." Shucard noted this tendency particularly in Peters' novels chronicling the Felse family, as well as her popular series featuring sleuth Brother Cadfael, and remarked that this optimistic outlook was one shared by her many fans.

■ Works Cited

Altner, Patricia, "Edith Pargeter," in *Twentieth-Century Romance and Historical Writers,* St. James Press, 1994, pp. 503-4.

Binyon, T. J., "Criminal Proceedings," in *Times Literary Supplement,* October 16, 1981, p. 1219.

Feder, Sue, "Ellis Peters," in *Twentieth-Century Crime and Mystery Writers,* third edition, St. James Press, 1989, pp. 846-49.

Review of *The Heaven Tree Trilogy,* in *Publishers Weekly,* September 6, 1993, p. 83.

James, Dean, review of *The Heaven Tree Trilogy,* in *Library Journal,* October 1, 1993, p. 128.

Melton, Emily, review of *The Heaven Tree Trilogy,* in *Booklist,* October 1, 1993, p. 255.

Peters, Ellis, introduction to *A Rare Benedictine: The Advent of Brother Cadfael,* Mysterious Press, 1989.

Review of *Monk's-Hood,* in *Publishers Weekly,* April 10, 1981, p. 61.

Peters, Ellis, introduction to *The Benediction of Brother Cadfael,* Mysterious Press, 1993.

Shucard, Alan, "Edith Pargeter," in *Contemporary Novelists,* sixth edition, St. James Press, 1996, pp. 791-93.

White, Jean M., review of *One Corpse Too Many,* in *Washington Post Book World,* May 18, 1980, p. 6.

White, Jean M., review of *Monk's-Hood,* in *Washington Post Book World,* June 21, 1981, p. 6.

Williams, Nick B., "Bloody Sunday," in *Los Angeles Times Book Review,* February 26, 1984, p. 6.

■ For More Information See

BOOKS

Whiteman, Robin, *The Cadfael Companion: The World of Brother Cadfael,* Macdonald, 1991.

PERIODICALS

America, April 16, 1994, p. 19.

Armchair Detective, summer, 1985, pp. 238-245.

Best Sellers, October 1, 1966; August 1, 1967; June 1, 1968; April 15, 1969; March 15, 1970; February, 1984; July, 1984; March, 1986; August, 1986; February, 1987.

Booklist, March 1, 1979, p. 1048; October 1, 1993, p. 263.

Books and Bookmen, April, 1965; December, 1967; June, 1968; June, 1969; August, 1970.

Globe and Mail (Toronto), May 5, 1984; July 5, 1986; December 13, 1986.

Listener, December 17, 1981, p. 794; May 19, 1983.

Los Angeles Times Book Review, January 31, 1982; October 27, 1985, p. 6.

National Review, December 5, 1986.

New Yorker, June 20, 1983; November 5, 1984.

New York Times Book Review, May 9, 1965; November 6, 1966; August 13, 1967; May 26, 1968; June 28, 1981, p. 33; September 26, 1982, p. 41.

Observer, February 14, 1965; May 15, 1966; September 17, 1967; April 21, 1968; January 23, 1983, p. 46; August 4, 1985, p. 23.

Publishers Weekly, October 16, 1978, p. 108; March 19, 1982, p. 58; February 8, 1985, p. 67.

Spectator, March 5, 1965; June 3, 1966.

Time, August 17, 1987.

Times (London), January 21, 1983; July 11, 1985.

Times Literary Supplement, February 25, 1965; June 2, 1966; September 21, 1967; July 18, 1968; October 3, 1980, p. 1118; August 14, 1981, p. 943; February 18, 1983; July 13, 1984, p. 790; January 11, 1985, p. 42; October 3, 1986, p. 1115; January 30, 1987, p. 108.

Village Voice, July 16, 1985.

Voice of Youth Advocates, October, 1983, p. 206.
Washington Post Book World, January 31, 1981; May 16, 1982.
Wilson Library Bulletin, October, 1983.

■ Obituaries

PERIODICALS

Chicago Tribune, October 16, 1995, sec. 1, p. 10.
Facts on File, October 19, 1995, p. 792.*

—Sketch by Susan K. Smith

Rodman Philbrick

Young Readers Award, Maryland Children's Middle School Book Award, and Charlotte Award, New York State Reading Association, and best Young Adult book of the year and recommended book for the Young Adult reluctant reader designations, both American Library Association, all for *Freak the Mighty.*

■ Personal

Born in 1951, in Boston, MA; married Lynn Harnett (a novelist and journalist). *Hobbies and other interests:* Fishing.

■ Addresses

Home--P.O. Box 4149, Portsmouth, NH 03802-4149. *E-mail*—Philbrick@earthlink.net.

■ Career

Writer. Formerly worked as a longshoreman and boat builder. Full-time writer, 1987—.

■ Awards, Honors

Best Novel award, Private Eye Writers of America, 1993, for *Brothers and Sinners;* Judy Lopez Memorial award honor book, 1994, Nebraska Golden Sower Award, Wyoming Soaring Eagle Award, 1997, California Young Readers' award, Arizona

■ Writings

YOUNG ADULT NOVELS

Freak the Mighty, Blue Sky Press, 1993, published as *The Mighty,* Scholastic, Inc., 1997.
The Fire Pony, Scholastic, Inc. (New York City), 1996.
Max the Mighty, Scholastic, Inc., 1998.

MYSTERY NOVELS FOR ADULTS

(As W. R. Philbrick) *Shooting Star,* St. Martin's Press (New York City), 1982.
(As W. R. Philbrick) *Slow Dancer: A Connie Kale Investigation,* St. Martin's Press, 1984.
(As W. R. Philbrick) *Shadow Kills,* Beaufort (New York City), 1985.
(As W. R. Philbrick) *Ice for the Eskimo: A J. D. Hawkins Mystery,* Beaufort, 1986.
(As W. R. Philbrick) *Paint It Black: A J. D. Hawkins Mystery,* St. Martin's Press, 1989.
(As W. R. Philbrick) *The Big Chip,* illustrated by Bruce Jensen, Microsoft Press, 1990.

(As W. R. Philbrick) *Walk on the Water,* St. Martin's Press, 1991.
Brothers and Sinners, Dutton (New York City), 1993.

Also author of novels *The Crystal Blue Persuasion, The Neon Flamingo,* and *Tough Enough.* Author of novels under pseudonym William R. Danse, including *Pulse, The Seventh Sleeper, Hunger,* and *Nine Levels Down.*

"WEREWOLF CHRONICLES" JUVENILE NOVEL SERIES

Night Creature, Scholastic, Inc., 1996.
Children of the Wolf, Scholastic, Inc., 1996.
The Wereing, Scholastic, Inc., 1996.

"HOUSE ON CHERRY STREET" JUVENILE NOVEL SERIES

(With wife, Lynn Harnett) *The Haunting,* Scholastic, Inc., 1995.
(With Lynn Harnett) *The Horror,* Scholastic, Inc., 1995.
(With Lynn Harnett) *The Final Nightmare,* Scholastic, Inc., 1995.

The Haunting was translated into French.

"VISITORS" SERIES; SCIENCE FICTION NOVELS

(With Lynn Harnett) *Strange Invaders,* Scholastic, Inc., 1997.
(With Lynn Harnett) *Things,* Scholastic, Inc., 1997.
(With Lynn Harnett) *Brain Stealers,* Scholastic, Inc., 1997.
(With Lynn Harnett) *Abduction,* Scholastic, Inc., 1998.

■ **Adaptations**

The motion picture *The Mighty* was adapted from Philbrick's novel *Freak the Mighty* and produced by Miramax in 1998.

■ **Work in Progress**

Two young adult novels: *Spaz* and *Rem World.*

■ **Sidelights**

Rodman Philbrick, a screenwriter as well as a novelist, started his career as an author of adult

NOW A MAJOR MOTION PICTURE FROM MIRAMAX FILMS
S T A R R I N G   S H A R O N   S T O N E

Originally published as *Freak the Mighty*

THE
MIGHTY
R O D M A N   P H I L B R I C K

Max and Kevin, two boys labeled as misfits, combine their unique strengths to help others in Philbrick's award-winning novel.

thrillers before shifting his interest to young-adult fiction. Gaining national accolades for his debut novel for teen readers, *Freak the Mighty,* Philbrick has gone on to lead a double life, continuing to pen adult mysteries while also adding to the body of fiction available to younger readers, sometimes in collaboration with his wife, journalist and author Lynn Harnett. Among Philbrick's novels for teens are *The Fire Pony* and *Max the Mighty,* while his works for adults include such works as *Brothers and Sinners,* winner of the Private Eye Writers of America's best novel award in 1993.

Born in Boston, Massachusetts, Philbrick grew up close to the New England coast, where one of his hobbies, fishing, is a prominent regional industry. Asked when he started his career as a writer, Philbrick explained to *Authors and Artists for Young Adults* (*AAYA*): "I got the 'bug' in about sixth grade, when I started writing short stories. Later I wrote a novel-length work while in high school, although it was never published." Although he had proved he had the ability to complete an entire novel-length work without giving up, adulthood meant focusing on the day-to-day necessities of life, and Philbrick devoted much of his attention to earning a living. Drawing his livelihood from the sea in traditional New England fashion, he worked as both a longshoreman and a boatbuilder, but still found enough time to complete several novels. Unfortunately those works were not accepted for publication. In 1982, however, the author made his literary debut with *Shooting Star*, published under the name W. R. Philbrick.

First Book Encourages Further Efforts

Philbrick's *Slow Dancer*, the first of two novels featuring female sleuth Connie Kale, was released by St. Martin's Press two years later, and by 1987 the writer had left his other occupations behind to devote himself to novel-writing full time. Working out the twists and turns of plots to mysteries and detective novels now became his stock in trade, with some of his work published under the pseudonym William R. Dantz. The prolific Philbrick would write more than a dozen mystery novels for adults before moving into the Young Adult market in the early 1990s.

The move from adult whodunits to teen fiction happened, as Philbrick recalled, "more or less by accident." It was inspired by a boy from his own neighborhood, the novelist explained to *AAYA*. "I used to see two kids walking down the street near

Kieran Culkin and Elden Henson play Max and Kevin in *The Mighty*, released by Miramax in 1998.

our apartment. One of them was a big guy and he sometimes carried the small kid on his shoulders. Later my wife and I became friends with the small boy's mother. We discovered that the small boy had Morquio Syndrome, which meant he would never grow to be more than three feet tall. He was extraordinarily bright, had a love for words and books, and an interest in sci-fi and Arthurian legends. About a year after his tragic death, I got an idea for a story inspired by his very special personality. The story is fiction, but I never would have written it if I hadn't known the boy himself."

Inspired by the imagination and courage of his young neighbor, Philbrick was moved to write *Freak the Mighty,* which was published in 1993. An award-winning work that has been translated into

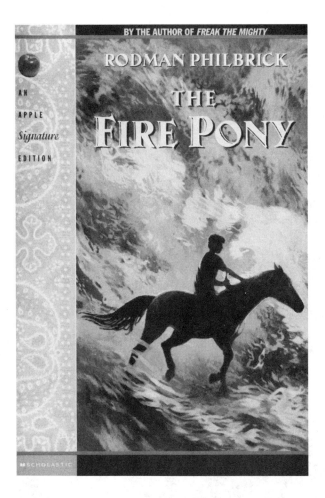

In this 1996 novel, two half-brothers drift from ranch to ranch until they find a home at the Bar None Ranch—where their past catches up with them.

numerous languages and is now read in schools throughout the world, the novel is described by *School Library Journal* contributor Libby K. White as "a wonderful story of triumph over imperfection, shame, and loss." In the book middle-school narrator Maxwell Kane feels doubly cursed. Not only is he clumsy, big boned, and condemned to an academic life of torment as a learning-disabled kid, but his dad is in prison for killing Maxwell's mom and the whole town knows about it. A loner, he spends much of his time in his room in the basement of his grandparents' house. Then something happens to change the dull despair of each passing day: a new boy moves in next door whom Max recognizes from his day-care days. The new boy, Kevin, is wheelchair-bound due to a birth defect that has prevented him from growing physically; however, he has an imagination and an energy that allow him to soar mentally. Soon Max and "Freak"—Kevin's name for himself—are the best of friends. With Kevin sitting astride Max's broad shoulders, the two dub their joint self "Freak the Mighty," channeling the one's strength and the other's intelligence to confront the taunting of other children and get out and explore the world. Caught up in the legend of King Arthur and his noble knights, the two boys search for causes to battle, one of which proves scary: "Killer" Kane returns and kidnaps Max, who escapes only with Kevin's help. Sadly, the effects of Morquio Syndrome begin to overtake Kevin, and he finally dies. Left to continue on his own, Max "is left with the memory of an extraordinary relationship," as well as a heightened sense of his own worth and a more optimistic outlook on his future, according to White.

Freak Draws National Acclaim

The winner of numerous awards, *Freak the Mighty* has been lauded by reviewers for its sensitivity and ability to appeal to more reluctant readers. *Bulletin of the Center for Children's Books* reviewer Deborah Stevenson praises Philbrick's novel as "a sentimental story written with energy and goofy humor instead of sentimentality; . . . kids will be drawn in by the idea and appreciate the story of an unusual relationship. In *Horn Book,* contributor Nancy Vasilakis calls *Freak the Mighty* "A fascinating excursion into the lives of people whose freakishness proves to be a thin cover for their very human existence," while Stephanie Zvirin labels it "both riveting and poignant, with solid

POINT · SIGNATURE

RODMAN PHILBRICK

In search of the truth.
No matter where
it leads.

MAX THE MIGHTY

■ SCHOLASTIC   A NOVEL

In this 1998 novel, Max and his new friend, a girl nicknamed Worm, travel across America after Max is accused of a serious crime.

son. Unlike some novelists who see their work transformed by others' hands onto the screen, Philbrick found the experience a positive one. "I'm quite pleased with the movie version—it reflects the emotional content and suspense of the novel," he told *AAYA*.

Freak the Mighty also sparked a sequel, *Max the Mighty*, which was published in 1998. Reuniting with narrator Max Kane now that he is on his own, readers are introduced to Max's new friend, Rachel, a pre-teen who has escaped so far into her hobby of reading that fellow students now refer to her as the "Worm." What prompts Rachel's reading is her need to mentally escape from the abusive household in which she has found herself since her Mom's remarriage. Unfortunately, her books can't save her from her unstable stepdad, dubbed the "Undertaker" because of his creepy demeanor, and the much older Max—he's now fourteen—eventually agrees to help Rachel run away and find her real father. On their way to Chivalry, Montana, in search of Rachel's real dad, the pair encounter a colorful cast of characters ranging from wild dogs to con artists, and have numerous adventures, all the while trying to elude both the Undertaker, who follows in pursuit, and the police, who are hunting Max in response to the kidnapping charges filed by Rachel's stepfather. Noting that the novel's ending is filled with "surprises" and is "more upbeat" than Philbrick's previous YA novel, a *Publishers Weekly* reviewer calls *Max the Mighty* a "rip-roaring, heartwarming escapade." Although Nancy Vasilakis notes that several of the story's zany characters "sometimes threaten[s] to stretch the reader's sense of reality to its limits," she concludes in her *Horn Book* review that Max and Rachel "grab our attention and engage your heart."

Novels Find Fans in New Territory

While *Freak* and its sequel are very "issue-oriented" novels—learning disabilities, single parenting, and family violence are just a few of the subjects covered—Philbrick's more recent books for younger readers, particularly those written with his wife, are fun reads, while also containing a salting of typical teen concerns in their plots. Because of the fast-paced action and the relatively simple vocabulary in such books as *The Haunting, Abduction,* and *Children of the Wolf,* they have been

characters, brisk pacing, and even a little humor to carry us along" in her Booklist review.

Freak the Mighty soon became a project that grew far beyond Philbrick's original novel. "*Freak the Mighty* was optioned by Scholastic Productions before the book was published," recalled the novelist. Philbrick was asked to adapt his novel into a screenplay, which he did; "but the producers thought it was too close to the original novel and hired another screenwriter," he explained. In 1998 *Freak the Mighty* made it into theatres, where it proved a success with young audiences as *The Mighty,* starring Sharon Stone and Gillian Ander-

If you enjoy the works of Rodman Philbrick, you may also want to check out the following books and films:

Sue Ellen Bridgers, *All Together Now,* 1979.
Betsy Byars, *The Summer of the Swans,* 1970.
M. E. Kerr, *Little Little,* 1981.
Simon Birch, a film starring Ian Michael Smith and Ashley Judd, 1998.

praised for their ability to motivate even reluctant readers to turn the page and see what happens next.

"I don't have any 'lessons' in mind when I write about adolescent kids," Philbrick explained in response to a question regarding his opinion on the importance of inserting a "message" in books for young adult readers. "Most of what I write, and the first person 'voice' I use, comes out of my own memories of being that age. The books Lynn Harnett and I collaborate on are intended to be easy-reading mass market paperbacks. My own work might be considered slightly more 'serious', but, I hope, still entertaining enough to hold a reader's attention. For the most part I find that all young readers really want is a good story, of whatever type." However, Philbrick also expressed delight that the techniques he uses in creating his adult mysteries—"how to keep a reader turning pages to find out what happens next," for example—have been of value in his YA projects.

Fire Pony Reflects Ranch Life

Philbrick's 1996 novel, *Fire Pony,* which would be his second written for a younger readership, also uses Montana as its setting and features a young man as its narrator. In the story, half-brothers Joe and Roy Dilly are on their own, having fled from ranch to ranch after the habits of arsonist Joe put an end to job after job. Now Joe has found work at the Bar None Ranch, where the owner, Nick Jessup, raises Arabian horses. The older of the two brothers, Joe has a talent for both blacksmithing and saddle-breaking horses and soon becomes a prized employee. Meanwhile, eleven-year-old Roy, while remaining concerned that his older brother's fascination with fire will ultimately force the two to go on the run again, begins to settle in at the ranch. Trying to follow in Joe's footsteps, he at-tempts to break a palomino filly named Lady Luck, which Jessup has promised to Roy if he is successful. Ultimately, Roy rides Lady Luck to glory at a rodeo, despite the efforts of another man named Mullins to thwart the boy's success and get the horse for himself. Older brother Joe, angered at Mullins, first accosts the man, then goes into a hay field and sets a fire which quickly grows out of control and ultimately threatens the life of Roy and Lady Luck. Noting the complex personalities of the two brothers, *Horn Book* contributor Martha V. Parravano comments that Philbrick's portrait of "the scarred but spirited Roy is near flawless"; likewise, Joe is "loving and funny and talented even as he is scary and unpredictable and disturbed." Praising Joe's rescue effort as the high point of the novel, *School Library Journal* contributor Christina Linz notes that *The Fire Pony* "has plenty of action and suspense and is a good choice for reluctant readers."

"The idea for *The Fire Pony* came while Lynn and I were driving across the Southwest," Philbrick explained of the novel's inspiration. "I loved the landscape, and when we got to California the state was suffering from a rash of fires. The two ideas combined into a story about a boy and his older brother, who is not only a talented farrier, but a sometimes arsonist. The idea from that part may have been inspired by my love of Faulkner, in particular his story 'The Barn Burner.'"

Husband-and-Wife Writing Team

Continuing his prolific career as an author of adult mysteries, Philbrick and his wife Lynn Harnett collaborate on mass-market paperbacks for school-age readers, and have begun several novel series in the horror and science fiction genres. Their novels appeal to even reluctant readers due to their fast-paced plots, with many chapters coming to a cliff-hanger conclusion that keep teens captivated—and reading. Part of their success may be credited to their ability to devise a system of working together that seems to work well. As Philbrick explained, "Lynn and I discuss story ideas. Then I write an outline and Lynn does all the heavy lifting, writing the first draft of the chapters. After more discussion we polish up a finished draft."

As far as his own projects go, Philbrick remains constantly busy, reserving his mornings for his craft, and rewarding himself with a chance to go fishing in the afternoon. One of his forthcoming books, titled *Spaz,* is a YA novel set in the future; next on the list is an adult thriller. Another teen novel, *Rem World,* is scheduled to be published in the spring of 2000. "I've never stopped writing for adults," Philbrick explained to *AAYA,* "although I spend more time writing YA novels these days. I've also written a number of screenplays, but none of them have been produced yet! I doubt I'll ever write much nonfiction, as I have a bad habit of making things up."

A voracious reader for many years, Philbrick counts among his favorite authors suspense novelist Elmore Leonard, as well as writers like Mark Twain and Joseph Conrad. Perhaps because of his roots in the seafaring culture of the New England shoreline, Philbrick also enjoys the seagoing fiction of Patrick O'Brien. He and his wife divide their time between their home in Maine and the Florida Keys.

■ Works Cited

Linz, Christina, review of *The Fire Pony,* in *School Library Journal,* September, 1996, p. 206.

Review of *Max the Mighty,* in *Publishers Weekly,* January 26, 1998, p. 91.

Parravano, Martha V., review of *The Fire Pony,* in *Horn Book,* July/August, 1996, p. 464.

Philbrick, Rodman, interview with *Authors and Artists for Young Adults,* June, 1999.

Stevenson, Deborah, review of *Freak the Mighty,* in *Bulletin of the Center for Children's Books,* January, 1994, p. 165.

Vasilakis, Nancy, review of *Freak the Mighty,* in *Horn Book,* January-February, 1994, p. 74.

Vasilakis, Nancy, review of *Max the Mighty,* in *Horn Book,* July/August, 1998, p. 495.

White, Libby K., review of *Freak the Mighty,* in *School Library Journal,* December, 1993, p. 137.

Zvirin, Stephanie, review of *Freak the Mighty,* in *Booklist,* December 15, 1993, p. 748.

■ For More Information See

PERIODICALS

ALAN Review, Winter, 1999.

Bulletin of the Center for Children's Books, July/August, 1996, p. 383; April, 1998, p. 291.

Kirkus Reviews, February 15, 1998, p. 272.

New Yorker, December 13, 1993, pp. 115-116.

School Library Journal, April, 1998, p. 136.

Voice of Youth Advocates, April, 1994, p. 30; October, 1996, p. 212; June, 1998, p. 124.

ON-LINE

Rodman Philbrick's Web site, located at http://www.rodmanphilbrick.com.

—Sketch by Pamela L. Shelton

Arthur Rackham

■ Personal

Born September 19, 1867, in London, England; died September 6, 1939; son of Alfred Thomas (a civil servant; Marshal of the Admiralty Court) and Anne (Stevenson) Rackham; married Edyth Starkie (an artist), July 16, 1903 (died March, 1941); children: Barbara Rackham Edwards. *Education:* Attended Lambeth School of Art.

■ Career

Artist and illustrator. While studying art in night school, worked in an insurance office, 1885-92; staff artist for the *Westminster Budget* (newspaper); free-lance illustrator, 1893—. *Exhibitions:* Rackham's drawings are exhibited in public collections in Barcelona, Melbourne, Paris, Vienna, and London. *Member:* Royal Water-Colour Society, Societe Nationale des Beaux Arts (associate).

■ Awards, Honors

Gold medal winner at exhibitions in Milan, Italy, 1906, in Barcelona, Spain, 1911, and in Paris, France; master of the Art Workers' Guild, 1919.

■ Illustrator

Anthony Hope (pseudonym of Anthony Hope Hawkins), *The Dolly Dialogues*, Westminster Gazette, 1894.

S. J. Adair-Fitzgerald, *The Zankiwank and the Bletherwitch*, Dutton, 1896.

Henry Seton Merriman (pseudonym of Hugh Stowell Scott) and S. G. Tallantyre, *The Money-Spinner and Other Character Notes*, Smith, Elder, 1896.

H. S. Merriman, *The Grey Lady*, Smith, Elder, 1897.

Charles Lever, *Charles O'Malley, the Irish Dragoon*, Putnam, 1897.

Maggie Browne (pseudonym of Margaret Hamer Andrewes), *Two Old Ladies, Two Foolish Fairies and a Tom Cat: The Surprising Adventures of Tuppy and Tue*, Cassell, 1897, published as *The Surprising Adventures of Tuppy and Tue*, 1904.

Frances Burney, *Evalina; or, The History of a Young Lady's Entrance into the World*, Newnes, 1898.

R. H. Barham, *The Ingoldsby Legends; or, Mirth and Marvels*, Dent, 1898.

Harriet Martineau, *Feats on the Fjord: A Tale*, Dent, 1899.

Charles and Mary Lamb, *Tales from Shakespeare*, Dent, 1899.

Jonathan Swift, *Gulliver's Travels into Several Remote Nations of the World*, Dent, 1900.

Jacob and Wilhelm Grimm, *Fairy Tales*, translated by Mrs. Edgar Lucas, Freemantle, 1900, twenty-five tales from a 1909 edition reprinted as *Snow-*

drop and Other Tales, Dutton, 1920, revised edition published as *Grimm's Fairy Tales: Twenty Stories*, Viking, 1973.

Agnes Grozier Herbertson, *The Bee-Blowaways*, Cassell, 1900.

C. R. Kenyon, *The Argonauts of the Amazon*, Dutton, 1901.

B. G. Niebuhr, *The Greek Heroes*, Cassell, 1903.

Greene, *The Grey House on the Hill*, Thomas Nelson, 1903.

Mary Cholmondeley, *Red Pottage*, Newnes, 1904.

W. P. Drury, *The Peradventures of Private Paget*, Chapman & Hall, 1904.

Henry Harbour, *Where Flies the Flag*, Collins, 1904.

Richard Henry Dana, *Two Years before the Mast*, Winston, 1904.

Washington Irving, *Rip Van Winkle*, Doubleday, Page, 1905.

A. L. Haydon, *Stories of King Arthur*, Cassell, 1905.

(With H. R. Millars and others) Myra Hamilton, *Kingdoms Curious*, Heinemann, 1905.

James M. Barrie, *Peter Pan in Kensington Gardens*, Scribner, 1906, published in an edition retold by May C. Gillington Byron, Scribner, 1930.

Rudyard Kipling, *Puck of Pook's Hill*, Doubleday, Page, 1906.

Lewis Carroll (pseudonym of Charles L. Dodgson), *Alice's Adventures in Wonderland*, Doubleday, Page, 1907.

A. E. Bonser, B. Sidney Woolf, and E. S. Buchleim, *The Land of Enchantment*, Cassell, 1907.

Eleanor Gates, *Good Night*, Crowell, 1907.

William Shakespeare, *A Midsummer-Night's Dream*, Doubleday, Page, 1908, published with new illustrations, Limited Editions Club, 1939.

De La Motte Fouque, *Undine*, adapted from the German by W. L. Courteney, Doubleday, Page, 1909.

Maggie Browne, *The Book of Betty Barber*, Duckworth, 1910.

Richard Wagner, *The Rhinegold and the Valkyrie*, Doubleday, Page, 1910.

Wagner, *Siegfried* [and] *The Twilight of the Gods*, Doubleday, Page, 1911.

Aesop, *Aesop's Fables*, translated by V. S. Vernon Jones, Doubleday, Page, 1912.

Mother Goose, *The Old Nursery Rhymes*, Heinemann, 1913, published as *Mother Goose Nursery Rhymes*, Viking, 1975.

Arthur Rackham's Book of Pictures, Century, 1913.

Charles Dickens, *A Christmas Carol*, Lippincott, 1915.

The Allies' Fairy Book, Lippincott, 1916, published as *A Fairy Book*, Doubleday, Page, 1923, published as *Fairy Tales from Many Lands*, Viking, 1974.

J. and W. Grimm, *Little Brother and Little Sister*, Dodd, 1917.

Thomas Malory, *The Romance of King Arthur and His Knights of the Round Table* (abridged from Malory's *Morte d'Arthur* by Alfred Pollard), Macmillan, 1917.

Flora A. Steel, *English Fairy Tales Retold*, Macmillan, 1918.

Algernon C. Swinburne, *The Springtide of Life: Poems of Childhood*, Lippincott, 1918.

Charles Seddon Evans, reteller, *Cinderella*, Lippincott, 1919.

Julia Ellsworth Ford, *Snickety Nick: Rhymes of Witter Bynner*, Moffat, Yard, 1919.

Some British Ballads, Dodd, 1919.

Evans, reteller, *The Sleeping Beauty*, Lippincott, 1920.

Irish Fairy Tales, Macmillan, 1920.

Eden Phillpotts, *A Dish of Apples*, Hodder & Stoughton, 1921.

John Milton, *Comus*, Doubleday, Page, 1921.

Nathaniel Hawthorne, *A Wonder Book*, G. H. Doran, 1922.

Christopher Morley, *Where the Blue Begins*, Doubleday, Page, 1925.

Margery Williams Bianco, *Poor Cecco*, G. H. Doran, 1925.

Shakespeare, *The Tempest*, Doubleday, Page, 1926.

Abbie Farwell Brown, *The Lonesomest Doll*, new edition, Houghton, 1928.

Irving, *The Legend of Sleepy Hollow*, McKay, 1928.

Oliver Goldsmith, *The Vicar of Wakefield*, McKay, 1929.

Izaak Walton, *The Compleat Angler*, McKay, 1931.

Clement C. Moore, *The Night Before Christmas*, Lippincott, 1931.

Dickens, *The Chimes*, Limited Editions Club, 1931.

John Ruskin, *The King of the Golden River*, Lippincott, 1932.

Hans Christian Andersen, *Fairy Tales*, McKay, 1932.

Christina Rossetti, *Goblin Market*, Lippincott, 1933.

The Arthur Rackham Fairy Book, Lippincott, 1933.

Robert Browning, *The Pied Piper of Hamelin*, Lippincott, 1934.

Edgar Allen Poe, *Tales of Mystery and Imagination*, Lippincott, 1935.

Henrik Ibsen, *Peer Gynt*, Lippincott, 1936.

Kenneth Grahame, *The Wind in the Willows*, Limited Editions Club, 1940.

Contributor of drawings to numerous periodicals, including the *Westminster Gazette, Scraps, Illustrated*

Bits, Daily Graphic, Pall Mall Budget, The Ladies' Field, Cassell's Magazine, Little Folks, Punch, and *St. Nicholas.*

■ Sidelights

Though his father planned a business career for him, renowned illustrator Arthur Rackham worked in an insurance office for seven years while he attended art school at night and began to get established in the profession he had leaned toward since childhood. His legacy is a long list of highly regarded books, many classics among them—including *Gulliver's Travels, Rip Van Winkle,* and *Peter Pan*—graced with the imaginative illustrations

Rackham's illustration of Gulliver fighting off a swarm of wasps comes from Jonathan Swift's *Gulliver's Travels into Several Remote Nations of the World,* published in 1900.

that earned him critical acclaim and a wide following in his lifetime. After his death, Rackham's early works became collectors' treasures.

Rackham was born on September 19, 1867, in London, to Alfred Thomas Rackham, a civil servant, and Anne Stevenson Rackham. There were twelve children in the family; Rackham told *The Junior Book of Authors* that his boyhood "was spent in a noisy, merry, busy little community of work and play almost large enough to be independent of outside engagements."

Artwork Gains Acceptance

After his years in the insurance office, Rackham joined the staff of the newspaper, *Westminster Budget,* where he worked from 1892 to 1896 and became known for his feature, "Sketches from the Life." At the same time, he was doing freelance work. The year 1899 was a difficult period for him—the "worst time in my life," as he described it in *Bookman*—because of changing values in art and the growing popularity of photography. But his unique talent began to gain recognition from other artists, and soon he was sought by art societies, dealers, and publishers. His work in *Fairy Tales of the Brothers Grimm,* published in 1900, marked the beginning of his fame as an illustrator.

By 1910 Rackham was regarded as a leading illustrator. He had been "elected an associate member of the Royal Society of Painters in Water Colours in 1902 and was promoted to full membership six years later," according to *Fantastic Illustration and Design in Britain, 1850-1930.* He had become a member of the Art Workers' Guild in 1909 and was very active in that organization during the years from 1917 to 1919; in 1919 he held the master's chair. He spoke publicly about art and illustration, and in the 1920s he visited the United States more thanonce to meet some of his following here. In 1923 he addressed a high school class in New Jersey, and during his 1929 trip he was discomfited by the noise of New York but pleased by the warm reception he was given.

Rackham's immediate family was involved in art, too. He married the portrait painter Edyth Starkie in 1903, and their daughter, Barbara, born in 1908, was sometimes a model for her father. Much later, in 1931, she traveled to Denmark with him on

Rackham illustrated scenes from various Shakespearian plays, including this one from *A Midsummer's Night Dream*, published in 1908.

his search for illustrations for Hans Christian Andersen's *Fairy Tales*. After the Rackhams built a house at Limpsfield, Surrey, their garden provided inspiration for Rackham's work, especially a favorite old beech tree that served as a model for some of the many trees with gnarled branches and human-like faces that were hallmarks of his work.

If you enjoy the works of Arthur Rackham, you may also want to check out the following:

The illustrations of nineteenth-century English artists Walter Crane, Kate Greenaway, and Randolph Caldecott.

The artwork of American painter Michael Hague, including his illustrations for Kenneth Grahame's *The Wind and the Willows*, 1980.

Illustrates Classic Work

Early in Rackham's career, according to a *Horn Book* article by George Macy, Kenneth Grahame asked Rackham to illustrate his book, *The Wind in the Willows*. Rackham had been too busy to accept the invitation and had regretted it for nearly thirty years. In 1936, Macy visited Rackham to persuade him to illustrate another book, but the outcome of the visit was an agreement that Rackham would illustrate *The Wind in the Willows* first.

It was the last book Rackham illustrated. He had agreed to deliver the watercolors to the publisher in the spring of 1938, but at that time he had to undergo surgery for cancer. He continued the job nevertheless, able toward the end to work only half an hour a day, and finished in the late summer of 1939, just before England declared war on Germany. On September 7, he died.

Robert Lawson paid this tribute to the artist in *Horn Book* in 1940: "The appreciation of Rackham's genius has suffered, I think, by its complete perfection. All his drawings appear so polished, so finished, so graceful, that many fail to realize the great strength and firm knowledge that underlie this seeming ease." And in October, 1967, Ellen Shaffer also said in *Horn Book*, "It has been nearly thirty years since the death of Arthur Rackham; a whole new generation has reached maturity in that period and been charmed by his work, as were their parents and their grandparents before them. Their children, too, are delighting in the books he illustrated, and their appreciation of his art will grow with the years."

■ Works Cited

Johnson, Diana L., *Fantastic Illustration and Design in Britain, 1850- 1930*, Museum of Art, Rhode Island School of Design, 1979, pp. 82-85.

Kunitz, Stanley J., and Howard Haycraft, editors, *The Junior Book of Authors*, 2nd edition, H. W. Wilson, 1951, pp. 252-53.

Lawson, Robert, "The Genius of Arthur Rackham," *Horn Book*, May-June, 1940, pp. 147-51.

Macy, George, "Arthur Rackham and 'The Wind in the Willows,'" *Horn Book*, May-June, 1940, pp. 153-58.

Rackham, Arthur, "The Worst Time in My Life," *Bookman*, October, 1925.

Shaffer, Ellen, "Arthur Rackham, 1867-1939," *Horn Book*, October, 1967, pp. 617-21.

■ For More Information See

BOOKS

Children's Books and Their Creators, edited by Anita Silvey, Houghton, 1995.

Dictionary of Literary Biography, Volume 141: *British Children's Writers, 1880-1914*, Gale, 1994, pp. 249-60.

Hudson, Derek, *Arthur Rackham, His Life and Work*, Scribners, 1960.

Hamilton, James, *Arthur Rackham*, Arcade, 1990.*

Chap Reaver

■ Personal

Given name is Herbert R. Reaver; born June 10, 1935, in Cincinnati, OH; died January 11, 1993, in Marietta, GA; son of Herbert R. (a chiropractor) and Mildred (Vordenburg) Reaver; married Dixie Reece (a realtor), September 3, 1959; children: Chappie, Scott. *Education:* Palmer College of Chiropractic, D.C., 1957. *Politics:* Republican. *Religion:* "No preference." *Hobbies and other interests:* Racquet sports, fishing, gardening.

■ Career

Private practice in chiropractic, Cincinnati, OH, 1957-80, Marietta, GA, 1980-93; writer. Part-time writing instructor at Marietta Junior High School, in association with the Marietta Community School Program. *Military service:* Served in the Air Force Reserve.

■ Awards, Honors

Delacorte Press Prize for an Outstanding First Young Adult Novel, 1990, and Edgar Allan Poe Award for best young adult mystery, Mystery Writers of America, 1991, both for *Mote*; Hugo Award nomination for short story, World Science Fiction Society, 1992, for "Feel Good Stuff."

■ Writings

Mote (young adult mystery), Delacorte, 1990.
A Little Bit Dead (young adult western), Delacorte, 1992.
Bill, Delacorte, 1994.

Contributor of articles and short stories to periodicals, including *Amazing Stories* and several humor publications.

■ Sidelights

Chap Reaver is best remembered for his 1990 young adult mystery, *Mote*, which won the Edgar Allan Poe Award. Reaver began a career in chiropractic medicine in Ohio in 1957, continuing his practice in Georgia after his family's move there in 1980. After his relocation Reaver also began dabbling in writing, penning *Mote* and contributing articles and short stories to periodicals. In addition, he found time to teach writing classes at Marietta Junior High School. In 1992, he saw publication of his young adult western *A Little Bit Dead*. He had completed a third novel, entitled *Bill*, before his death.

Reaver never planned to become a writer. He was perfectly contented with his private practice as a chiropractor and active family life. But then in 1980 he moved with his wife and two children to Marietta, Georgia, where they did not have many friends or relations. Reaver decided to use some of his free time for writing. After publishing only a few short stories and articles, his first novel, *Mote*, won the most prestigious prize for mystery fiction in the United States—the Edgar Allan Poe Award. "What is nice is that it does happen," Reaver once stated. "I'm a real ordinary guy who wrote a book, and the long shot came and got it published, which is a thousand to one or whatever. Not only got published, but got

After Reece saves the life of Shanti, a Yahi brave, Reece must clear his name of murder with Shanti's help in this 1992 novel set in the old West.

nominated for an Edgar; not only got nominated, but won the damn thing. It can happen; so keep your courage up."

Reaver—who's given name is Herbert—got his nickname the day he was born in his family's home in Cincinnati, Ohio. "Dad said, 'What a cute little chap,'" the author recalled. "And I take his word for it; I've been Chap as long as I know." Like his father, Reaver received his degree in chiropractic and established a private practice. He would have remained in his home town, except that his wife, whom Reaver first met when he was stationed at an Air Force base in Georgia, missed living in the South. After moving to Georgia, Reaver drew on his wife's career as a source of inspiration: "I did a few pieces about my wife's real estate activities from the standpoint of the long-suffering husband. Then I did a lot of humor pieces in professional magazines like problems of ethics and morals. It is always with a light approach, hopefully to entertain, because if I don't keep that in mind I tend to start preaching."

Fast Start in Publishing

Unlike many beginning writers, Reaver had little trouble getting his articles published. "It really helped that I was ignorant," he explained. "I didn't know that it was hard to do, and that you had to get three hundred rejections. So I just wrote a story and sold it, and then they wanted some more and I sold the first five or six before I got a rejection slip. So I guess I've got some kind of natural storytelling ability." Before his novel *Mote* was accepted by a publisher, Reaver received a scant eight rejections, an unusually low amount. Nevertheless, he asserted: "What I've learned is that the publishing business doesn't seem like a very nice business to me. The people in children's and young adults' publishing seem like the cream of the crop. They really seem well motivated; they're not just—I don't think—in it for the money. They're really trying to write good books for kids."

Reaver had originally planned *Mote* to be for an adult audience, but after it was written he and his editor decided it was more suited to young adults. "My vocabulary is about that level," the author confessed. "That's kind of my natural voice." Reaver also commented, "I find that to be

Reaver completed this novel about Jess, a motherless girl whose father is a bootlegger and whose best friend, Bill, is a dog, just before his death in 1993.

a very interesting time of life anyway and set it there."

Award-winning Novel

Mote concerns a teenager named Chris and his investigation of the murder of one of his teachers. The police believe that Chris's friend, a vagabond Vietnam veteran nicknamed "Mote," is responsible because one of his knives was found at the scene. Chris, however, is certain that Mote could never commit murder. With the help of a black police detective named Steinert, Chris conducts a search for the killer that leads him into the hands of a white supremacist group called Equal Rights for White Americans and its African American counterpart, the Black Brigade. Racism, then, becomes one of the important themes in the story.

Reaver's concern about this topic dated back to an experience he had as a child. One day his father, who had a dark complexion and had gotten very tan after a trip to Florida, was refused a ticket to the theater. "He looked dark enough that the ticket seller was in doubt and refused seating," Reaver recalled. "It really had an effect on my father who up to that time had never given a thought to racial matters. He became very active in the NAACP, and rose to national vice president, and we had meetings in our house. I think I grew up in as racially liberal an atmosphere as possible." Reaver's background made him impatient with prejudiced people. "When I see racism it seems like such a waste of time. We should have been through that a long time ago."

Because the author considers the viewpoints of racist people to be ridiculous, their ideas can seem laughable until he becomes aware of "their potential for harm and unhappiness." Then he would get angry. Still, Reaver acknowledged, "I tend to deal with them in a humorous way. I think it's more effective." "I think that my best thing is to write with a humorous approach to serious problems," Reaver revealed at one point. In addition to the issue of racism, *Mote* deals with other serious matters like divorce and the tragic memories of Vietnam.

Despite the presence of themes like divorce and racism, the main focus of *Mote*, Reaver once revealed, concerns "coming of age. I think it's more a book about friendship, bonding and friendship between the kid and Steinert, and the kid and Mote, cross-cultural and cross-racial friendships, and the commonality of that." Reaver also admitted that there are autobiographical elements in *Mote*. For one thing, Chris and the author both enjoy fly fishing and are avid tennis players. But more than this, Reaver said that all the main characters in the story express some side of himself. "This was a wonderful vehicle for me because I think, like most males, part of me is still very immature and stuck in this childish mode of being sixteen. So it's not a problem for me to speak in that voice. I think Chris's narrative sounds like a sixteen-year old. It was not hard for me to duplicate that because part of me is still there. Part of my emotional reactions are still very little-boyish. But then part of me is Mote's stuff too. I know what's important now. When I had something to say that needed a wiser, more experienced voice, I had Mote, or when I needed kind of a street wise thing to say, I had Steinert, and when I had a juvenile thing to say, or a little uncertain thing to say, I had Chris or Billy. And so I had all the various parts of myself, the parent and the child. I think there's some kind of psychological system that talks about that, that we each have a parent side and a child side. I had mouths through which to speak all the sides of myself."

Because the characters and their relationships in the book are what was important to Reaver, he was surprised *Mote* was considered for the Edgar Allan Poe Award. "I never figured the who-done-it aspect was its strongest point." But winning an Edgar did not change Reaver's attitude toward writing in any way. As he once remarked, "People pay a little bit more attention to you now that you've got an award that says you wrote a good book. . . . I'm glad I won, but I wish the system would allow a little bit of something for second and third. Just being nominated is a marvelous honor with all the mysteries that are written every year." The book was also popular with critics; *Wilson Library Bulletin* reviewer Cathi MacRae called the work "an exceptional first novel of riveting suspense and sly humor."

Young Protagonists Face Danger

Reaver's second work, *A Little Bit Dead,* tells a story of the old West. When Reece, a fur trader, comes across a lynching party, he rescues the intended victim, a young Indian named Shanti. The lynchers want to exact revenge, however, and they accuse Reece of a murder, burn down his house, and kill Shanti's family. Reece and Shanti are forced into a confrontation with the men a bloody shoot-out at a hidden goldmine. A *Publishers Weekly* reviewer declared thatReaver "has fashioned a complex, tightly woven tale that moves through scene after gripping scene with sure-footed grace," and a contributor in *Kirkus Reviews* found the work "violent but well-crafted, with a thoughtful, clear-eyed protagonist."

Bill, the author's final novel, concerns a motherless teenage girl in rural Kentucky. Jess Gates carves out a living with her often absent, alco-

If you enjoy the works of Chap Reaver, you may also want to check out the following books and films:

Robbie Branscum, *The Murder of Hound Dog Bates,* 1982.
A. E. Cannon, *The Shadow Brothers,* 1990.
Pieter Van Raven, *Pickle and Price,* 1990.
True Grit, a film starring John Wayne, 1969.

holic father, Leonard, and her dog, Bill. Jess' life undergoes a profound change when "Wrong Man" Shaft Dudley, the local Alcohol Beverage Control agent, appears, determined to shut down Leonard's still. Her life is further complicated when Leonard reveals the whereabouts of a hidden treasure to both Jess and the villainous Hawkins. "Reaver's story is filled with great humor and affection, wonderful, well-realized characters, and enough action to please even reluctant readers," stated Chris Sherman in *Booklist.* According to a critic in the *Bulletin of the Center for Children's Books,* the author's "perfect sense of pace, flawless downhome style, humorously individualized characterizations, and absolute fidelity to the protagonist's viewpoint make for unique reading."

As a writer for young adults, Reaver felt a certain obligation toward his audience. "It's important that I remind myself to entertain because if I don't I'm going to go to preaching, and the kids are going to turn me off and I don't blame them. I don't want to be preached to either. I'm old enough! And I didn't like it back then and that's what everybody's doing. I think the kids need to learn that they're okay." He then added, "I think it's a greater responsibility writing for teens or young adults than it is writing for adults because their values have not all been shaped yet and you'll have a greater influence. You have to be more careful and you have to feel that responsibility more and really think about what you're doing. Those are young precious lives, and it's an honor if you can just have their attention for a while, much less have any influence. You don't want to squander that."

Reaver also had an influence on teenagers as a creative writing teacher for high school students.

"I really get a kick out of it. I would like to do more, but there are some educators here that are a little bit afraid of Mote. It's a little bit too provocative for them, and it's got the F-word in there, and it's got racial epithets." Reaver later observed, "I think a lot of people write down to kids. I think it's a terrible mistake. They pick that up so quick, and I think that a lot of people try to moralize to them. They don't need that."

■ Works Cited

Review of *Bill, Bulletin of the Center for Children's Books,* May, 1994, pp. 299-300.

Review of *A Little Bit Dead, Kirkus Reviews,* October 1, 1992, p. 1259.

Review of *A Little Bit Dead, Publishers Weekly,* October 26, 1992, p. 72.

MacRae, Cathi, review of *Mote, Wilson Library Bulletin,* March, 1991, p. 112.

Sherman, Chris, review of *Bill, Booklist,* April 1, 1994, p. 1441.

■ For More Information See

PERIODICALS

Booklist, September 1, 1992.
Horn Book, September-October, 1994, p. 591.
Kirkus Reviews, June 1, 1994.
Publishers Weekly, July 13, 1990, p. 57; April 4, 1994.
School Library Journal, September, 1992, p. 279.
Voice of Youth Advocates, February, 1991, pp. 355-56; October, 1992; June, 1994.
Wilson Library Bulletin, November, 1994, pp. 120-21.

■ Obituaries

PERIODICALS

School Library Journal, May, 1993, p. 20.*

—Sketch by Kevin S. Hile

R. A. Salvatore

■ Personal

Born in Massachusetts, in 1959; married, wife's name, Diane; children: Bryan, Geno, Caitlin. *Education:* Fitchburg State College, B.S. (communications), 1981, B.A. (English).

■ Addresses

Home—Massachusetts. *Agent*—Scott Siegel, P.O. Box 20340, New York, NY 10017.

■ Career

Fantasy writer. Worked at various jobs to support writing habit, 1982-90. Creator, with others, of game modules for "Fantasy Realms" computer game, TSR, 1999.

■ Writings

"FORGOTTEN REALM" SERIES

The Crystal Shard (first volume of "Icewind Dale" trilogy), TSR, 1988.

Streams of Silver (second volume of "Icewind Dale" trilogy), TSR, 1989.

The Halfling's Gem (third volume of "Icewind Dale" trilogy), TSR, 1990.

Homeland (first volume of "Dark Elf" trilogy), TSR, 1990.

Exile (second volume of "Dark Elf" trilogy), TSR, 1990.

Sojourn (third volume of "Dark Elf" trilogy), TSR, 1991.

Canticle (first volume of "Cleric Quintet"), TSR, 1991.

In Sylvan Shadows (second volume of "Cleric Quintet"), TSR, 1992.

The Legacy, TSR, 1992.

Night Masks (third volume of "Cleric Quintet"), TSR, 1992.

The Fallen Fortress (fourth volume of "Cleric Quintet"), TSR, 1993.

Starless Night, TSR, 1993.

The Chaos Curse (fifth volume of "Cleric Quintet"), TSR, 1994.

Siege of Darkness, TSR, 1994.

Passage to Dawn, TSR, 1996.

The Dark Elf Trilogy (compilation; contains *Homeland, Exile,* and *Sojourn*), TSR, 1998.

The Silent Blade, TSR, 1998.

The Spine of the World, TSR, 1999.

The Cleric Quintet (compilation; contains *Canticle, In Sylvan Shadows, Night Masks, The Fallen Fortress,* and *The Chaos Curse*), TSR, 1999.

"SPEARWIELDER'S TALE" TRILOGY

The Woods out Back, Ace, 1993.
The Dragon's Dagger, Ace, 1994.
Dragonslayer's Return, Ace, 1995.

"CRIMSON SHADOW" TRILOGY

The Sword of Bedwyr, Warner, 1995.
Luthien's Gamble, Warner, 1996.
The Dragon King, Warner, 1996.

"DEMON WARS" SERIES

The Demon Awakens, Ballantine, 1997.
The Demon Spirit, Ballantine, 1998.
The Demon Apostle, Ballantine, 1999.

OTHER

Echoes of the Fourth Magic, Roc, 1990.
The Witch's Daughter, Roc, 1991, updated, 1999.
Tarzan: The Epic Adventures (based on a character by Edgar Rice Burroughs), Ballantine, 1997.
The New Jedi Order: Vector Prime (part of "Star Wars" series), Del Rey, 1999.

Contributor to anthologies, including *Halflings, Hobbits, Warrows, and Weefolk,* Warner, 1992; and *Otherwere,* Putnam, 1999. Contributor to magazines, including *Dragon.*

■ Sidelights

The creator of fantasy novels that appeal to a young adult audience, R. A. Salvatore takes his inspiration from varied sources as the legends of Robin Hood and the writings of J. R. R. Tolkien. Developer of such popular protagonists as the elf Drizzt Do'Urden and others, Salvatore has been commended by critics for crafting battle scenes that are integral to much of his work. His "Forgotten Realms" novels, which include the bestselling *Halfling's Gem, Sojourn,* and *The Legacy,* take place within the fantasy world created by publisher TSR for its popular Advanced Dungeons and Dragons (AD&D) role-playing game. However, Salvatore's work has captured the imagination of more than AD&D enthusiasts, often reaching bestseller status among mainstream fantasy and science-fiction fans. The prolific Salvatore has also penned a number of other novels in addition to the Forgotten Realms books, among them the "Spearwielder's Tales" trilogy, which follows a twentieth-century factory employee as he is transported from his quiet suburban neighborhood into a Faerie land that requires him to hone his little-used warrior instincts, and the "Demon Wars" trilogy, a sophisticated fantasy epic published in the late 1990s.

Born in New England in 1959, Salvatore was raised in Massachusetts, where he attended college and still makes his home. As a youngster, reading was a favorite pastime, with the "Peanuts" comics and "Charlie Brown" books by Charles Schultz being Salvatore's number-one choice. But the junior high and high school "required reading" lists turned that former pleasure into a chore, and books ceased to spark his imagination. After graduating from high school, Salvatore enrolled in Fitchburg State College with the intention of studying something practical like computer science. However, when a February blizzard during his freshman year found him literally snowed in with the fantasy literature of British writer J. R. R. Tolkien, *The Lord of the Rings* changed Salvatore's life. Excited by the prospect of writing his own fantasy novels but yet unwilling to throw all practicality to the winds, Salvatore changed his major to journalism and graduated with a B.S. in communications in 1981. While he would later return to Fitchburg to earn an undergraduate English degree, he didn't let the lack of that training stop him; by 1982 Salvatore was hard at work on a manuscript about the Bermuda Triangle that would eventually become the fantasy/mystery novel *Echoes of the Fourth Magic.*

Brings Life to "Forgotten Realms"

Like many writers, Salvatore's first writing project did not result in a published book. Taking editorial feedback he received along with publisher' rejection of his first manuscript to heart, he put *Echoes of the Fourth Magic* aside temporarily—it would be published in 1990—and started to work on another book. In 1987 *The Crystal Shard* was accepted by fantasy publisher TSR and reached bookstore shelves a year later. The first installment in Salvatore's "Forgotten Realms" series, the novel's plot turns on Akar Kessell, a murderous apprentice mage who gains power by using a magic crystal known to all as Crenshinibon. Representing the forces of good is the hulking human Wulfgar, who is trained by an elf named

Drizzt and ultimately able to harness his own magic against the seemingly invincible Kessell. Reviewing the novel in *Voice of Youth Advocates*, Ruth Cline notes that *The Crystal Shard* "is a book about power and different ways men try to become powerful, some with magic and magic weapons, some through physical force, and others through alliances." Remarking on the large cast of elves, dwarves, orcs, humans, and other strange characters that are assembled in Salvatore's debut, Cline adds that "many gruesome death scenes . . . [and] violent battles" punctuate the storyline.

The Crystal Shard marks the first appearance of one of Salvatore's most popular fictional creations in the dark elf Drizzt. Destined to take a central role in future installments of the Forgotten Realm books, such as *Streams of Sliver, The Halfling's Gem, Homeland, The Legacy,* and *The Spine of the World,* Drizzt is a member of one of the leading families of the drow, a race of dark-skinned elves who live in the underground city of Mezoberranzan. As a member of the prestigious House Do'Urden, Drizzt is expected to cultivate his aggressive and violent tendencies—he is an expert swordsman—through such socially acceptable methods as bribery, blackmail, murder, and the like. But after learning about the relatively peaceful society of elves, dwarves, and humans that exists on the surface, Drizzt decides to rally against both nature and nurture and fight his darker side, all the while forced to mask his new approach to life from his evil mother and siblings. Drizzt is an "angst-ridden hero," in the opinion of *St. James Guide to Fantasy Writers* essayist Lucya Szachnowski, who notes that the elf "struggles against using his instinctive and deadly fighting abilities, fearing that by killing he will become as evil as the others of his race." As the series winds on, Drizzt is shunned by his drow fellows, but is also looked upon with suspicion by surface-dwellers due to his dark coloring and strange ways.

The Crystal Shard, together with *Streams of Silver* and *The Halfling's Gem,* comprise the "Icewind Dale" trilogy within the Fantasy Realms novel sequence. Salvatore would create other novel groupings within the ever-growing list of AD&D-based novels, among them the "Cleric Quintet" and the "Dark Elf" trilogy. The Dark Elf books draw readers back to the years of Drizzt's birth and childhood, as, in *Homeland* the political machinations of the matriarchal Mezoberranzan dynasty are revealed. Matron Malice, the leader of the

house of Do'Urden, gives birth to Drizzt, intending to sacrifice the boy-dwarf to Loth, Demon Queen of Spiders and ruler over Menzoberranzan, as a way to ensure victory in her upcoming battle against a rival family. However, plottings within her own home cause Malice to preserve Drizzt's life, and the dwarf is eventually trained in the art of fighting upon reaching his sixteenth year. Ultimately, his father, who secretly shares his son's peaceful outlook, is killed by the family's evil matriarch, and Drizzt flees Mezoberranzan for the surface and the winter vista depicted in the "Icewind Dale" books.

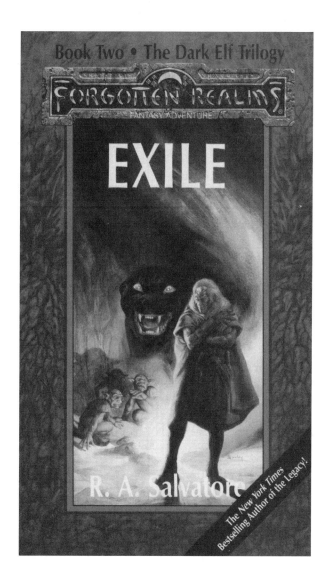

Drizzt Do'Urden, along with his magical cat, Guenhwyvar, searches for a new home in the tunnel-mazes of the Underdark in this 1990 novel.

Good vs. Evil

In 1992's *The Legacy,* Salvatore's first hardcover novel, sibling rivalry is taken to the extreme as surface-dwelling Drizzt is hunted by his sister, Vierna, after he has dishonored the family through his peace-loving ways. Risen to a high rank as priestess to Loth, Vierna seeks to use her brother as a sacrifice in one of her religious rituals. A *Rapport* reviewer calls *The Legacy* "an adventure story with a heart. . . . Whether you've gamed in the Forgotten Realms or not, you'll feel a great familiarity with its territory and a fondness for many of its inhabitants." And a subsequent installation, *Siege of Darkness,* is deemed a "powerful tale of intrigue and danger" by a *Rapport* reviewer.

Also within the Forgotten Realms series is Salvatore's "Cleric Quintet," a five-volume series that follows the adventures of a young priest-scholar named Cadderly as he resists the rule of chaos. Using his increasingly effective magical powers—as well as the help of his "cheerleader-look-alike martial-artist girlfriend," according to Szachnowski—Cadderly defuses the machinations of a group of evil priests who are in league with a vampiric living-dead phenomenon called "Ghost" which can enter the bodies of others and use them like puppets in pursuing its own evil ends. While praising the novel as "tightly plotted," Leslie S. J. Farmer, reviewing the third volume, *Night Masks,* in *Kliatt,* comments that battle scenes "dominate the story to the detriment of character development." While Farmer finds the next Cleric entry, *The Fallen Fortress,* "not breathtaking wizardry, but . . . pleasantly entertaining," the series finale *The Chaos Curse* wins the critic's highest praise. Maintaining that Salvatore's Cleric Quintet "may prove to be a standard set within the fantasy genre," Farmer praises what she deems "the tightest plot and clearest writing of the quintet" in a novel that finds Cadderly drawing on his personal faith and the help of loyal friends in his final battle against evil.

After the Cleric books, Salvatore has continued to unfold the saga of the Forgotten Realms, with such books as *The Silent Blade* and *The Spine of the World,* which feature the return of both the popular Drizzt and the barbarian Wulfgar, as each battle for survival against overwhelming odds in the sometimes hostile environs of the Forgotten Realm. In *The Silent Blade,* published in 1998, Drizzt, now exiled from the subterranean Mezo-

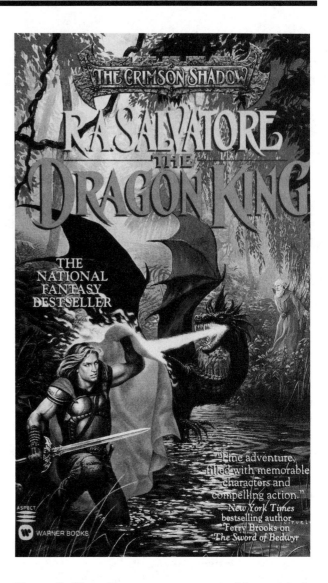

The evil King Greensparrow meets his match in Luthien Bedwyr, also known as the Crimson Shadow, in this final book of the "Crimson Shadow" trilogy.

berranzan, attempts to destroy the powerful, and troublesome crystal, while a confused Wulfgar fights the temptations of drink while attempting to gain a grip on reality after his release from a psychologically and physically debilitating six-year thraldom at the hands of the evil Ertu. Meanwhile, the villainous Artemis Entreri, whose machinations overshadow all in the realm, plots his path to supremacy by taking advantage of the factions among the region's now-warring houses. While noting that Salvatore makes use of many traditional characters and archetypes within his writing, a *Publishers Weekly* contributor cites "intelligence in using the classic elements, a pleasant dry wit and a narrative gift that make [*The Silent Blade*] certain to keep . . . readers turning pages."

Salvatore straddled the line between the real world and the world of Faerie to create his Spearwielder series. The trilogy begins with 1993's *The Woods out Back,* as recent college graduate Gary Leger wakes from one of the many naps that highlight his humdrum existence working in an English plastics factory to find that he has been kidnapped by the leprechaun Mickey McMickey, who involves Leger in a quest by elf Kelsey Gil-Ravadry to repair an ancient magical spear once owned by Faerie king Cedric Donigarten. While Leger accompanies his faerie captors under duress—not a particularly heroic individual, he was selected by McMickey solelybecause he fit the armor of King Cedric—he is gradually won over to their aims, and joins them to fight all-out attempts by the sorceress Ceridwen to prevent the spear's repair. A *Publishers Weekly* contributor finds troubling the lack of explanation given for the story's premise—"for what purposes Kelsey wants the spear or why Ceridwen opposes him"—as well as the lack of a likeable female character. *Voice of Youth Advocates* contributor Deborah L. Dubois cites Salvatore's premise of positing a character from the modern world within his fantasy word "a clever one," and notes that "it provides for a bit of comedy in the attitude and ideas of Gary and how he perceives this [Faerie] world." In *Locus,* contributor Scott Winnett praises *The Woods out Back* as "an enjoyable light read that moves like the wind." *The Dragon's Dagger* finds Gary once again returned to the land of Faerie to battle a dragon named Robert, who is under the sway of the evil Ceridwen, and the trilogy concludes with 1995's *The Dragonslayer's Return,* as Ceridwen and Gary have their final confrontation.

With *The Sword of Bedwyr,* published in 1995, Salvatore inaugurated yet another fantasy series. The "Robin Hood-like" character of Luthien Bedwyr—the "Crimson Shadow"—is a young nobleman exiled from the lands of Bedwydr after a close friend is murdered and his father, whom he formerly worshiped, will do nothing to avenge the death or fight other evils perpetrated upon the kingdom of Eriador by its ruling wizard King Greensparrow and his henchman, the evil Duke of Montfort. Deciding to take matters into his own inexperienced hands, the wide-eyed Luthien assembles a rag-tag band of followers that includes the charismatic Gascan thief Oliver DeBurrows,

dons a magical cloak that makes him invisible, and becomes the Crimson Shadow, crusading for justice for his people. Replete with "an overabundance of swordplay," according to *Library Journal* contributor Jackie Cassada, *The Sword of Bedwyr* still offers fantasy fans a "fast- paced" read. A *Publishers Weekly* critic views the novel's action sequences on a more positive note, commenting that "Salvatore describes and choreographs battle scenes better than any other contemporary fantasist." Praising the "great bantering dialogue" of the novel's action sequences, *Voice of Youth Advocates* contributor Dorothy M. Thompson notes of the Shadow's tendency to "rob from the rich, evil dukes and give to the poor" that Salvatore "prove[s] . . . once again that justice and right prevail."

In the sequel, *Luthien's Gamble,* Luthien continues his efforts to oust the evil Greensparrow, aided by the street-smart DeBurrows, an elven beauty named Sioban, and Brind'Amour, a good but aged wizard. Reviewing the novel, in which the band must fight both an army of cyclopians and a powerful dragon-like creature, a *Publishers Weekly* contributor states that in this "fitfully rousing" work the "battle scenes are robust, but [Salvatore's] fantasy is dully derivative." Ultimately reaching a truce with Greensparrow, Brind'Amour is appointed king, but the peace in Eriador is short-lived. In *The Dragon King,* the trilogy's conclusion, swords are again drawn, as a host of combatants assemble on either side of the line separating good from evil. While a *Publishers Weekly* contributor dubs *The Dragon King,* "pseudo-Tolkien" with "plenty of sound and fury but precious little fire," *Booklist* contributor Roland Green opines that "Salvatore reliably delivers intelligent, fast-moving, entertaining fantasy." Commenting on the Crimson Shadow trilogy, *Kliatt* contributor Hugh M. Flick Jr. calls the author "a veteran fantasy writer whose characters are always interesting and well portrayed."

Breaks New Ground with Demon Awakens

The first volume of his "Demon Wars" trilogy, *The Demon Awakens* gives Salvatore yet another opportunity to leave the Forgotten Realm of AD&D and enter new territory of his own making. Salvatore's new world is home to humans, elves, goblins, giants, and other mythic creatures. It is also home

---

If you enjoy the works of R. A. Salvatore, you may also want to check out the following books:

Stephen R. Donaldson, *Lord Foul's Bane,* 1977.
Diane Duane, *High Wizardry,* 1990.
Terry Goodkind, *Wizard's First Rule,* 1994.
J. R. R. Tolkien, *The Hobbit; or, There and Back Again,* 1937.
Joan D. Vinge, *The Snow Queen,* 1980.

---

to a demon dactyl named Bestesbulzibar, a "dark force of insidious subtlety," in the opinion of *Library Journal* reviewer Jackie Cassada. The evil dragon-like creature marshals a horde of goblins, giants, and "powries"—evil dwarves—in an assault on the peaceful village of Corona, where a young ranger named Elbryan Wyndon and his wizard girlfriend Pony live. The pair are orphaned during the conflict, and find themselves the only ones able to defend their home against the evil Bestesbulzibar. Trained by elves, Elbryan feels up to the task; he acquires a magical amethyst from the noble Avelyn Desbris, and join forces with several other courageous souls in fighting the dactyl. While noting that the novel is not "superlatively original" in its concept, *Booklist* contributor Roland Green calls *The Demon Awakens* Salvatore's "most ambitious book to date" and praises it as "certainly very readable."

While their mission was seemingly accomplished in the first Demon Wars installment, readers anticipating the remainder of the trilogy are not surprised when Elbryan and Pony discover that the evil force of the vanquished Bestesbulzibar finds a new and powerful host. Corona has become a desolate battleground, and the lawless spirit encourages flawed individuals like Abellican Father Abbot Markwart to take advantage of the situation. Making his bid for power in *The Demon Spirit,* Markwart gains control of Desbris' magic stone, and swords must again be drawn. While noting that this second installment of the trilogy might be difficult for newcomers to follow, *Booklist* critic Green notes that the author "has lost none of his skill for weaving classic fantasy elements into a fast-moving tale featuring touches of wit." Praising the novel's pacing and likeable char-

acters, a *Publishers Weekly* contributor goes on to maintain that "the intrigues and literally murderous rivalries within the Abellican Church form the more original and absorbing part" of *The Demon Spirit.* In *The Demon Apostle,* published in 1999, the trilogy comes to a fitting conclusion, as the powers of good finally prove triumphant over what seems to Elbryan and Pony to have become almost a deathless malignancy.

While Salvatore considers the new fantasy world that houses Corona to be his "new home," as he told an interviewer for the R. A. Salvatore Web site, "I think of Drizzt and his friends as family. So while I love my new home, I can go back and visit my family from time to time." In his negotiations within the real world—in between writing projects and exploring new worlds via computer and role playing games—Salvatore enjoys bicycling and spending time with his wife and three growing children in the Massachusetts home the family shares with their assorted pets. Salvatore's letters, manuscripts, and professional papers were donated to his alma mater, Fitchburg State College, in 1997.

■ Works Cited

Cassada, Jackie, review of *The Sword of Bedwyr,* in *Library Journal,* December, 1994, p. 19.

Cassada, Jackie, review of *The Demon Spirit,* in *Library Journal,* March 15, 1998, p. 99.

Cline, Ruth, review of *The Crystal Shard,* in *Voice of Youth Advocates,* August, 1988, p. 140.

Review of *The Demon Spirit,* in *Publishers Weekly,* March 9, 1998, p. 53.

Dubois, Deborah L., review of *The Woods out Back,* in *Voice of Youth Advocates,* February,1994, p. 385.

Review of *The Dragon King,* in *Publishers Weekly,* October 12, 1996, pp. 74-75.

Farmer, Leslie S. J., review of *Night Masks,* in *Kliatt,* November, 1992, p. 19.

Farmer, Leslie S. J., review of *The Chaos Curse,* in *Kliatt,* November, 1994, p. 24.

Flick, Hugh M., Jr., review of *Luthien's Gamble,* in *Kliatt,* March, 1997, p. 21.

Green, Roland, review of *The Dragon King,* in *Booklist,* October 1, 1996, p. 326.

Green, Roland, review of *The Demon Awakens,* in *Booklist,* May 1, 1997, p. 1483.

Green, Roland, review of *The Demon Spirit,* in *Booklist,* March 15, 1998, p. 1207.

Review of *Luthien's Gamble,* in *Publishers Weekly,* January 29, 1996, p. 88.

Salvatore, R. A., interview at R. A. Salvatore Web site, http://www.rasalvatore.com/interview.html (June 14, 1999).

Review of *The Sword of Bedwyr,* in *Publishers Weekly,* January 2, 1995, p. 63.

Review of *The Silent Blade,* in *Publishers Weekly,* September 28, 1998, p. 78.

Szachnowski, Lucya, "R. A. Salvatore," in *St. James Guide to Fantasy Writers,* edited by David Pringle, St. James Press, 1996, pp. 510-12.

Thompson, Dorothy M., review of *The Sword of Bedwyr,* in *Voice of Youth Advocates,* April, 1995, p. 39.

Winnett, Scott, review of *The Woods out Back,* in *Locus,* November, 1993, pp. 56-57.

Review of *The Woods out Back,* in *Publishers Weekly,* September 6, 1993, p. 88.

■ **For More Information See**

PERIODICALS

Booklist, October 15, 1993, p. 422; August, 1994, p. 2030; January 15, 1995, p. 901.

Kirkus Reviews, December 1, 1995, pp. 1673-74; September 1, 1996, p. 1282; March 15, 1997, p. 423.

Kliatt, November, 1992, p. 19; November, 1993, p. 18; March, 1994, p. 20; January, 1995, p. 19; November, 1995, p. 20.

Library Journal, August, 1993, p. 160; November 14, 1993, p. 118; February 15, 1996, p. 179; April, 1997, p. 124.

Publishers Weekly, June 28, 1993, p. 61.

Rapport, Volume 17, 1992, p. 26; May, 1995, p. 20.

Voice of Youth Advocates, December, 1994, p. 289; October, 1996, p. 220.*

—Sketch by Pamela L. Shelton

Dana Stabenow

■ Personal

Born March 27, 1952, in Anchorage, AK; daughter of a master mechanic and a bookkeeper. *Education:* University of Alaska, B.A. (journalism), 1973, M.F.A., 1985.

■ Addresses

Agent—Richard Henshaw Group, 264 West 734th St., New York, NY 10023.

■ Career

Science-fiction and mystery writer. Previously worked as a gofer for Cook Inlet Aviation, Seldovia, AK; worked variously as an egg-grader, bookkeeper, and expediter for Whitney-Fidalgo Seafoods, Anchorage, 1969-73; employee of Alyeska Pipeline, Galbraith Lake, AK, beginning 1975, and British Petroleum, Prudhoe Bay, AK, until 1982.

■ Awards, Honors

Edgar Award, 1993, for *A Cold Day for Murder.*

■ Writings

"STAR SVENSDOTTER" SERIES

Second Star, Berkley/Ace, 1991.
A Handful of Stars, Ace, 1991.
Red Planet Run, Berkley/Ace, 1995.

"KATE SHUGAK" SERIES

A Cold Day for Murder, Berkley, 1992.
A Fatal Thaw, Berkley, 1993.
Dead in the Water, Berkley, 1993.
A Cold-Blooded Business, Berkley, 1994.
Play with Fire, Berkley, 1995.
Blood Will Tell, Putnam, 1996.
Breakup, Putnam, 1997.
Killing Grounds, Putnam, 1998.
Hunter's Moon, Putnam, 1999.
Midnight Come Again, St. Martin's Press, in press.

"LIAM CAMPBELL" SERIES

Fire and Ice, Dutton (New York City), 1998.
So Sure of Death, Dutton, 1999.
Nothing Gold Can Stay, Dutton, in press.

Contributor of short fiction to anthologies.

■ Sidelights

Drawing on her familiarity with life in the frozen north, Dana Stabenow wields the pen behind several fictional series known for their courageous, independent female protagonists.Beginning her writing career in 1991 with the first installment in a science-fiction series about space pioneer Star Svensdotter, Stabenow has also earned a large fan following among mystery buffs for her series detailing the exploits of likeable Alaskan P.I. Kate Shugak. Both series have been praised by critics for their author's deft characterizations, insightful use of detail, and briskly unfolding plots. In a review of Stabenow's debut novel, *Second Star* for *Booklist*, Roland Green cited the author's "almost cinematic vividness" in describing her futuristic setting. With her third novel series, a sequence of mysteries featuring an Alaskan state trooper and his high-flying love interest, critical reaction has proven once again that a fast-moving story and interesting settings are characteristic Stabenow.

Stabenow was born in Anchorage, Alaska in the spring of 1952. She spent most of her early years afloat in the Gulf of Alaska aboard her father's fishing boat, the *Celtic,* a 75-foot fish tender on which her mother was deckhand. For company she had her parents, as well as several cats her mother brought home to keep young Dana company. As the novelist remarked on her Web page, "When I wasn't seasick, I wrote stories about NORMAL children who lived on SHORE, and made my mother read them." These early efforts at fiction Stabenow would later judge, tongue-in-cheek, as "Probably some of my best work."

While Stabenow enjoyed writing as a way to disembark—at least in her imagination—she didn't grow up intending to become a writer. However, she gained a sense that her life held some specific purpose when, on her twelfth birthday in 1964, a huge earthquake shook the city of Anchorage and the surrounding area. "It was then that I realize I was destined for greatness," Stabenow later recalled, "always supposing I survived the day."

Academic Interests Put on Back Burner

While Stabenow was home-schooled during her elementary years, attending her community's high school finally provided her with an opportunity to spend some quality time on solid ground. She graduated from Seldovia High School in 1969. While attending college was always her goal, Stabenow had to earn money in order to afford

it, which meant putting in long hours as an egg-grader, a bookkeeper, and an expeditor at a local seafood packager in Anchorage. The added temptations offered by the active social life at the University of Alaska made Stabenow's actual graduation in 1973 with a B.A. in journalism truly an accomplishment.

With her degree finally in hand, Stabenow and her college roommate took a well-earned four-month backpacking trip to Europe, and "discovered English pubs, German Beer and Irish men," as she later reminisced. Finally forced to return home to Alaska due to lack of funds, Stabenow found herself with a degree but with neither a job nor cash in her pocket. Fortunately for her, the same run of luck that had let her survive the earthquake of 1964 placed Stabenow squarely in the biggest economic boom in modern Alaskan history: the construction of the TransAlaska Oil Pipeline. Jobs were easy to come by, and Stabenow quickly found herself at work at Alyeska Pipeline, moving from there to British Petroleum. The years passed relatively event-free, and by the time her thirtieth birthday rolled around in 1982, Stabenow had begun to question what it was she really wanted to do with her life. Coming to the realization that working on the pipeline, partying, and taking periodic trips to Hawaii, while fun for the time being, might not translate well into her more mature years, she quit her job and enrolled in the University of Alaska's M.F.A. program, funding her degree with money saved from her well-paying pipeline job.

After earning her master's degree in 1985, Stabenow was determined to take her best shot at becoming a writer. Still with some money in the bank, she decided upon a specific goal: to write, market, and sell at least one book-length manuscript before her savings ran out. "I just barely made it," the author recalled on her Web site, noting that her first novel, *Second Star,* was sold to science-fiction publishers Ace Books in 1990.

Makes Publishing Debut

Reaching bookstore shelves in 1991, Stabenow's *Second Star* introduces readers to space scientist Esther Natasha "Star" Svensdotter. The inhabitants of Earth are packing their bags for a move to an L-5 space colony, and Star has been appointed director of the operation to construct L-5. It is a challenging task made more difficult by obstacles that include terrorists, an attempted military takeover, computers with a mind of their own, and antagonistic aliens. An Alaskan native like her creator, Star "runs the operation with a firm hand, brilliant mind, and well- conditioned body," according to *Locus* contributor Carolyn Cushman in her favorable appraisal of Stabenow's fiction debut. While the ultra-competent heroine takes coupe d'etat and assassination attempts in stride as she completes her mission, she also has time for a romantic interest in the form of L-5's hunky chief of security, and family responsibilities in the form

of her young niece, Elizabeth. While *Analog* reviewer Tom Easton praised *Second Star* as "a pleasant evening's read" and commended its author's "good sense of pacing and plotting," he added that Stabenow would "do much better once she escapes her influences and begins to invent worlds and situations that are more her own."

Several critics commented on references to works by the late, great science-fiction writer Robert A. Heinlein that dot Stabenow's Star Svensdotter novels, and Heinlein is an influence that the author readily acknowledges; in fact she dedicated *Second Star* to him. The sequel to that work, *A Handful of Stars*, finds world-builder Svensdotter still at work at what she does best, this time setting up a supervisory base of operations within the asteroid belt orbiting Earth's solar system. Taking place over five years, the book recounts Star's progress in detail, an aspect of the novel that some critics felt detracts from the story's action. *Voice of Youth Advocates* contributor Vicky Burkholder found *A Handful of Stars* to be less satisfying and more confusing than *Second Star*, and its reading "more like a diary than a novel, full of the details of mundane day-to-day problems." While agreeing that the novel was problematic on several levels, contributor Carolyn Cushman pointed out in *Locus* that *A Handful of Stars* "is a tale of the Yukon gold rush, translated to space, complete with whorehouse, saloons, and a plague of gold fever" that "has its entertaining moments."

Red Planet Run, the third book in the Svensdotter series, is set in part on Mars, where Star—now a mother juggling the demands of her high-power space colonization enterprise with raising twin teens—survives a crash landing and discovers the existence of a previously unknown settlement. Problems again enter the picture, this time in the form of space pirates who threaten the integrity of an archeological dig tracking the Red Planet's habitation history. Green praised the work as a "rousing success" in *Booklist*, calling the storyline and pacing "brisk, the characters engaging, the many details well chosen and frequently humorous."

Aleut detective Kate Shugak investigates the disappearance of two persons believed dead in the Alaskan wilderness in this Edgar Award-winning mystery.

Mystery Moves to Northern Climes

While the Svensdotter stories appeared first, Stabenow's books featuring savvy sleuth Kate

A KATE SHUGAK MYSTERY

DANA STABENOW

EDGAR AWARD–WINNING AUTHOR OF *BLOOD WILL TELL*

"Exciting... Stabenow writes lively, intriguing descriptions of the magnificence of the Alaska wilderness."
—*PUBLISHERS WEEKLY*

BREAKUP

Kate Shugak appears in this 1997 mystery about a dead body that turns up in the detective's own yard during spring thaw, a time of year also called "breakup."

Shugak have surpassed them both in number and, arguably, in overall popularity. Stabenow's first Kate Shugak mystery was the Edgar Award-winning *A Cold Day for Murder*. Written shortly after the first Svensdotter novel, *A Cold Day* was published in 1992; Stabenow's editor was so taken by its main character that she immediately signed Stabenow to a three-book contract featuring her sleuth. Shugak, a thirty-something Aleut, shares her cabin on her 160-acre homestead in the Alaskan wilderness with Mutt, a loyal wolf-husky crossbreed. While she retired from her job as an investigator for Anchorage's District Attorney's

office, the disappearance of the son of a U.S. Congressman in a 200-million-acre national wilderness park necessitates her return to work. Shugak's investigative prowess, hard-edged survival skills, and knowledge of the Alaskan wilderness make her "one of the toughest detectives in fiction," in the opinion of *Kliatt* reviewer Claire Rosser. While full of fictional elements—the national wilderness park setting, the author noted in her Web page, if it "really existed, would take up two-thirds of the entire state of Alaska"—the series and its protagonist have allowed Stabenow to examine the realities of Aleutian culture and the pressure to assimilate into white society that Native Americans experience.

In the third installment in the Shugak series, *Dead in the Water*, Kate is once again working for the DA's office, where she reports to on-again, off-again romantic interest Jack Morgan. Her assignment this go-round: to go undercover as a crew member of a crabbing boat to discover the whereabouts of a pair of missing fishermen, a task that ultimately finds her afloat on the Bering Sea with not-so-comforting company. "Down-to-earth, feisty, and funny, Kate is a fine guide to life and crime in the North," maintained *Wilson Library Bulletin* reviewer Gail Pool. Discussing the series overall, Allen J. Hubin agreed in *Armchair Detective*: "Kate is a striking figure," noted the reviewer, "and the wryly observed Alaskan scene is beautifully captured in its many aspects—political, economic, geographic, meteorological, and cultural."

As the series continues, Stabenow develops Shugak's character, and readers watch as she grows in appreciation of the native Aleut culture that she shunned during her younger, more rebellious days. In *A Cold-Blooded Business* Shugak comes face to face with the reality that this culture may be disappearing as she stumbles upon a black market in Native American artifacts while hunting down a notorious drug dealer. Later novels find the wilderness-wise sleuth gaining some social skills as she is encouraged to take more of an interest in the politics of her region, particularly as they impact the Aleut people.

Other novels in the Kate Shugak series include *Play with Fire*, which finds Kate piecing together the deadly practices of a modern ultra-conservative religious cult in what *Booklist* contributor Emily Melton called "a mesmerizing story that's intriguingly plotted and chockful of suspense."

If you enjoy the works of Dana Stabenow, you may also want to check out the following books:

Robert A. Heinlein, *Red Planet*, 1949.
Tony Hillerman, *People of Darkness*, 1990.
Valerie Wilson Wesley, *When Death Comes Stealing*, 1994.
Fargo, a film by the Coen brothers, 1996.

Blood Will Tell, the sixth installment in the series, finds Indian lands threatened, a string of accidental deaths raising eyebrows, and Kate in the middle of a debate over preserving the old ways of living versus cashing in on the region's vast natural resources. Fishing again becomes a background for trouble in *Killing Ground* as a local fisherman winds up dead and floating in the bay, leaving in his wake a town full of folks who disliked him enough to want him out of the picture. "In powerful prose, Stabenow evokes Alaska's rugged physical splendors and the tolltaken on the humans who live there," commented a *Publishers Weekly* contributor in a review of Shugak's eighth mystery novel.

With *Hunter's Moon* rounding out the total number of Kate Shugak mysteries to nine by 1999 and with more in the works, Stabenow continues to offer mystery lovers a welcome change of pace from the tough inner cities and the dilettante-ridden wealthy suburbs. Critics have also remarked that Stabenow's knowledge of native Alaskan people—the Aleuts, Athabascans, and Tlingits—her intimate familiarity with the beauty of the Alaskan wilderness, and her understanding of wildlife work to enhance her novels' descriptive passages. Books in the series pick up common settings and themes, as well as the hunting, crab fishing, oil fields, wilderness exploration, and logging that characterize life in the United States' northernmost territory. Stabenow's ability to make this region come alive for readers reflects her own experiences living and working in Alaska, including her varied jobs held before she became a full-time writer. In *Hunter's Moon*, as in other series installments, Stabenow posits her protagonist's current quandary—in this case, an invasion by a group of German businessmen that turns a hunting holiday into homicide—amid the day-to-day

episodes encountered by ordinary Alaskans, showing these native northerners to be people either toughened by their wild surroundings or broken by them. Combining such realism with a compelling mystery drew praise from Emily Melton in a *Booklist* review of the author's hard-cover debut, *A Cold-Blooded Business*. Melton added, "Shugak is an uncommonly charismatic heroine . . . and Stabenow is a splendid writer who knows how to hook her readers with an exciting blend of thrills, danger, humor, pathos, fact, and fable."

New Sleuth Takes to the Alaskan Skies

Stabenow's new mystery series featuring protagonists Liam Campbell, a handsome and dedicated Alaska state trooper recovering from the tragic death of his wife and son, and his former—soon to be current—flame, bush pilot Wyanet Chouinard, debuted with 1998's *Fire and Ice*. The setting this time is the town of Newenham, a settlement on Bristol Bay that serves as the newly demoted Campbell's "beat" while he recovers from alcoholism and depression. The character of Wyanet was inspired by Stabenow's fascination with aviation, not to mention the fact that many of her relatives are pilots who transport people and supplies across long expanses of wilderness to bush settlements. Noting that many native Alaskans living in outlying areas spend more time in planes than they do in cars, Stabenow commented on her Web site: "Aviation is as much or more a part of Alaskan history as the Gold Rush, and I wouldn't be doing my job if I didn't write about flying." Judging from reviews of the first installment—"the mystery is hard to solve, the plot fast moving . . ., the Arctic landscape stunning, and the characters vivid and sympathetic," *Booklist* contributor John Rowen noted of *Fire and Ice*. Critics and readers could anticipate that future novels in the Liam Campbell series, which include *So Sure of Death* and *Nothing Gold Can Stay*, will command as loyal a following as the Shugak books.

■ Works Cited

Burkholder, Vicky, review of *A Handful of Stars*, in *Voice of Youth Advocates*, February, 1992, p. 387.

Cushman, Carolyn, review of *Second Star*, in *Locus*, June, 1991, p. 27.

Cushman, Carolyn, review of *A Handful of Stars*, in *Locus*, November, 1991, p. 27.

Easton, Tom, review of *Second Star,* in *Analog Science Fiction/Science Fact,* December, 1991, pp. 163-64.

Green, Roland, review of *Second Star,* in *Booklist,* June 1, 1991, p. 1861.

Green, Roland, review of *Red Planet Run,* in *Booklist,* January, 1995, pp. 1312, 1317.

Hubin, Allen J., review of *Blood Will Tell,* in *Armchair Detective,* summer, 1997, p. 343.

Review of *Killing Grounds,* in *Publishers Weekly,* January 19, 1998, p. 375.

Melton, Emily, review of *A Cold-Blooded Business,* in *Booklist,* March 1, 1994, pp. 1183, 1188.

Melton, Emily, review of *Play with Fire,* in *Booklist,* March 15, 1995, p. 1312.

Pool, Gail, review of *Dead in the Winter,* in *Wilson Library Bulletin,* November, 1993, pp. 86-87.

Rosser, Claire, review of *A Cold Day for Murder,* in *Kliatt,* September, 1992, p. 16.

Rowen, John, review of *Fire and Ice,* in *Booklist,* September 1, 1998.

Stabenow, Dana, Web site commentary, located at http://www.stabenow.com (February 9, 1999).

■ **For More Information See**

PERIODICALS

Alaska, September, 1996, p. 70.

Armchair Detective, fall, 1992, p. 433; summer, 1994, p. 373; fall, 1995, p. 456; fall, 1996, p. 495; summer, 1997, p. 345.

Booklist, March 15, 1995, pp. 1312, 1317; April 15, 1996, pp. 1424, 1428; May 15, 1997, p. 1567; February 15, 1998, p. 989.

Kirkus Reviews, January 1, 1994, p. 22; February 15, 1995, p. 186; April 1, 1996, p. 492; May 1, 1997, p. 684; February 1, 1998, p. 158; March 19, 1999; April 1, 1999, p. 492.

Kliatt, March, 1993, p. 10; September, 1993, p. 14; May, 1995, p. 11.

Library Journal, March 1, 1994, p. 123; February 1, 1995, p. 103; September 1, 1995, p. 236; May 1, 1996, p. 137.

Locus, July, 1991, p. 48; January, 1992, p. 60; February, 1995, p. 58.

New York Times Book Review, April 3, 1994, p. 22.

Publishers Weekly, May 18, 1992, p. 64; June 14, 1993, p. 64; January 17, 1994, p. 410; February 6, 1995, p. 79; April 1, 1996, p. 59; April 21, 1997, p. 64; April 19, 1999, p. 64.

School Library Journal, November, 1992, p. 147; September, 1994, p. 256.

Science Fiction Chronicles, January, 1995, p. 37.

Voice of Youth Advocates, August, 1991, p. 182; April, 1992, p. 11; June, 1995, p. 110.

Washington Post Book World, July 26, 1992, p. 1; July 20, 1997, p. 10.

Wilson Library Bulletin, June, 1995, p. 98.

—Sketch by Pamela L. Shelton

Megan Whalen Turner

■ Personal

Born November 21, 1965, in Fort Sill, OK; daughter of Donald Peyton (a soldier in the U.S. Army) and Nora Courtenay (Green) Whalen; married Mark Bernard Turner (a professor of English), June 20, 1987; children: John Whalen, Donald Peyton, another son. *Education:* University of Chicago, B.A. (with honors), 1987.

■ Addresses

Agent—c/o Greenwillow Books, 1350 Avenue of the Americas, New York, NY 10019. *E-mail*—mwturner@worldnet.att.net.

■ Career

Writer. Harper Court Bookstore, Chicago, IL, children's book buyer, 1988-89; Bick's Books, Washington, DC, children's book buyer, 1991-92. *Member:* Authors Guild.

■ Awards, Honors

Dorothy Canfield Fisher Children's Book Award master list, 1996-97, for *Instead of Three Wishes;* Newbery Honor Book, Notable Book, and Best Book for Young Adults designations, all American Library Association, all 1997, all for *The Thief.*

■ Writings

Instead of Three Wishes, Greenwillow (New York City), 1995.
The Thief, Greenwillow, 1996.

■ Work in Progress

The Queen of Attolia, for Greenwillow, expected 2000.

■ Sidelights

With a whimsical approach to children's literature that has been compared by critics to that of Joan Aiken, Anne Lindbergh, and E. L. Konigsburg, Megan Whelan Turner has found fans among readers and critics alike. With only two published books to her credit, Turner might be considered a novice, except for the fact that she has already

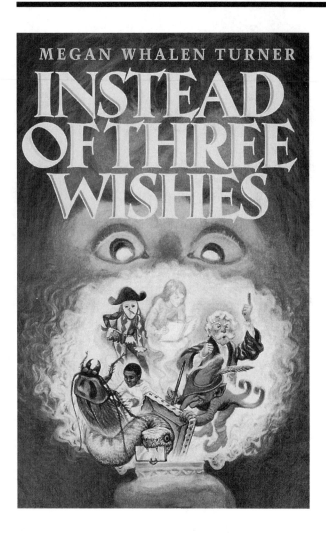

MEGAN WHALEN TURNER

INSTEAD OF THREE WISHES

Magic and a bit of fantasy appear in the seven short stories presented in this collection.

cept for my poor brother who was forced to wait patiently, bored out of his mind, while we browsed in bookstores for hours," the author recalled to *Authors and Artists for Young Adults* (*AAYA*). Although she loved to disappear between the covers of a book whenever possible,Turner didn't fit any of the established criteria for being a full-fledged writer. "I did not tell stories from birth. So far as I remember, I didn't tell stories at all." When she was ten any hopes she still had of becoming a writer when she grew up were quickly dashed after a reading of Joan Aiken's short story collection *Not What You Expected*. As Turner recalled: "The author's bio in the back said that Aiken had ALWAYS told stories and had written her first novel in Latin class at age seventeen. She said she saw stories everywhere she looked; I looked everywhere and couldn't find one. . . . I was ten, and I thought I was all washed up. I really thought that if I didn't have notebooks filled with idle but brilliant poems and stories, I obviously didn't have the gift."

Reconsiders Fate in College

Reconciling herself to a life of non-writing, but continuing to indulge her love of reading, Turner enrolled at the University of Chicago in 1983, intending to major in English language and literature. "At that time they had one of the largest private collections of children's books because of the Center for Children's Books," Turner recalled. "I hadn't realized until I was wandering through the collection that anybody but me was interested in children's books. I enrolled in a couple of graduate classes with Betsy Hearne, who was the editor of the Center's *Bulletin* then. I asked if I could do my senior project with her and if she would accept fiction." Though Turner admits to writing "AWFUL fiction" for Hearne in the form of short stories, she received A's on her papers and graduated with honors.

After college Turner married Mark Turner, who had a position as a professor of English at the University of Maryland. In between short stints working as a children's book buyer, first in Chicago and then again in Washington, D.C., Turner and her husband began to travel extensively in response to Mark's need to do academic research, and spent time in areas such as Princeton, New Jersey, as well as San Diego and Stanford, California. It was on a trip to Del Mar, California,

garnered one of the highest awards that the American Library Association can bestow upon a children's book writer. In 1997 her novel *The Thief* would be one of four books designated as a Newbery Honor title; it would also receive the American Library Association's Notable Book and Best Book for Young Adults designations. Reassuring readers that Turner's talent is no one-time affair is her short-story collection *Instead of Three Wishes*. These seven imaginative tales again showcase their author's light, yet deliberate touch, introducing readers to likeable, realistic characters that deal with their dose of the fantastic using down-to-earth common sense.

Born in Oklahoma in 1965, Turner was the last of four children. "All of us read constantly exwhile her husband was a visiting researcher at the University of California at San Diego that Turner penned many of the short stories that would appear in her first published work.

"I wrote the stories in *Instead of Three Wishes* because my husband Mark had heard them told aloud and he wanted to see them written down," the author recalled. "In 1992 he received a Guggenheim fellowship and I quit my job as a children's book buyer in Washington, D.C., to spend a year in California with him while he did research, and I decided it would be my year to write. I was pregnant with my first child and my schedule was not so full then. After Jack came along, Mark agreed to take him for long stretches

The scholarly Magus uses Gen, an expert thief, to steal a legendary stone that contains magical powers in this Newbery Honor Book set in Greece.

so that I could write, but that was all I was supposed to do. NO DISHES."

Captivates Critics with *Three Wishes*

Although there were probably a few interruptions involving dishes, to say the least, Turner completed the text of *Instead of Three Wishes* and it was snapped up by Greenwillow Books for publication in 1995. Aimed at middle-grade readers, Turner's collection contains seven stories in which an unexpected dollop of magic changes the lives of ordinary people. In "Factory," a young man attempting to escape into a good book during his lunch hour meets up with a ghostly bookworm at the factory where he works, while in the title story a no-nonsense teen tries to brush aside an elf prince's inconvenient and insistent efforts to repay her kindness. And "Leroy Roachbane" finds a young black boy from an inner-city neighborhood transported back to prehistoric Sweden after slipping on the ice on his way home from an errand to buy boric acid and Roach Motels.

The collection received consistent praise from reviewers for what *School Library Journal* contributor Jane Gardner Connor called "a mild humor that will elicit gentle chuckles and smiles." Hailing *Instead of Three Wishes* as "a fine debut," Sarah Guille noted in her *Horn Book* appraisal that Turner "combines a shrewd wit with an eye for the endearingly absurd." And Carolyn Phelan remarked in *Booklist* that while Turner's tales are imbued with a strong sense of history and "eternal truths," the "real magic" wrought is her "ability to convince readers that the realms of fairy tales can intersect with contemporary life."

The process of selecting and completing the stories for *Instead of Three Wishes* involved some difficult decisions on Turner's part. One story in particular, "Leroy Roachbane," was a questionable inclusion because it went against the current trends in children's literature. She recalled to *AAYA:* "I wasn't sure that "Leroy" was going to go over well . . . [because it developed out of the fact that] I was irritated and dissatisfied by some politically correct or what I called 'RSV' (redeeming social value) stories that I had been reading. It seemed to me that, in books, white kids from the suburbs could save the world, solve the murder, travel through space, be transported through time, and essentially do anything, while

---

If you enjoy the works of Megan Whalen Turner, you may also want to check out the following books:

Joan Aiken, *Up the Chimney Down, and Other Stories*, 1984.

Vivien Alcock, *Singer to the Sea God*, 1993.

Paul Jennings, *Unmentionable! More Amazing Stories*, 1993.

John Rowe Townsend, *The Fortunate Isles*, 1989.

Robert Westall, *The Call and Other Stories*, 1993.

---

black kids lived the tough life in the inner city. I'd only found one author, Virginia Hamilton, who offered a picture of black children doing something else." Turner remembered encountering books by Judy Blume when she was a grade-schooler. "Judy Blume had perfectly captured my life," she recalled. "I was living it; why would I want to read about it?"

Turner became inspired: "Surely, I thought, there should be African American characters who are free to do something completely UNLIKE living life in the inner city. Surely if they fall asleep and dream they don't HAVE to dream about going to Africa. They could dream about Boise. They could dream anything they wanted." So, "Leroy Roachbane" was written down; bundled up and armed with boric acid and Roach Motels, he arrived in ancient Sweden where he saved a local tribe from a nasty bug infestation occurring in the lodge of their leader, Wiglaff, before returning to his home in the South Side of Chicago. "I think Leroy is the only time I've been deliberately polemical in my stories," maintained Turner. "The rest of the characters in my stories, handicapped and otherwise, just appear because they need to be there."

"I had the idea for 'Leroy Roachbane' when I was in college," Turner continued. "That was in the early eighties before the experiences of African American characters started to broaden dramatically. I included it in Three Wishes because I liked it and thought that there might be some readers who liked it as well—even if there were others who didn't. My stories do come out of my own

experience. That apartment that Leroy lived in was mine. I lived there with my neighbors, roaches, and a kitchen covered in boric acid."

Novel Inspired by Travels in Greece

While attending the University of Chicago, Turner studied Greek history, and was particularly influenced by *The Peloponnesian War* by Greek historian Thucydides. "Mygrounding in Greek history is a result of Chicago's common core curriculum," Turner remarked. "Greek Thought and Literature is a core course for freshman." Turner and her husband also traveled to Greece during a summer vacation. With this background in the history and landscape of the Mediterranean, the sight of some olive trees while in California inspired Turner to set a novel amid a Greek setting. That novel would be *The Thief*.

Turner's intricately plotted *The Thief* introduces readers to the enigmatic Gen, an expert thief living in a country that could be ancient Greece, but isn't—Turner made up all the details, even the kingdom's pantheon of gods and goddesses. Imprisoned for making a public bet that he could steal anything, even if it belonged to the king, Gen is unexpectedly released from the dungeon where he has been chained, the orders for his release issued by none other than the scholarly Magus to the greedy King of Sounis. The Magus's interest in Gen is that he wants to use the young thief's talents to steal a legendary stone known as Hamiathes' Gift, which will give to its owner control of a neighboring kingdom.

Imbedded within Gen's narrative are the feelings of humiliation that lurk below his confident, sometimes rebellious exterior—a result of the mistreatment and ridicule he receives at the hands of his fellow travelers, which include the magus, soldiers, and several aristocrats—as well as the myths and legends recited by the travelers on their journey to their goal—a temple maze that remains hidden under water for all but two days each year. Meanwhile, *The Thief* moves toward what a *Publishers Weekly* reviewer called "one of the most valuable treasures of all—a twinkling jewel of a surprise ending."

Winning numerous awards, Turner's fantasy novel also received positive critical notice, and many reviewers encouraged young fans to read the novel a second time for added fun. *School Library*

Journal contributor Patricia A. Dollisch had praise for the book's clever protagonist, adding that the author "does a phenomenal job of creating real people to range through her well- plotted, evenly paced story." Citing "believable characters" and a "well-realized setting," Carolyn Phelan wrote in her *Booklist* review that *The Thief* "offers a refreshing change of pace for readers who enjoy adventure stories with a touch of magic." In her appraisal of the novel for *Horn Book*, Martha V. Parravano added special praise for Turner's portrayal of the character Gen, writing that "[He] is simply superb: she lets the reader know so much about him—his sense of humor, his egotism, his loyalty, his forthrightness, his tendency to sulk," all the while "manag[ing] to hide the most essential information" to keep the denouement in shadow. And a Kirkus contributor maintained that "No adolescent will be able to ignore Gen's resentment, embarrassment, and pain, made palpable through Turner's compassion and crystalline prose."

Commitment to Writing Supported by Family

While Turner's successes in the children's book field have encouraged her to continue writing her imaginative tales, the challenges continue to mount. Chief among them is life with three energetic boys, which makes each day fly by, and opportunities for quiet time to sit and write almost nonexistent. Fortunately for Turner, her husband is supportive of her creative efforts; in fact, she dedicated her first book to him. As she revealed to *AAYA:* "My husband reminds me that it is easy to think that all the recurring chores of the house are more important than writing, and that just means the writing never gets done. So I try to get some time in theschedule when—no matter what—the writing is the thing at the top of the priority list." Still, even the best-laid plans have flaws; as Turner admitted, "It doesn't always work. Those children creep up to the top of the list no matter how hard I try to slide them down again. I am lucky that I can work while they play with babysitters nearby. I am reassured that they are well taken care of and can work undistracted . . . except when they climb upstairs and ask me when they can use the computer."

■ Works Cited

Connor, Jane Gardner, review of *Instead of Three Wishes, School Library Journal,* September, 1995, p. 204.

Dollisch, Patricia A., review of *The Thief, School Library Journal,* October, 1996, p. 150.

Guille, Sarah, review of Instead of *Three Wishes, Horn Book,* May-June, 1996, p. 337.

Parravano, Martha V., review of *The Thief, Horn Book,* December, 1996, p. 747.

Phelan, Carolyn, review of Instead of *Three Wishes, Booklist,* October 1, 1995, p. 309.

Phelan, Carolyn, review of *The Thief, Horn Book,* January 1, 1997, p. 863.

Review of *The Thief, Kirkus Reviews,* June 15, 1996.

Review of *The Thief, Publishers Weekly,* October 21, 1996, p. 84.

Turner, Megan Whelan, interview with *Authors and Artists for Young Adults,* July, 1999.

■ For More Information See

PERIODICALS

Booklist, October 1, 1995, p. 309.

Bulletin of the Center for Children's Books, October, 1995, p. 72; November, 1996, pp. 117-18.

Kirkus Reviews, July 1, 1995, p. 954.

New York Times Book Review, November 5, 1995, p. 31.

Publishers Weekly, July 24, 1995, p. 66.

Voice of Youth Advocates, June, 1997, p. 114.

—Sketch by Pamela L. Shelton

Tad Williams

Personal

Born in 1957; married Deborah Beale, 1994.

Addresses

Home—San Francisco Bay area, CA; London. *Office*—c/o DAW Books, 375 Hudson St., 3rd Floor, New York, NY 10014-3658.

Career

Writer. Apple Computers, Knowledge Engineering department, technical writer; host of *One Step Beyond* (syndicated radio talk show), KFKC Radio. Author and co-producer of *Valleyvision* (television series); also worked variously as a musician and songwriter for a rock band, as an illustrator, and as a teacher in public schools and colleges.

Awards, Honors

John W. Campbell Award nomination for Best Newcomer in Science Fiction and Fantasy, 1986, for *Tailchaser's Song*.

Writings

Tailchaser's Song, DAW (New York City), 1985.
(With Nina Kiriki Hoffman) *Child of an Ancient City*, illustrated by Greg Hildebrandt, Atheneum (New York City), 1992.
(And illustrator) *Caliban's Hour*, HarperPrism (New York City), 1994.
(Editor) *Mirror World: An Illustrated Novel*, HarperPrism, 1998.

Also author of comic books.

"MEMORY, SORROW, AND THORN" TRILOGY

The Dragonbone Chair, DAW, 1988.
Stone of Farewell, DAW, 1990.
To Green Angel Tower, DAW, 1993.

"OTHERLAND" SERIES

City of Golden Shadow, DAW, 1996.
River of Blue Fire, DAW, 1998.
Mountain of Black Glass, DAW, 1999.

Sidelights

Fantasy writer Tad Williams has travelled a very colorful career path on his way to—and in addition to—becoming a successful author of novels for fans of imaginative fiction. Singing in a rock band, teaching school, working on the crew of both theatre and television productions, designing manuals for the U.S. military: the wide-ranging interests and talents Williams developed from these varied pursuits now enrich his fictional worlds. With such popular novel series as "Memory, Sorrow, and Thorn" and "Otherland" to his credit, Williams has also found time to write comic books and film and television scripts, as well as serve as co-founder of an interactive television company. His writing has in particular been praised for the small but telling moments set within his descriptive prose. As Williams himself

Only Simon, a young kitchen hand, can save the Osten Ard kingdom from the ancient and evil Sisthi Storm King in this first book from the "Memory, Sorrow, and Thorn" trilogy.

commented on his Web site: "most of the people who like vast fantasies, and even a lot of the people who like mine, seem to enjoy the big sweeping stuff most—battles, magic, things like that. But when I look at what I myself am proudest of, it's usually small stuff—a nice turn of phrase, a touch of transcendence, a character who becomes suddenly real, or just a weird little idea that does nothing but sit in the middle of a chapter and make people stop and stare."

Born in 1957, Williams was raised in Palo Alto, California. "My parents never had much money—we were not on the wealthy side of town—but we never suffered (except existentially) and were always encouraged, especially in our creativity," he explained on his Web site. The writer credits his mother in particular with encouraging creativity in her children. "She made up odd Pooh-bear-type songs about things we were doing, and improvised great Halloween costumes—she made me a Viking suit one year with a wooden coat hanger for the helmet-horns and a furry bathmat for the vest. Way cool."

After high school graduation, Williams broke away from the path to college and toward the "good job" that many of his friends were following. "I was more interested in living on my own and supporting myself," he recalled, "so after high school I began the series of pretty hideous jobs that has so tragically shaped my outlook on life. I stacked tiles, made tacos, sold shoes, peddled insurance, collected loans . . . and worked at other things in my free moments." Among his more interesting avocations was a stint as singer/songwriter in a rock band called Idiot that incorporated such things as exploding objects as part of their stage show. As Williams fondly recalled, "We wrote songs about bowling and voles and luxury camper vans and the end of the world. We were a little ahead of out time. It was fun."

While he was engaged in this succession of jobs, Williams also had a hope that the writing skills he had been trying to develop would ultimately provide him with a long-term career. In his free time Williams put together the manuscript for one novel, a work of science fiction that he quickly packed away in the back of the closet. He completed a second novel, sent it out to several publishers, and in January of 1985 New York-based DAW picked it up. *Tailchaser's Song* was in book stores by the fall of that year, and Williams' entire life was transformed: He was now a published author. "When I received the letter from DAW that they were going to buy my novel I was excited and relieved," he later recalled; "somehow, the idea that my published books might totally fail to sell never occurred to me that first day, although it was and always is a possibility."

Felines Featured in Debut Work

Tailchaser's Song was inspired by "the shock of living with cats for the first time," as its author recalled. "I had one particular cat, a splendid . . . [orange] male named Fever. I could never get over the incredible scam he and the other cats had going. Dogs WORK for their living, fetching, guarding, wagging, drooling, making it clear how much they love humans. Cats think you should feel lucky to be slaving at a horrible job so you can buy them food." Williams began imagining a "cat-o-centric" world: "How would they see things? What kind of stories and folktales would they have? What part would humans play? (Answer: Meal Ticket.)" A few years later, when he decided to begin his first novel-length work, Williams recalled the idea of the cat-centered world.

In *Tailchaser's Song* Williams introduces readers to Fritti Tailchaser, a courageous orange tom cat who senses that all is not well; his fellow felines are disappearing at an alarming rate. When his friend Hushpad suddenly joins the ranks of the disappeared, Tailchaser goes out in search of his intended mate. The search for a friend is soon transformed into an heroic quest, as Tailchaser finds himself on a mission to thward the machinations of an evil cat god. Along the way, he makes the acquaintance of several other cats, including the Queen of the entire species, and learns a great deal of cat lore. While a contributor to *Kirkus Reviews* faulted the book for portraying cats as "thoroughly un-catlike"—as the reviewer noted, "they gather in cities and hunt in groups"—a *Publishers Weekly* critic lauded Williams' debut as an "extravagantly detailed fantasy" that "should engage the fancy of cat lovers." The book's popularity among readers was reflected by its author's nomination for the 1986 John W. Campbell Award for best newcomer in science fiction and fantasy.

In addition to being strongly influenced by the "Lord of the Rings" trilogy by British fantasy author J.R.R. Tolkien, *Tailchaser's Song* includes

While searching for a pair of swords that will help free his kingdom, Simon becomes the first mortal to enter the Sisthi tribe.

several other themes, according to its author. "The distrust of easy and/or dramatic solutions is one of them," Williams explained. "The love for stories of the past, but also a certain skepticism about history, is another. And, most importantly, the need to learn about oneself, to find out who you are before you can expect to change things in this or any world, is something I still work with all the time, in my books and my life."

Introduces Fantasy World of Osten Ard

After the success of his debut novel, Williams decided to undertake a more complex work: a fantasy series that would span several volumes and again allow him to create a unique world with its own legends, history, and problems. Beginning with a hundred-page outline of this world, which he named Osten Ard, he embarked upon the "Memory, Sorrow, and Thorn" trilogy, releasing *The Dragonbone Chair* in 1988. The novel's protagonist is Simon, a young scullion working in the kitchens of the castle of John, ruler of Osten Ard. With dreams of someday finding fame and fortune through courage and valor, Simon becomes the apprentice of Morgenes, a healer and magician. However, John is soon dead, and his throne is taken by John's son, Prince Elias. Under the influence of a malevolent magician-counselor named Pryates, Elias is in league with members of an immortal race of elves called Sithi who had formerly ruled this land. Soon, the kingdom of Osten Ard is threatened by the rebirth of the ancient Sithi Storm King, Ineluki, through the machinations of Pryates, a rebirth preceded by a civil war in which even the land begins to wither in the climate of hatred and fear. Now, Simon gets his chance at demonstrating his courage, as he rescues Elias's younger brother Prince Josua from the dungeon prison where Elias has locked him, then sets out to locate three magic swords that legend holds possess the key to vanquishing the Sithi ruler. Only one of these swords will be discovered by the novel's end. On his quest he gains several companions, including the wolf Qantaqa, the princess Miriamele, a Sithi named Jiriki, and the troll Binabik.

Compared by some critics with J.R.R. Tolkien's "Lord of the Rings" trilogy, as well as with the epic *War and Peace* penned by nineteenth-century Russian novelist Leo Tolstoy, *The Dragonbone Chair* was hailed as a "must-read for Tolkien fans" and a work "far superior to much popular fantasy" by *Voice of Youth Advocates* contributor Susan Williamson. While a *Publishers Weekly* critic dubbed the novel "derivative," the reviewer also called it "richly detailed, sweeping," and "colorfully characterized." Noting that the novel contains "several moments of genuine richness and strangeness," *St. James Guide to Fantasy Writers* contributor Wendy Bradley added that "Williams seems to have a particular talent for the arresting moment when something utterly surprising is revealed."

On his Web site, Williams commented that "there were a lot of things I didn't know when I started

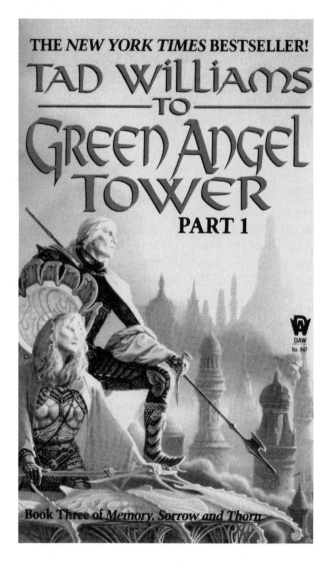

THE *NEW YORK TIMES* BESTSELLER!

TAD WILLIAMS
TO
GREEN ANGEL TOWER
PART 1

Book Three of *Memory, Sorrow and Thorn*

In this 1993 work, Prince Joshua, with the help of Simon and others, battles the Sisthi tribe to preserve the Osten Ard kingdom.

Dragonbone, and I just had to trust I would find out along the way. Lots of characters who eventually became very important didn't mean much to begin with. . . . Every book has a life of its own to the writer." Recalling his relative inexperience at the start of what would become a three thousand-page opus: "If you'd told me when I started writing the first paragraph of *The Dragonbone Chair* that I wouldn't finish the story for eight years, I'd have thought you were absolutely barking mad."

In *Stone of Farewell* Williams returns to Osten Ard and follows Simon as he becomes the first mortal to enter the realm of the ancient Sithi tribe. Still searching for the remaining two swords of power—Memory and Sorrow—he hopes will vanquish the corrupted undead Sithi king Ineluki from Simon's homeland, Simon now wields the sword Thorn, gained in the previous novel. He also gains the alliance of many living Sithi elves in the battle against King Elias and Ineluki and their evil minions.

While several critics commented on the complexity of the plot and the preponderance of characters in this middle volume of the series, a *Library Journal* reviewer applauded the second book's "vivid, likeable characters and exotic cultures," and a *Publishers Weekly* critic deemed it "panoramic, vigorous," and "often moving." Noting that the efforts of protagonist Simon to aid his friends and rendezvous at the haven offered by the *Stone of Farewell* "provide a strong core for this rather typical middle book of a trilogy," *Locus* contributor Carolyn Cushman added that the "huge scale" of the "Memory, Sorrow, and Thorn" books "provides an epic fantasy that you can get lost in for days, not just hours." "Middle volumes are always a problem," admitted Williams on his Web site. "They're not the ending and they're not the beginning. Things have to happen, but nothing really resolves."

Epic Finish to an Epic Saga

Partway through the ambitious undertaking of creating and preserving the threatened kingdom of Osten Ard, Williams began to confront the perplexing problems posed by creating such a lengthy work. The fact that the first and second novel were in print as he was completing the final volume made it "too late to go back and alter [something], as you could do before printing a stand alone novel. So—and this is a general tip useful to anyone writing very long fiction—I left some things open-ended in the first two volumes, so I could enforce a different interpretation once the book was in print, if necessary." "Memory, Sorrow, and Thorn" came to a close in 1993 with *To Green Angel Tower*, as Simon and his allies recover each of the three swords prophesied to be able to preserve their kingdom, the evil factions supporting Ineluki unite, and the warring parties finally confront each other in the inevitable ultimate showdown between good and evil. Prince Josua, aided by the powerful knight Camaris, Simon, and

Josua's niece Miriamele are confronted by not only above-ground evils, but also by subterranean swamp creatures and other tunnel-dwelling fiends before the final, surprising ending to this epic adventure. Noting that the work "weaves together a multitude of intricate strands, building to a suitably apocalyptic conclusion," a reviewer for *Publishers Weekly* also praised "the extraordinary tension built up in the book's closing pages." Citing Williams' novel as "well-written," *Library Journal* contributor Jackie Cassada opines that the "panoramic" trilogy comes to a close "in grand style."

> "... the need to learn about oneself, to find out who you are before you can expect to change things in this or any world, is something I still work with all the time, in my books and my life."
> —Tad Williams

To Green Angel Tower spent five weeks on the *New York Times* bestseller list, attesting to Williams' popularity among fantasy fans of the "Memory, Sorrow, and Thorn" series. This must have been a consolation of sorts for its author, who had dubbed *To Green Angel Tower* "The Book That Ate My Life" in his list of printed acknowledgments. As Williams later remarked on his Web site, for one thing, he had no way of knowing, when embarking on his own journey into Osten Ard, that his story would take shape in such a long, complex manner, or with as many characters. Although, he added in hindsight, "I guess I should have figured it out when I wrote a hundred-page outline for what I thought was a single-volume novel." The novel also was written during a tumultuous time in the author's personal life, as the stresses of a divorce from his first wife took its toll on his writerly focus. "Last but not least," Williams explained, "I had set up a very complex story and promised to finish it in one more volume. . . . When I finished it, the manuscript was 1,650 pages, a stack of paper over a foot tall. It barely made it into hardcover binding, and was so large it had to be published in two volumes in paperback."

Begins Otherworldly "Otherland" Novels

Completing "Memory, Sorrow, and Thorn" was a monumental achievement for Williams, a writer whose ambition far outweighed the number of published works to his credit, but whose efforts had been met with success. Starting—and finishing—such a vast undertaking, Williams took on a responsibility, not only to the many readers waiting to see what happened next, but also to his characters. "I . . . feel like I took responsibility for a world and for a lot of people in it," he explained, "and gave those characters and their world respect, and paid attention to what happened to all of them, and allowed each one the room to have his or her own story." Interestingly, within a few short years he would have accepted such a responsibility again; *City of Golden Shadow,* the first volume of a proposed tetralogy, "Otherland" was published in 1996.

As readers delve into *City of Golden Shadow* they find an infantryman named Paul Jonas hoping to survive the hellfire raining down on the trenches of France during World War I. But as the novel progresses, Paul is revealed to be not what he seems, as an explosion throws him not into death but into another place in time and space. Paul's story is followed by several more seemingly unrelated events until Williams moves his storyline to the near future and a classroom in South Africa, where teacher Renie Sulaweyo educates her students about virtual reality. When use of virtual reality equipment by her younger brother leaves the boy comatose, Renie begins a search for a cure that uncovers a plot whereby a secret worldwide group, the Grail Brotherhood, has conspired to steal the minds of young people and transfer them to a virtual world called Otherland. Calling *City of Golden Shadow* "a true mind bender," *Voice of Youth Advocates* contributor Kevin S. Beach added that while the novel's more than seven hundred pages of text might prove daunting to some readers, Williams' "research, writing, and character development are all remarkably well done." Writing in *Booklist,* critic Roland Green hailed the novelist for "bring[ing] the virtues of historical literacy and more than competent prose to his massive undertaking," and added that the first volume of "Otherland" is "well launched."

Joined by Paul Jonas, the infantryman from *City of Golden Shadow,* and others in 1998's *River of Blue Fire,* Renie continues her efforts to both thwart the efforts of the Brotherhood to depopulate the earth and save her brother's life. Now trapped on-line in Otherland, where anything is possible due to the nature of virtual reality, each member of the group must search for a way back to earth amid "a kaleidoscopic array of dreamscapes and nightmare worlds," as well as ferret out the spy for the Brotherhood who lurks within their midst, according to Cassada in *Library Journal.* The reviewer also had praise for Williams and his ability to move between reality and created worlds, as well as for "spinning multiple variations on a theme." While opining that *River of Blue Fire*

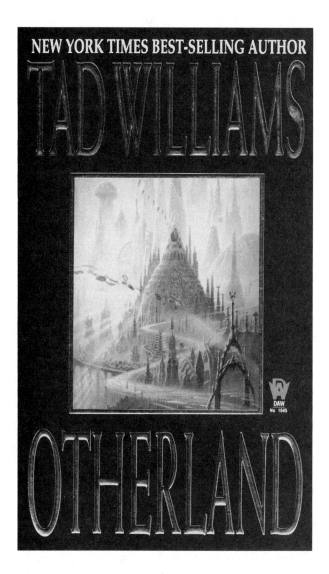

After a bomb explodes near him during World War I, Paul Jonas is blown into another world of virtual reality in Williams's "Otherland" series.

"would have profited from trimming," *Booklist* reviewer Green notes that this novel "is the work of a powerful imagination and high-class world builder." Attracting a large following of fantasy and science-fiction fans, the ongoing "Otherland" series has sparked a Web site where readers can trade theories and opinions, and receive information about the two concluding volumes. The third series installment, *Mountain of Black Glass,* was published in 1999.

Takes a Break from Epic Works

During a hiatus from his "Memory, Sorrow, and Thorn" series, Williams collaborated with fellow author Nina Kiriki Hoffman on *Child of an Ancient City,* part of an illustrated, multi-author series called "Dragonflight." In this work, published in 1992 and using the *1001 Arabian Nights* motif, a group of Muslim travelers passing through the Caucasian Mountains find themselves ambushed by bandits and then pursued by a "vampyr" during their attempt to return back through the mountains to Bagdad. After several members of their tattered party are waylaid by the vampyr, the remaining members of the group challenge the fiend to a story contest. If the travelers can tell the saddest tale, they will be allowed to continue their journey; otherwise, the vampyr will deal with them. The vampyr's tale recounts his own downfall from humanity many years ago; it is up to the travellers to top the sadness of this personal tragedy. Sally Estes, writing in *Booklist,* hailed *Child of an Ancient City* as "a haunting fantasy in which the ill-fated 'monster' is as sad to behold as Dr. Frankenstein's creation." And Cathi Dunn MacRae added in *Wilson Library Bulletin* that "The Arabic flavor of each man's story-within-a-story melds with the atmosphere of menace," making *Child of an Ancient City* a book sure to "spellbind" teen readers enamored of tales about the undead.

The novel *Caliban's Hour,* which Williams published in 1994, looks at what might have happened after the close of William Shakespeare's play *The Tempest.* Taking place two decades after the events of the play, the lowly, deformed figure of Caliban arrives in Italy in search of Miranda, the beautiful daughter of the exiled Prospero. Having long since fled the island on which she and her father had made their home in exile, Miranda is now a woman in mid-life with a husband and daughter; Caliban, also aged and hard-

". . . when I look at what I myself am proudest of, it's usually small stuff—a nice turn of phrase, a touch of transcendence, a character who becomes suddenly real, or just a weird little idea that does nothing but sit in the middle of a chapter and make people stop and stare."

—Tad Williams

ened in his bitterness for the unkind treatment she once exacted upon him, still seeks revenge and vows to tell Miranda of his pain before he kills her.

"Tad Williams's Caliban is not some Conan-esque noble savage," noted Joe Mahew in reviewing the novel for the *Washington Post Book World,* "or an anachronistically sullen egalitarian voice from below the stairs. He speaks, despite all his monstrosity, for what is decent and honorable in man, and in a manner appropriate to the Renaissance as well as to the age in which we live." According to a reviewer in *Publishers Weekly,* Williams' "prose is lucid and smooth" and "puts a very different spin on events." Bestowing equal praise upon the novelist for his "marvelous job of bringing Caliban to life for modern readers," *Analog* reviewer Tom Easton noted that *Caliban's Hour* is "strong and warm and deeply felt, a charmer that should appeal to fans of both Shakespeare and fantasy."

"The Tempest has always been one of my favorite plays," the novelist once commented in *Locus.* Williams' interpretation of Shakespeare's play includes uncovering pointed remarks made by several characters regarding the evils of imperialism, the same attitudes that Williams maintains are responsible for much of the bloodshed that continues to occur around the world. "What got me going on that in the first place was that in the play Caliban says, in effect, 'This was my island first. I was here first, and you came along and basically tricked me. . . . You treated me well for a while, and then you turned me into a servant.'" "Of course," Williams added, "by the end of the play, not only have they turned him into a servant, they've chastised him for wanting his independence back again."

If you enjoy the works of Tad Williams, you may also want to check out the following books and films:

Terry Goodkind, *Wizard's First Rule*, 1994.
Brian Jacques, *Salamandastron*, 1993.
Robert Jordan, *The Fires of Heaven*, 1993.
Willow, a film directed by Ron Howard, 1988.

Speaks Frankly about Writer's Life

"The simple fact is, no one writes two or three thousand pages of story without thinking they've got a story worth telling," Williams commented on his Web site, discussing the craft of fiction and the difference between success and failure at making a career out of it. "No one makes a living from writing without having at least a little confidence in what they do." However, he is always quick to admit that writing is not always a task over which the author has complete control. "[In completing "Otherland,"] some things will not be as wonderful as I'd envisioned . . . (that's the sad fact of writing: your best hope of what something can be doesn't always make it to paper), but other elements . . . come as happy surprises, and nobody sensible is allergic to serendipity."

Despite the ups and downs of the business, however, Williams wouldn't trade it for any of the other jobs he has had—or could have had, for that matter. "I am deliriously grateful every day that I get to do what I want to do for a living," he concluded. "Whenever the pressures of work and life start to make me cranky, I just remind myself of managing the art store next to the freeway . . . or being smacked with a $3.99 sale slipper by an irate Kinney's Shoes customer who refused to believe I didn't know where the other half of the pair was, and I suddenly feel much better about everything."

■ Works Cited

Beach, Kevin S., review of *Otherland*, *Voice of Youth Advocates*, June, 1997, p. 122.
Bradley, Wendy, "Tad Williams," *St. James Guide to Fantasy Writers*, St. James Press, 1994, pp. 618-19.

Review of *Caliban, Locus*, January, 1995, pp. 4-5, 73.
Cassada, Jackie, review of *To Green Angel Tower, Library Journal*, March 15, 1993, p. 111.
Cassada, Jackie, review of *River of Blue Fire, Library Journal*, July, 1998, p. 142.
Cushman, Carolyn, review of *Stone of Farewell, Locus*, July, 1990, p. 57.
Review of *The Dragonbone Chair, Publishers Weekly*, August 19, 1988, p. 58.
Easton, Tom, review of *Caliban's Hour, Analog*, August, 1995, p. 168.
Estes, Sally, review of *Child of an Ancient City, Booklist*, December 1, 1992, p. 662.
Green, Roland, review of *City of Golden Shadow, Booklist*, October 1, 1996, p. 292.
Green, Roland, review of *River of Blue Fire, Booklist*, May 15, 1998, p. 1566.
MacRae, Cathi Dunn, review of *Child of an Ancient City, Wilson Library Bulletin*, October, 1993, p. 125.
Mahew, Joe, "Tempest-Tost," *Washington Post Book World*, January 29, 1995, p. 11.
Review of *Stone of Farewell, Library Journal*, June 15, 1990, p. 139.
Review of *Tailchaser's Song, Kirkus Reviews*, September 15, 1985, p. 980.
Review of *Tailchaser's Song, Publishers Weekly*, September 27, 1985, p. 84.
Review of *To Green Angel Tower, Publishers Weekly*, January 11, 1993, p. 56.
Williams, Tad, commentary from his personal Web site, located at http://www.tadwilliams.com (July 24, 1999).
Williamson, Susan, review of *The Dragonbone Chair, Voice of Youth Advocates*, February, 1989, p. 296.

■ For More Information See

BOOKS

Contemporary Authors, Volume 146, Gale, 1995.

PERIODICALS

Analog Science Fiction/Science Fact, July, 1986.
Booklist, August, 1990, p. 2124; February 1, 1993, p. 955.
Kirkus Reviews, September 15, 1985, p. 980; May 15, 1998, p. 702.
Publishers Weekly, June 1, 1990, p. 51; January 11, 1993, p. 56; November 28, 1994.

School Library Journal, January, 1993, p. 134.
Voice of Youth Advocates, December, 1993, p. 304; April, 1993, p. 48; October, 1998, p. 290; December, 1998, p. 374.
Wilson Library Bulletin, March, 1995, p. 86.

—Sketch by Pamela L. Shelton

Tennessee Williams

Letters, American Society of Composers, Authors, and Publishers (ASCAP), American Automatic Control Council (president, 1965-67), Alpha Tau Omega.

■ Personal

Born Thomas Lanier Williams, March 26, 1911, in Columbus, MI; choked to death February 24, 1983, in his suite at Hotel Elysee, New York, NY; buried in St. Louis, MO; son of Cornelius Coffin (a traveling salesperson) and Edwina (Dakin) Williams. *Education:* Attended University of Missouri, 1931-33, and Washington University, St. Louis, MO, 1936-37; University of Iowa, A.B., 1938. *Religion:* Roman Catholic.

■ Career

Playwright, novelist, short story writer, and poet; full-time writer, 1944-83; International Shoe Co., St. Louis, MO, clerical worker and manual laborer, 1934-36; worked at various jobs, including waiter and hotel elevator operator, New Orleans, LA, 1939; teletype operator, Jacksonville, FL, 1940; worked at various jobs, including waiter and theatre usher, New York City, 1942; Metro-Goldwyn-Mayer, Hollywood, screen writer, 1943. *Member:* Dramatists Guild, National Institute of Arts and

■ Awards, Honors

Group Theatre Award, 1939, for *American Blues;* Rockefeller Foundation fellowship, 1940; American Academy and National Institute of Arts and Letters grant, 1943; New York Drama Critics Circle Award, Donaldson Award, and Sidney Howard Memorial Award, all 1945, all for *The Glass Menagerie;* New York Drama Critics Circle Award, Pulitzer Prize, and Donaldson Award, all 1948, all for *A Streetcar Named Desire;* elected to National Institute of Arts and Letters, 1952; New York Drama Critics Circle Award and Pulitzer Prize, both 1955, and London *Evening Standard* Award, 1958, all for *Cat on a Hot Tin Roof;* New York Drama Critics Circle Award, 1962, and first place for best new foreign play, London Critics' Poll, 1964-65, both for *The Night of the Iguana;* creative arts medal, Brandeis University, 1964-65; National Institute of Arts and Letters Gold Medal, 1969; received first centennial medal of Cathedral of St. John the Divine, 1973; elected to Theatre Hall of Fame, 1979; Kennedy Honors Award, 1979; Common Wealth Award for Distinguished Service in Dramatic Arts, 1981.

■ Writings

PLAYS

Cairo, Shanghai, Bombay! (comedy), produced in Memphis, TN, 1935.

Headlines, produced in St. Louis, MO, 1936.

Candles to the Sun, produced in St. Louis, 1936.

The Magic Tower, produced in St. Louis, 1936.

The Fugitive Kind (also see below), produced in St. Louis, 1937.

Spring Song, produced in Iowa City, IA, 1938.

The Long Goodbye (also see below), produced in New York City, 1940.

Battle of Angels (also see below; produced in Boston, MA, 1940), New Directions (New York City), 1945.

Stairs to the Roof, produced in Pasadena, CA, 1944.

The Glass Menagerie (two-act; also see below; produced in Chicago, 1944; produced on Broadway, 1945), Random House (New York City), 1945.

(With Donald Windham) *You Touched Me!: A Romantic Comedy in Three Acts* (three act; produced on Broadway, 1945), S. French (New York City), 1947.

Twenty-seven Wagons Full of Cotton (also see below; part of triple bill "All in One"; produced on Broadway, 1955), in *The Best One-Act Plays of 1944,* Dodd (New York City), 1945.

This Property Is Condemned (also see below), produced Off-Broadway, 1946.

Moony's Kids Don't Cry (also see below; produced in Los Angeles, 1946), in *The Best One-Act Plays of 1940,* Dodd, 1941.

Portrait of a Madonna (also see below), produced in Los Angeles, 1946, produced in New York City as part of "Triple Play," 1959.

The Last of My Solid Gold Watches (also see below), produced in Los Angeles, 1946.

Twenty-seven Wagons Full of Cotton, and Other One-Act Plays (includes *The Long Goodbye, This Property Is Condemned, Portrait of a Madonna, The Last of My Solid Gold Watches, Auto-da-Fe, The Lady of Larkspur Lotion, The Purification, Hello from Bertha, The Strangest Kind of Romance,* and *Lord Byron's Love Letter* [also see below]), New Directions, 1946, 3rd edition with preface by Williams (contains two new plays, *Talk to Me like the Rain* and *Let Me Listen and Something Unspoken* [also see below]), 1953.

Lord Byron's Love Letter (also see below), produced in New York City, 1947, revised version produced in London, 1964.

Auto-da-Fe, produced in New York City, 1947, produced in Bromley, Kent, England, 1961.

The Gnadiges Fraulein, Dramatists Play Service, 1967.

The Lady of Larkspur Lotion, produced in New York City, 1947, produced in London, 1968.

Summer and Smoke (produced in Dallas, 1947; produced on Broadway, 1948; revised version produced as *Eccentricities of a Nightingale* in Washington, DC, 1966), New Directions, 1948, in *The Eccentricities of a Nightingale, and Summer and Smoke: Two Plays,* New Directions, 1964.

A Streetcar Named Desire (three-act; also see below; produced on Broadway, 1947), New Directions, 1947, with preface by Williams, 1951, revised edition, Dramatists Play Service, 1953, with foreword by Jessica Tandy and introduction by Williams, Limited Editions Club, 1982.

American Blues: Five Short Plays (contains *Moony's Kids Don't Cry, The Dark Room, The Case of the Crushed Petunias, The Long Stay Cut Short; or, the Unsatisfactory Supper,* and *Ten Blocks on the Camino Real;* also see below), Dramatists Play Service, 1948.

Camino Real (also see below; in expanded version as *Ten Blocks on the Camino Real,* produced in New York City, 1953), with foreword and afterword by Williams, New Directions, 1953.

The Rose Tattoo (also see below; produced in New York City, 1951), with preface by Williams, New Directions, 1951.

Cat on a Hot Tin Roof (three-act; also see below; produced on Broadway, 1955), with preface by Williams, New Directions, 1955.

Three Players of a Summer Game (produced in Westport, CT, 1955), Secker & Warburg (London), 1960.

(Librettist) Raffaello de Banfield, *Lord Byron's Love Letter* (one-act opera), Ricordi, 1955.

The Case of the Crushed Petunias, produced in Cleveland, OH, 1957, produced in New York City, 1958.

Orpheus Descending (three-act; also see below; revision of *Battle of Angels;* produced in New York City, 1957; produced Off-Broadway, 1959), New Directions, 1959.

Orpheus Descending, with Battle of Angels: Two Plays, with preface by Williams, New Directions, 1958.

A Perfect Analysis Given by a Parrot: A Comedy in One Act (also see below), Dramatists Play Service, 1958.

The Rose Tattoo and Camino Real, introduced and edited by E. Martin Browne, Penguin, 1958.

Garden District: Two Plays; Something Unspoken and Suddenly Last Summer (also see below; produced Off-Broadway, 1958), Secker & Warburg, 1959.

Suddenly Last Summer, New Directions, 1958.

Talk to Me like the Rain and Let Me Listen, produced in Westport, CT, 1958, produced in New York City, 1967.

I Rise in Flame, Cried the Phoenix: A Play about D. H. Lawrence (produced Off-Broadway, 1958-59), with a note by Frieda Lawrence, New Directions, 1951.

Sweet Bird of Youth (produced at Martin Beck Theatre, 1959), edition with foreword by Williams, New Directions, 1959, revised edition, Dramatists Play Service, 1962.

Period of Adjustment; High Point over a Cavern: A Serious Comedy (produced in Miami, FL, 1959; produced on Broadway, 1960), New Directions, 1960, as *Period of Adjustment; or, High Point Is Built on a Cavern,* Dramatists Play Service, 1961.

The Night of the Iguana (also see below; from Williams's short story of the same title; short version produced in Spoleto, Italy, 1960, expanded version produced on Broadway, 1961), New Directions, 1961.

The Purification, produced Off-Broadway, 1959.

Hello from Bertha, produced in Bromley, 1961.

To Heaven in a Golden Coach, produced in Bromley, 1961.

The Milk Train Doesn't Stop Here Anymore (also see below; produced as one-act in *Spoleto,* at Festival of Two Worlds, 1962, expanded version produced on Broadway, 1963, revision produced on Broadway, 1964), New Directions, 1964.

Slapstick Tragedy (contains *The Mutilated* and *The Gnaediges Fraulein;* also see below; produced on Broadway, 1966.

The Dark Room, produced in London, 1966.

The Mutilated (one-act), Dramatists Play Service, 1967.

The Gnaediges Fraulein (one-act), Dramatists Play Service, 1967, revised as *The Latter Days of a Celebrated Soubrette,* produced in New York City, 1974.

Kingdom of Earth: The Seven Descents of Myrtle (originally appeared in *Esquire* as *Kingdom of Earth,* 1967; as *The Seven Descents of Myrtle,* produced on Broadway, 1968, revised as *Kingdom of Earth,* produced in Princeton, NJ, 1975), New Directions, 1968.

The Two-Character Play (produced in London, 1967), revised as *Out Cry* (produced in Chicago, 1971, produced on Broadway, 1973), New Directions, 1969.

In the Bar of a Tokyo Hotel (produced Off-Broadway, 1969), Dramatists Play Service, 1969.

The Strangest Kind of Romance, produced in London, 1969.

(Contributor) *Oh! Calcutta!,* produced Off-Broadway at Eden Theatre, 1969.

The Frosted Glass Coffin [and] *A Perfect Analysis Given by a Parrot,* produced in Key West, FL, 1970.

The Long Stay Cut Short; or, The Unsatisfactory Supper (also see below), produced in London, 1971.

I Can't Imagine Tomorrow [and] *Confessional,* produced in Bar Harbor, ME, 1971.

Small Craft Warnings (produced Off-Broadway, 1972), New Directions, 1972.

The Red Devil Battery Sign (produced in Boston, 1975; revised version produced in Vienna, Austria, 1976), New Directions, 1988.

Demolition Downtown: Count Ten in Arabic, produced in London, 1976.

This Is (an Entertainment), produced in San Francisco, 1976.

Vieux Carre (produced on Broadway, 1977), New Directions, 1979.

A Lovely Sunday for Creve Coeur (produced under title *Creve Coeur* in Charleston, SC, at Spoleto Festival, 1978, produced Off-Broadway, 1979), New Directions, 1980.

Clothes for a Summer Hotel: A Ghost Play (produced on Broadway, 1980), Dramatists Play Service, 1981.

Steps Must Be Gentle: A Dramatic Reading for Two Performers, Targ Editions, 1980.

It Happened the Day the Sun Rose, Sylvester & Orphanos, 1981.

The Remarkable Rooming-House of Mme. Le Monde, Albondocani Press, 1984.

Something Cloudy, Something Clear (produced Off-Off Broadway, 1981), introduction by Eve Adamson, New Directions, 1995.

Not about Nightingales, 1939.

The Notebook of Trigorin: A Free Adaptation of Anton Chekhov's The Sea Gull, New Directions, 1997.

Also author of *Me, Vashya, Kirche, Kutchen und Kinder, Life Boat Drill, Will Mr. Merriwether Return from Memphis?, Of Masks Outrageous and Austere,* and *A House Not Meant to Stand.* Also author of television play, *I Can't Imagine Tomorrow.* Contributor to anthologies. Contributor to periodicals, including *Esquire.*

Williams's plays appear in numerous foreign languages.

COLLECTIONS

Four Plays (contains *The Glass Menagerie, A Streetcar Named Desire, Summer and Smoke,* and *Camino Real*), Secker & Warburg, 1956.

Five Plays (contains *Cat on a Hot Tin Roof, The Rose Tattoo, Something Unspoken, Suddenly Last Summer,* and *Orpheus Descending*), Secker & Warburg, 1962.

Three Plays: The Rose Tattoo, Camino Real, Sweet Bird of Youth, New Directions, 1964.

Baby Doll: The Script for the Film [and] *Something Unspoken* [and] *Suddenly Last Summer,* Penguin, 1968.

The Night of the Iguana [and] *Orpheus Descending,* Penguin, 1968.

The Milk Train Doesn't Stop Here Anymore [and] *Cat on a Hot Tin Roof,* Penguin, 1969.

Dragon Country: A Book of Plays, New Directions, 1970.

Battle of Angels [and] *The Glass Menagerie* [and] *A Streetcar Named Desire,* New Directions, 1971.

Cat on a Hot Tin Roof [and] *Orpheus Descending* [and] *Suddenly Last Summer,* New Directions, 1971.

The Eccentricities of a Nightingale [and] *Summer and Smoke* [and] *The Rose Tattoo* [and] *Camino Real,* New Directions, 1971.

The Theatre of Tennessee Williams, New Directions, Volume 1, 1971, Volume 2, 1971, Volume 3, 1971, Volume 4, 1972, Volume 5, 1976, Volume 6, 1981, Volume 7, 1981.

Three by Tennessee Williams, New American Library, 1976.

Cat on a Hot Tin Roof [and] *The Milk Train Doesn't Stop Here Anymore* [and] *The Night of theIguana,* Penguin, 1976.

Selected Plays, illustrations by Jerry Pinkney, Franklin Library, 1977.

Tennessee Williams: Eight Plays, introduction by Harold Clurman, Doubleday, 1979.

Selected Plays, illustrations by Herbert Tauss, Franklin Library, 1980.

Ten by Tennessee (one-act plays), produced in New York City at Lucille Lortel Theatre, May, 1986.

SCREENPLAYS

(With Gore Vidal) *Senso,* Luchino Visconti, c. 1949.

(With Oscar Saul) *The Glass Menagerie,* Warner Bros., 1950.

A Streetcar Named Desire, 20th Century-Fox, 1951.

(With Hal Kanter) *The Rose Tattoo,* Paramount, 1955.

Baby Doll, Warner Bros., 1956, published as *Baby Doll: The Script for the Film,* New American Library, 1956, published as *Baby Doll; the Script for the Film, Incorporating the Two One-Act Plays which Suggested It: 27 Wagons Full of Cotton* [and] *The Long Stay Cut Short; or, The Unsatisfactory Supper,* New Directions, 1956.

(With Vidal) *Suddenly Last Summer,* Columbia, 1959.

(With Meade Roberts) *The Fugitive Kind* (based on *Orpheus Descending*), United Artists, 1959, published as *The Fugitive Kind,* Signet, 1960.

Boom (based on *The Milk Train Doesn't Stop Here Anymore*), Universal, 1968.

Stopped Rocking and Other Screenplays (contains All Gaul Is Divided, The Loss of a Teardrop Diamond, One Arm, and *Stopped Rocking*), introduced by Richard Gilman, New Directions, 1984.

A Streetcar Named Desire: A Screen Adaptation Directed by Elia Kazan, Irvington, 1989.

Baby Doll and Tiger Tail, New Directions, 1991.

Also author, with Paul Bowles, of *The Wanton Countess* (English-language version), filmed in 1954.

STORIES

One Arm, and Other Stories (includes *The Night of the Iguana*), New Directions, 1948.

Hard Candy: A Book of Stories, New Directions, 1954.

Man Brings This up Road: A Short Story, Street & Smith, 1959.

Three Players of a Summer Game, and Other Stories, Secker & Warburg, 1960.

Grand, House of Books, 1964.

The Knightly Quest: A Novella and Four Short Stories, New Directions, 1967.

Eight Mortal Ladies Possessed: A Book of Stories, New Directions, 1974.

Collected Stories, introduction by Gore Vidal, New Directions, 1985.

Contributor of short stories to *Esquire.*

OTHER

The Roman Spring of Mrs. Stone (novel), New Directions, 1950.

In the Winter of Cities: Poems, New Directions, 1956.

(Author of introduction) Carson McCullers, *Reflections in a Golden Eye,* Bantam, 1961.

Memoirs, Doubleday, 1975.

Moise and the World of Reason (novel), Simon & Schuster, 1975.

Tennessee Williams's Letters to Donald Windham, 1940-65, edited with commentary by Windham, [Verona], 1976, Holt, 1977.

Androgyne, Mon Amour: Poems, New Directions, 1977.

Where I Live: Selected Essays, edited by Christine R. Day and Bob Woods, introduction by Day, New Directions, 1978.

Conversations with Tennessee Williams, edited by Albert J. Devlin, University Press of Mississippi, 1986.

Five o'Clock Angel: Letters of Tennessee Williams to Maria St. Just, 1948-1982, Knopf, 1990.

A collection of Williams' manuscripts and letters is located at the Humanities Research Center of the University of Texas at Austin.

■ Adaptations

The Roman Spring of Mrs. Stone was filmed by Warner Bros. in 1961; *Sweet Bird of Youth* was filmed in 1962; *Period of Adjustment* was filmed in 1962; *This Property Is Condemned* was filmed by Paramount in 1966; *I Can't Imagine Tomorrow* and *Talk to Me like the Rain and Let Me Listen* were jointly televised as *Dragon Country,* New York Television Theatre, 1970; *The Seven Descents of Myrtle* was filmed by Warner Bros. in 1970 as *The Last of the Mobile Hot-Shots; Summer and Smoke,* Belwin-Mills, 1972, was adapted from Williams' play, with music by Lee Hoiby and libretto by Lanford Wilson; *The Glass Menagerie* was filmed by Burt Harris for Cineplex Odeon in 1987; *A Streetcar Named Desire* was filmed for television in 1984 and broadcast on ABC-TV; *Cat on a Hot Tin Roof* was filmed for television in 1984 by International TV Group; *Summer and Smoke* was filmed for television in 1989 and broadcast on NBC-TV.

■ Sidelights

The Glass Menagerie, A Streetcar Named Desire, Cat on a Hot Tin Roof, and *Suddenly Last Summer:* these plays are considered among the classics of twentieth-century American theatre. Their author, Tennessee Williams, while benefiting from the success of these works during his lifetime, also suffered from their collective interpretation. Concentrating on the less than noble side of human emotions—rape, incest, self-delusion, homosexuality, drug abuse, cannibalism, castration, and murder among them—critics maintained that the plays were largely influenced by the playwright's own life in the American South, and theatergoers—used to the discrete sexuality and proper language common in the 1940s and 1950s—were shocked. Another aspect of Williams' life also affected his plays' reception. While openly admitting to being a homosexual since the 1950s, he focused many of his plays on sexual energy within a wide variety of human relationships, imbuing his plots with ambiguity and often leaving the sexual orientation of his characters open for interpretation. His characters, too, were drawn from the lower levels of society. "I have always been more interested in creating a character that contains something crippled," Williams once said. "I think nearly all of us have some kind of defect, anyway, and I suppose I have found it easier to identify with the characters who verge on hysteria, who were frightened of life, who were desperate to reach out to another person."

Despite the fact that Williams' works have endured their share of criticism, they have also won supporters among critics whose reviews summoned large audiences by praising Williams' unique insights into the growing isolation of life in the United States and the human condition in general. His works enjoyed lengthy runs on the New York stage, as well as in cities around the world, and they earned their author a number of prestigious awards. Film versions of Williams' works, as well as staged productions, have featured some of the most well-known actors of the mid-1900s, including Elizabeth Taylor, Maureen Stapleton, Paul Newman, Jessica Tandy, Geraldine Page, Bette Davis, and Marlon Brando. While best known for a few choice dramatic works, Williams was a prolific writer; he penned over sixty lesser-known plays, as well as seven volumes of short stories, three books of verse, several screenplays, a number of essays, and an autobiography during his more than fifty-year career.

Develops Close Family Ties

Born on March 26, 1911 in Columbus, Mississippi, Williams was the second of three children born to Cornelius Coffin and Edwina Dakin Williams. Named Thomas Lanier by his parents, the nickname "Tennessee" would come later, during his college days when fellow students were taken by his Southern drawl. In childhood, however, nicknames were more pointed and cutting, reflecting the unstable emotional relationships existing within the Williams family. Here young Thomas was dubbed "Miss Nancy" by an overbearing father who viewed his son as weak and feminine. Indeed, the young boy must have appeared weak; at a young age he contracted diphtheria, which caused partial paralysis in his legs and from which he almost died. Fear of a recurrence of this condition caused Williams to shy from sports and other "boy-like" activities through much of his childhood.

Williams and his sister were reared primarily by their mother. Their father, a salesman who was either on the road or at the bar, was an infrequent presence at the family's gracious home at the rectory of Grace Episcopal Church, where Edwina's father was a priest. The emotional climate in the Williams' household would become increasingly unhealthy after Williams' older sister Rose, imaginative and energetic as a child, began the periods of depression that caused her to be later diagnosed as schizophrenic. Williams was very close to his sister, despite her often erratic behavior, and remained concerned for her well-being. Rose's emotional decline was painful for him to observe, and he would later write about her mental illness in several works, including the plays *The Fugitive Kind* and *Candles in the Sun*.

Because of his physical disability and the fact that he was often ridiculed by other children, Williams kept to himself as a young boy, preferring to enjoy the gracious life at the rectory than the rambunctious life on the streets and fields of his rural Mississippi town. When he was eight, the family moved from their comfortable home to a small apartment in a crowded tenement located in the working-class portion of St. Louis, where Cornelius Williams found a job working in a shoe factory. In St. Louis Williams and Rose were joined by a younger brother, Dakin, but the appearance of a new child did little to improve the emotional life of the family. Ultimately, the overall malaise and unhappiness in Thomas Lanier's life led him to writing as an escape. Spending his days working on short stories, he began entering his work in contests.

The Appearance of Tennessee Williams

Williams' first published work, "Can a Good Wife Be a Good Sport?," appeared in the magazine *Smart Set* in 1927, winning third prize in that magazine's essay contest. The win encouraged the sixteen-year-old writer, and he continued his literary endeavors, publishing his first short story, "The Vengeance of Nitocris" in the pulp magazine *Weird Tales* in August of the following year. These and all other publications by Williams would feature the byline Thomas Lanier Williams; the name Tennessee Williams did not appear until the summer of 1939, when the author used it to end a short story in *Story* magazine. That story, "The Field of Blue Children," would signal the end of Thomas Lanier Williams and the birth of Tennessee Williams.

The Glass Menagerie

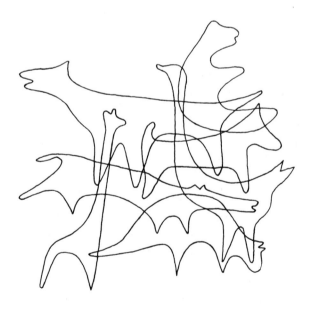

by Tennessee Williams

Originally published in 1944, this play became Williams's first popular and successful work and an American theater classic.

Tennessee Williams and Oscar Saul wrote the screen-play for this 1950 Warner Bros. film adaptation of *The Glass Menagerie*, featuring Jane Wyman and Kirk Douglas.

Meanwhile, enrolling at the University of Missouri in 1929 at the age of eighteen, Williams found his father's attitudes toward his more "feminine" nature and his dislike of sports reflected in that of his fraternity brothers at Alpha Tau Omega, who labeled him a "sissy." In addition to writing, his romantic relationship with Hazel Kramer, who Williams had been in love with since childhood, distracted the young man from his coursework, and his grades suffered. Bouts of heavy drinking quickly became Williams' means of finding solace amid the emotional turmoil presented by his first year of college. After watching his son fail the entrance exam into the college's military training program, a disgusted Cornelius Williams pulled the plug on his worthless son's education. Demanding that Williams return home to St. Louis, he found the young man a job at the International Shoe Company. Still using writing as a refuge, Williams worked in the factory by day and wrote by night, sometimes going without sleep to complete a story. Sleep deprivation eventually took its

toll, and Williams suffered his first nervous break-down in 1935, the result of exhaustion and frustration at his life.

To aid in his recuperation, the twenty-four-year-old Williams was sent to live with his maternal grandparents in Memphis. Here he would discover drama, when he met several people involved with local theatre groups. Persuaded to try his hand at play-writing, Williams penned *Cairo! Shanghai! Bombay!*, a play about sailors and prostitutes that would have a successful local run. Fueled by the reception to his work and determined that writing would be his career, Williams returned to St. Louis and enrolled at Washington University, where he began taking his writing more seriously, and became involved with a local amateur theatre group called the Mummers, which produced several of his early works.

In 1927, while pursuing his studies at Washington University, Williams again suffered as a result of the unfeeling actions of his father, this time through his sister, Rose. Increasingly unhappy since being forced to change colleges by the controlling Cornelius, Rose had sunk into a deep depression. Then the elder Williams accepted the advice of a psychiatrist: he had his daughter hospitalized and scheduled her for a prefrontal lobotomy. The procedure, then still in its nascent stages, left Rose mentally damaged and unable to interact with others for the rest of her life. Sickened by seeing his sister in her tragic condition and unable to witness her further deterioration, Williams left St. Louis. He entered the University of Iowa where he studied, wrote, and completed his bachelor's degree in 1938. During World War II he travelled around the United States and Mexico, writing and working at a variety of jobs to pay his way. These travels would provide him with a great deal of raw material about people and places that he would one day incorporate in his writings.

Gains Publicity—of a Sort—in Boston

Since his work with the Mummers in St. Louis, several of Williams' plays had made the rounds of community theatre groups across the country, attracting the notice of several in the literary world. Eventually he was approached by Audrey Wood, a literary agent who was impressed by the young playwright's talent. In 1939 Wood agreed to represent Williams as a playwright; she also found a way to harness grant monies and scholarships, enabling the playwright to continue writing while also seeing several of his plays produced. Among those grants was $1,000 from the Rockefeller Foundation, which enabled the playwright to complete *Battle of Angels* and achieve his first taste of the notoriety that would follow him throughout his career.

Reaching the Boston stage in 1940, *Battle of Angels* never completed its run, sparking as it did such public indignation over its treatment of sex and religion that it closed after just two weeks. The play, which follows the escapades of a young wanderer named Val Xavier as he seduces a succession of women in a small town, was ripe with symbolism in the fashion of D. H. Lawrence. The play contains several characteristics that would show themselves in much of Williams' later works, according to *Dictionary of Literary Biography* essayist Sally Johns: "it is set in a small Southern town, it presents the romantic theme of repressed passion and spiritual sterility, and it contains several sharply drawn minor characters."

Following the *Battle of Angels* debacle, Williams returned to the southern United States, discouraged. After a short stay in New Orleans, however, he returned to New York City and resumed his habit of working at a succession of menial jobs and accumulating material for his writing. Fortunately, Wood found her client a scriptwriting contract with Metro-Goldwyn- Mayer. It would be during this period that Williams completed his first major work, *The Gentleman Caller*, which, while rejected by M-G-M, would be reworked and gain prominence under the title its author bestowed upon it prior to its 1944 stage debut in Chicago: *The Glass Menagerie*.

The Glass Menagerie

Noting that an understanding of Williams and his work is best gained through the plays *The Glass Menagerie, A Streetcar Named Desire,* and *Cat on a Hot Tin Roof, Contemporary American Dramatists* contributor Dennis Welland noted that *The Glass Menagerie* "has a lyrical, sad gentleness that separates it from the savage cruelty of much of [Williams'] later work." Set amid the Depression years of the late 1930s, the play focuses on the relationships within a family living in working-class

St. Louis. But more importantly, it focuses on a withdrawn, emotionally crippled young woman named Laura Wingfield, whose treatment at the playwright's hands "shows the playwright's sympathetic insight into female psychology which, despite occasional sentimentalisation, is distinctive of Williams's dramas." In the play, it is Laura's birthday. Stout and disillusioned Amanda Wingfield, a former Southern belle who has long since been deserted by her husband, hopes that her reclusive daughter might marry into a family of stature as a means of both making Laura "whole" and eliminating the burden of her care from her mother. Laura's brother, Tom, resents his mother's intrusion, seeing his sister as a unique and valuable individual in her own way. The arrival of a gentleman caller named Jim O'Connor due to the mother's machinations sparks some hope in Amanda and some interest in Laura, but ultimately bothwomen's dreams are dashed when it is learned that the industrious and personable Mr. O'Connor is otherwise spoken for.

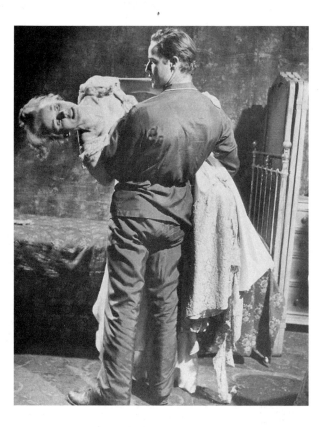

The career of Marlon Brando (shown here with Jessica Tandy) soared after he starred in the 1951 film adaptation of Williams's Pulitzer Prize-winning play *A Streetcar Named Desire.*

The response of critics to the first run of Williams' debut was, on the whole, positive; in the *New Yorker* reviewer Wolcott Gibbs called it "very touching," and noted that the playwright "has captured a brief but poignant period in four lives, no negligible accomplishment on any stage." However, several critics saw in Williams' work a tendency toward self-indulgence. Dubbing Williams "a playwright in *transition*," Kappo Phelan expressed concern over the conflicting details presented, via Williams' dialogue, as to the time period of the play's action, and commented in his *Commonweal* critique that "if [such] . . . complaint seem[s] unduly fractional, it must be remembered that the method Mr. Williams has chosen for his main play depends wholly upon the fractional, upon the building of infinitesimal pieces of observation to create men and women. And it is his extreme astuteness in handling this method which breeds suspicion in his audience when he veers into false or no detail, into abstraction." Reviewing *The Glass Menagerie* in *Nation*, critic Joseph Wood Crutch went so far as to say that Williams' "weaknesses are as patent as his gifts. . . . [While the] play has a hard, substantial core of shrewd observation and deft, economical characterization, ... this hard core is enveloped in a fuzzy haze of pretentious, sentimental, pseudo-poetic verbiage." Crutch even offered advice to the playwright: "whenever you have written a line you like especially well, strike it out."

Like most of Williams' oeuvre, *The Glass Menagerie* was interpreted by many critics as autobiographical, a point the playwright did not dispute. One entry point through which Williams' interjects his own life into his drama is via the play's narrator. Tom, a struggling writer working in the dust and din of a St. Louis shoe factory, lives a life that paralleled Williams' own during his early twenties. "Listen!," the character Tom exclaims to his mother at one point in the play. "You think I'm crazy about the warehouse? You think I'm in love with Continental Shoemakers? You think I want to spend fifty-five years down there in that—celotex interior! with—florescent—tubes! Look! I'd rather somebody picked up a crowbar and battered out my brains—than go back mornings. . . . For sixty-five dollars a month I give up all that I dream of doing and being ever!" Tom's sister Laura retires into the safe, sheltered world offered by her glass animals in much the same way as the playwright's sister Rose had perhaps retreated into her own collection of crystal crea-

tures during the early stages of her depression. The play is also imbued throughout with an aura of the Southern decadence that would attain an increasingly sinister tinge in Williams' later works.

Years of Success on Broadway

While his career would span over four decades, Williams composed his most critically acclaimed works for the stage during the twenty years following *The Glass Menagerie*. Williams' first major success, the play's Broadway run lasted for almost two years, and resulted in the New York Drama Critics Circle Award. However, the high that the playwright enjoyed as a result of *Menagerie* was short lived, and financial concerns soon began to consume him again. Williams would later chronicle this period of depression following his first stage success in "On a Streetcar Named Desire," an essay that would be published as an introduction to the 1947 play of the same name.

The stage version of *A Streetcar Named Desire*, which lasted through 855 performances on Broadway, would earn Williams another New York Drama Critics Circle Award, a Donaldson Award, and the first of two Pulitzer Prizes he would receive during his career. Perhaps more well known to U.S. audiences, the film version, directed, as was the stage version, by Elia Kazan and starring Marlon Brando as the coarse and illiterate Stanley Kowalski, would become an American classic. Williams, who took on the role of assistant screenwriter in most cases when his plays were first adapted for the screen, assisted in writing the screenplay adaptation.

The play's action takes place in the small, dingy New Orleans apartment of Stanley Kowalski and his pregnant wife, Stella. Stella, descended from an old Southern family, is a strong, stable young woman who seems undeterred by her shabby surroundings; her older sister Blanche, who arrives for a visit with the couple after the family's homestead is sold, is not. The high-minded yet oddly fragile Blanche takes an immediate dislike to the loutish, working-class Stanley, while Stanley immediately recognizes Blanche for what she has become: a woman who finds consolation in indiscriminate sex and alcohol. When Blanche threatens Stanley's marriage by cajoling her sister to abandon her husband, Stanley brandishes

Blanche's weaknesses for all to see in an effort to preserve his home and family.

Commenting on Williams' developing skills as a playwright since his first production, *The Glass Menagerie*, Irwin Shaw noted that *A Streetcar Named Desire* "is written with a triumphantly heightened naturalism, in which the rhythms and images of ordinary life are subtly combined and contrasted with a verselike elegance of phrase. . . . It finally has the surprising effect of seeming infinitely more real, more like life itself, than all the clipped banalities lesser playwrights put together in the dreary name of realism."

In *Streetcar* Williams again has a woman as a central character, but unlike Laura in *The Glass Menagerie*, the recently widowed Blanche DuBois is assertive, even brash. While noting that the focus is again "woman's self-destructive urge for sexual fulfillment," Welland characterized Blanche as "predatory and cruel—yet her vulnerable sensitivity is indisputable, and she too is the victim of others." Like Laura and Amanda before her, and like the other female characters that would follow, Blanche has a fantasy world as well: the way life was in the family's former plantation home, Belle Reve. Indeed, the character of Blanche echoes many facets of Williams' characterization of Amanda Wingfield from *The Glass Menagerie*.

Blanche, too, has been cited by critics as in many ways emblematic of Williams' focus. "Williams' people are all . . . solitary and in need of connection," noted Lois Gordon in *Contemporary Dramatists*. "They travel the wrong roads, repeat earlier failures, or take refuge in violence, sexuality, alcoholism, or paralyzing dreams. Blanche . . . depends upon the kindness of strangers, a memorable phrase that characterizes most of Williams's human connections. Of Blanche's real yearning for wholeness, she says: 'Sometimes—there's God—so quickly!' although 'intimacy with strangers' appears the only way to fill the 'empty heart.'"

Novels Continue Symbolism of Staged Works

In 1948 *American Blues: Five Short Plays*, the collection for which Williams was given a special Group Theatre Award, was published. Two years later, in 1950, his first novel-lengthwork, *The Roman Spring of Mrs. Stone*, appeared on bookstore shelves. The story, typical of Williams, focuses on a middle-aged married woman who proves susceptible to the charms of an attractive younger man during her holiday in Rome. Made into a film in 1961 starring Vivien Leigh and Warren Beatty, the novel would be followed twenty-five years later by *Moise and the World of Reason*, which focuses on the relationship between a bohemian woman artist and a homosexual who contemplates suicide after being abandoned by his current lover. Williams would also publish numerous volumes of short fiction, among them *Hard Candy*, released in 1954, and *Eight Mortal Ladies Possessed*, published in 1975.

While his novels and other fiction provided Williams with an outlet for his writing talent, it is as a writer for the stage that he comes into his own as a stylist. As William R. Mueller noted in an essay in *Christian Century*, one of the things Williams' dramas have in common with each other "is the quality of their prose. . . . though his language is without rhyme or regular meter, it is suffused with imagery and so phrased as to create a dreamlike state which is strangely hypnotic, suggesting the inner world of his characters and touching the inner world of his viewers. It is a tone gained in part through an impressively grotesque interplay of the tragic and the comic. As is true of much great theatre, Williams' theater keeps its audience nervously poised on the fine razor edge where tears and laughter meet."

Making a Comeback

Once again under the tutelage of director Elia Kazan, Williams' saw his new work, *Cat on a Hot Tin Roof*, open on Broadway in March of 1955. The work signalled a comeback of sorts for the playwright, whose *Streetcar* had been staged more than seven years earlier. Reviewed with glowing accolades, *Cat on a Hot Tin Roof* brought Williams another New York Drama Critics Circle Award and his second Pulitzer prize. The film version starred Paul Newman, Elizabeth Taylor, and Burl Ives.

In the play, Brick is a young man who, while married to Maggie, is haunted by the death of his best friend and their relationship's homosexual overtones. He currently indulges in excessive amounts of alcohol and constantly repels his wife's advances. Maggie, however, is a woman with a strong survival instinct; she is determined to re-

The 1958 film *Cat on a Hot Tin Roof* featured Burl Ives (left), Elizabeth Taylor, and Paul Newman.

kindle a romantic relationship with her husband in order to bear the child needed to inherit a sizeable estate from her father-in-law. Big Daddy, Brick's wealthy father, enters the action strenuously voicing his disappointment with members of his squabbling family, with society and the church, and with humanity in general. When his critical diatribe focuses on Brick, the son lashes out by confirming that Big Daddy is dying of cancer.

The fading days of the old, Southern world of gentility and decorum can be felt very keenly in *Cat on a Hot Tin Roof;* as Gordon noted: the world of the Old South and the "life of dreams, may bring some form of order and honor (rules), but they also carry with them sterility and conservatism. On the other hand, reality, like the modern world, is insensitive and cruel. Decadence, order, nostalgia, and rigidity vie in Williams with flux, physicality, cruelty, and absurdity." Interestingly, Kazan was thought to have had a strong effect on Williams' play, causing the work to adhere to a more structured, conventional form than had been seen before in Williams' writing. As Richard Hayes opined in *Commonweal,* the Broadway production was "full of a hard, richly wrought and fluent poetry of actuality, a vision of life arrested at the threshold of fantasy, fixed in time yet extended out of reality into dream." The script, as well as the production, was also more grounded in reality than Williams' earlier work, showing perhaps Kazan's influence. Hayes noted that, in contrast to the playwright's characteristic poetic and metaphysical approach, there was present, in *Cat on a Hot Tin Roof,* "a curious presence of an

---

If you enjoy the works of Tennessee Williams, you may also want to check out the following books and films:

Sherwood Anderson, *Winesburg, Ohio*, 1919.
Walter Dean Myers, *Somewhere in the Darkness*, 1992.
Carolyn Reeder, *Moonshiner's Son*, 1993.
Touch of Evil, a film by Orson Welles, 1956.

---

impulse, the burden of some serous concern and intention making itself felt through layers of modish sensibility and gratuitous shock."

Stage Successes Fail to Buoy Playwright

Despite his multiple stage successes, the pressures resulting from the associated acclaim and his need to re-experience the adulation of stage audiences led to depression and despondency, and Williams underwent psychoanalysis in 1957. Diagnosed as suffered from hypochondria, claustrophobia, and fears of suffocation, he was also gaining a growing dependency on alcohol. His father had died in 1957 and his grandfather two years earlier, in 1955; dealing with these losses, combined with the increasing tensions of daily life as a public figure, was beginning to overwhelm Williams, and his work became increasingly troubled, unfocused, and violent in nature as a result.

Freudian analysis, as well as a great deal of reading on the subject of psychoanalysis, filled Williams' time in the late 1950s. The play *Suddenly Last Summer*, as well as *Sweet Bird of Youth*, would be tinged with their creator's study, emerging as they did from this period in his life. Not surprisingly, *Suddenly Last Summer* was judged by many to be Williams' most shocking play. In spite of how "shocking" the play was, it was still a box-office success. Though it earned no awards, the work did enjoy a lengthy run of more than two hundred performances, caused in part by thrill-seekers who had heard that the play involved cannibalism.

Suddenly Last Summer takes place in a Gothic-styled mansion in the heart of New Orleans. More precisely, it takes place in the house's lush tropical garden, wherein sits elderly matron Violet Venable, talking with a young psychiatrist named Dr. Cucrowicz. Violet reminisces about her son, Sebastian, a poet, with whom she travelled continuously until his violent death a few months before at the age of forty, and then makes a strange request of the doctor. As a way to silence her niece, Catharine, from telling the truth about Sebastian's death, which Catharine witnessed, Violet wishes that a lobotomy be performed on the young woman. Catherine is brought to the house so that the doctor can see how unstable she is, and also to see if she will recant her story. Despite pressure from Violet and her own family—who stand to lose a large inheritance unless Catharine changes her tale—the young woman continues to tell the truth: That Sebastian was gay and used trips with his mother to attract young men. Catharine had gone with him on his last, fateful trip, and an horrific encounter with some beggar children had ended his life in a gruesome fashion.

Night of the Iguana

Williams enjoyed his last major recognition as a playwright with *The Night of the Iguana*, which opened in late December of 1961. Earning the playwright his fourth and final Drama Critics Circle Award, the play focuses on Shannon, a former minister who is now conducting literary tours in the Costa Verde. While staying at a local hotel, he meets Maxine, a hot-bloodedhotel owner who immediately sets her sights on capturing him. Also in the cast is Hannah, a strong, spiritual forty-something woman who is travelling with her elderly grandfather, a poet. Increasingly under stress due to a past that had involved bedding a succession of underage women, Shannon eventually ends up in the arms of Maxine, despite the fact that Hannah is the more noble character. Viewing *Night of the Iguana* within the context of all of Williams' work, reviewer M. A. Corrigan noted in *Renascence*: "the message . . . is the necessity of finding one's place in the present. The characters of the play, as Williams says, 'reach the point of utter despair and go past it with courage.' Their despair results from the burdens placed on them by their mortality and by the changes which accompany the passage of time. The drama consists in their clinging together, enlightening, and helping each other through this 'dark night of the soul'."

Even though he met with tepid and uneven critical success following the production of *Night of the Iguana,* Williams continued to write and his plays continued to find producers. The death of longtime lover Frank Merlo in 1963 saw the playwright slip again into depression, and again into a cycle of abuse of drugs and alcohol. The low point for Williams came in 1969 when his younger brother, Dakin, confined the Pulitzer Prize-winning playwright to the mental ward of a St. Louis hospital, fearful that his older brother would not otherwise survive.

Williams' later plays were often criticized for being thinly disguised reworkings of his earlier works, reworking that went beyond the playwright's characteristic obsession with re-examining a few particular themes and styles. Criticisms that had followed him throughout his career further added to what *Contemporary Dramatists* essayist Lois Gordon dubbed his "dubious reputation"; as she explained: "his more than a dozen plays since the early 1960s have been scrutinized as either watered down versions of earlier, more successful pieces, or as artless indulgences in . . . public psychotherapy." Several works composed into the 1970s featured a increasingly impressionistic approach by Williams, some, like *Small Craft Warning,* even enjoying a slight success in production. Williams' last full-length work, *A House Not Meant to Stand,* was produced at Chicago's Goodman Theatre in 1982 after requests to producers to stage this final work by the aging playwright in New York were ignored.

Autobiography Reflects Life on and Off-stage

Williams' *Memoirs,* published in 1975, is a stream-of-consciousness account of his life and many loves, as well as of the battle with mental illness he fought throughout his life. One of the most noted aspects of the work was its author's open discussion of his homosexuality, including his long relationship with Merlo. Indeed, the playwright's candid approach to his own life in this volume, and in other writings, as well as his insistence on the autobiographical nature of his plays and prose fiction, caused many critics to view Williams as a self-obsessed sensationalist. However, others saw the book as a candid confessional by its author. "For all its ornery formlessness, its stylistic self-indulgence, its avoidance of high drama, [*Memoirs*] has genuine rewards," maintained *New Re-public* contributor Foster Hirsch, citing "descriptive passages that remind us of Williams' special lyrical gifts and his distinctive personality. . . . Even when the narrate voice is whining or out of control, even when it is lazy and repetitive, it is still, manifestly, the voice of America's greatest playwright. There is bristling wit here, and charm, and temperament."

A year after *A House Not Meant to Stand* appeared on the Chicago stage, Williams died in his apartment in New York City on February 25, 1983. While suicide was suspected due to the quantity of alcohol and drugs found in the playwright's apartment, Williams was later shown to have died of natural causes. Wealthy because of the royalties generated by his most widely viewed works, Williams left the bulk of his estate to the University of the South, with future royalties to go toward replenishing a fund for writers. He also provided for his sister, Rose, who was still confined to a sanitarium at the time of her brother's death.

Like his life, Williams' career followed a complex path, characterized by monumental failures as much as by extraordinary successes. Taken as a whole, his contributions to American theatre have been placed on a par with those of Eugene O'Neill, and his best works have entered the nation's common cultural heritage through their transition from the stage to movies and television. As critic Harold Clurman wrote of the playwright in his the essay "Tennessee Williams: Poet and Puritan": Williams "has opened our eyes and hearts to the victims of our savagely mechanized society, the company of the 'somehow unfit,' the fragile, the frightened, the different, the odd and the lonely, whose presence in our world we have so long sought to avoid thinking about and recognizing as our kin."

■ Works Cited

Clurman, Harold, "Tennessee Williams: Poet and Puritan," in *The Divine Pastime: Theatre Essays,* Macmillan, 1974, pp. 230-31.

Corrigan, M.A., "Memory, Dream, and Myth in the Plays of Tennessee Williams," in *Renascence,* spring, 1976, pp. 155-67.

Hayes, Robert, review of *Cat on a Hot Tin Roof,* in *Commonweal,* June 3, 1955, pp. 230-31.

Hirsch, Foster, review of *Memoirs,* in *New Republic,* May 24, 1975.

Gibbs, Wolcott, "Such Nice People," in *New Yorker,* April 7, 1945, pp. 39-40.

Gordon, Lois, "Tennessee Williams," in *Contemporary Dramatists,* St. James Press, 1982, pp. 852-55.

Johns, Sally, "Tennessee Williams," in *Dictionary of Literary Biography,* Volume 7: *Twentieth-Century American Dramatists,* Gale, 1981.

Mueller, William R., "Tennessee Williams: A New Direction?," in *Christian Century,* October 14, 1964, pp. 1271-72.

Phelan, Kappo, review of *The Glass Menagerie,* in *Commonweal,* April 20, 1945, pp. 16-17.

Shaw, Irwin, review of *A Streetcar Named Desire,* in *New Republic,* December 22, 1947, pp. 34- 35.

Williams, Tennessee, *Tennessee Williams: Eight Plays,* introduction by Harold Clurman, Doubleday, 1979.

Welland, Dennis, "Tennessee Williams," in *Contemporary American Dramatists,* St. James Press, 1990.

■ For More Information See

BOOKS

Atkinson, Brooks, *Broadway,* revised edition, Macmillan, 1974.

Bentley, Eric, *What Is Theatre?,* Atheneum, 1968.

Bernstein, Samuel J., *The Strands Entwined: A New Direction in American Drama,* Northeastern University Press, 1980.

Bigsby, C. W. E., *A Critical Introduction to Twentieth-Century American Drama,* three volumes, Cambridge University Press, 1985.

Broussard, Louis, *American Drama: Contemporary Allegory from Eugene O'Neill to Tennessee Williams,* University of Oklahoma Press, 1962.

Brustein, Robert, *Seasons of Discontent: Dramatic Opinions 1959-1965,* Simon & Schuster, 1965.

Brustein, Robert, *Critical Moments: Reflections on Theatre and Society, 1973-1979,* Random House, 1980.

Cohn, Ruby, *Dialogue in American Drama,* Indiana University Press, 1971.

Concise Dictionary of American Literary Biography: The New Consciousness, 1941-1968, Gale, 1987.

Contemporary Literary Criticism, Gale, Volume 1, 1973, Volume 2, 1974, Volume 5, 1976, Volume 7, 1977, Volume 8, 1978, Volume 11, 1979, Volume 15, 1980, Volume 19, 1981, Volume 30, 1984, Volume 39, 1986, Volume 45, 1987.

Contemporary Novelists, St. James Press, 1981.

Crandell, George W., *Tennessee Williams: A Descriptive Bibliography,* University of Pittsburgh Press, 1995.

Crandell, George W., *The Critical Response to Tennessee Williams,* Greenwood Press, 1996.

Devlin, Albert J., editor, *Conversations with Tennessee Williams,* University Press of Mississippi, 1986.

Dickinson, Hugh, *Myth on the Modern Stage,* University of Illinois Press, 1969.

Dictionary of Literary Biography Documentary Series, Volume 4, Gale, 1984.

Dictionary of Literary Biography Yearbook: 1983, Gale, 1984.

Donahue, Francis, *The Dramatic World of Tennessee Williams,* Ungar, 1964.

Downer, Alan S., *Fifty Years of American Drama: 1900-1950,* Regnery, 1951.

Drama Criticism, Volume 4, Gale, 1994.

Falk, Signi, *Tennessee Williams,* 2nd edition, Twayne, 1978.

Fleche, Anne, *Mimetic Disillusion: Eugene O'Neill, Tennessee Williams, and U.S. Dramatic Realism,* University of Alabama Press, 1997.

Ganz, Arthur, *Realms of the Self: Variations on a Theme in Modern Drama,* New York University Press, 1980.

Gassner, John, *Theatre at the Crossroads: Plays and Playwrights of the Mid-Century American Stage,* Holt, 1960.

Gilman, Richard, *Common and Uncommon Masks: Writings on Theatre, 1961-1970,* Random House, 1971.

Gould, Jean, *Modern American Playwrights,* Dodd, 1966.

Griffin, Alice, *Understanding Tennessee Williams,* University of South Carolina Press, 1995.

Gunn, Drewey Wayne, *Tennessee Williams: A Bibliography,* Scarecrow Press, 1980.

Heilman, Robert Bechtold, *Tragedy and Melodrama: Versions of Experience,* University of Washington Press, 1968.

Herron, Ima Honaker, *The Small Town in American Drama,* Southern Methodist University Press, 1969.

Kerr, Walter, *The Theatre in Spite of Itself,* Simon & Schuster, 1963.

Kerr, Walter, *Journey to the Center of Theatre,* Knopf, 1979.

Langer, Lawrence, *The Magic Curtain,* Dutton, 1951.

Laughlin, James, editor, *Five Young American Poets,* New Directions, 1944.

Leavitt, Richard F., editor, *The World of Tennessee Williams,* Putnam, 1978.

Leverich, Lyle, *Tom: The Unknown Tennessee Williams*, Crown, 1995.

Leverich, Lyle, *Tenn: The Timeless World of Tennessee Williams*, Crown, 1997.

Lewis, Allan, *American Plays and Playwrights of the Contemporary Theatre*, Crown, 1965.

Little, Stuart W., and Arthur Cantor, *The Play-makers*, Norton, 1970.

Logan, Joshua, *Josh: My up and down, in and out Life*, Delacorte, 1976.

Londre, Felicia Hardison, *Tennessee Williams*, Ungar, 1979.

Lumley, Frederick, *New Trends in Twentieth-Century Drama: A Survey since Ibsen and Shaw*, Oxford University Press, 1967.

Martin, Robert A., editor, *Critical Essays on Tennessee Williams*, Prentice Hall, 1997.

Maxwell, Gilbert, *Tennessee Williams and Friends: An Informal Biography*, World, 1965.

McCann, John S., *The Critical Reputation of Tennessee Williams: A Reference Guide*, G. K. Hall, 1983.

McCarthy, Mary, *Theatre Chronicles: 1937-1962*, Farrar, Straus, 1963.

Miller, Arthur, *The Theatre Essays of Tennessee Williams*, edited by Robert A. Martin, Penguin, 1978.

Nathan, George Jean, *The Theatre Book of the Year*, Knopf, *1947-1948*, 1948, *1948-1949*, 1949.

O'Connor, Jacqueline, *Dramatizing Dementia: Madness in the Plays of Tennessee Williams*, Bowling Green State University Popular Press, 1997.

Phillips, Gene D., *The Films of Tennessee Williams*, Art Alliance Press, 1980.

Porter, Thomas E., *Myth and Modern American Drama*, Wayne State University Press, 1969.

Rabkin, Gerald, *Drama and Commitment: Politics in the American Theatre of the Thirties*, Indiana University Press, 1964.

Rasky, Harry, *Tennessee Williams: A Portrait in Laughter and Lamentation*, Dodd, 1986.

Roudane, Matthew C., editor, *The Cambridge Companion to Tennessee Williams*, Cambridge University Press, 1997.

Schlueter, June, *Dramatic Closure: Reading the End*, Associated University Presses, 1995.

Simon, John, *Acid Test*, Stein & Day, 1963.

Spoto, Donald, *The Kindness of Strangers: The Life of Tennessee Williams*, Little, Brown, 1985.

Steen, Mike, *A Look at Tennessee Williams*, Hawthorne, 1969.

Styan, J. L., *Modern Drama in Theory and Practice, Volume 1*, Cambridge University Press, 1981.

Tharpe, Jac, editor, *Tennessee Williams: A Tribute*, University Press of Mississippi, 1977.

Tischler, Nancy M., *Tennessee Williams: Rebellious Puritan*, Citadel, 1961.

Tynan, Kenneth, *Curtains*, Atheneum, 1961.

Weales, Gerald, *American Drama since World War II*, Harcourt, 1962.

Williams, Dakin, and Shepherd Mead, *Tennessee Williams: An Intimate Biography*, Arbor, 1983.

Williams, Edwina Dakin, as told to Lucy Freeman, *Remember Me to Tom*, Putnam, 1963.

Williams, Tennessee, *Memoirs*, Doubleday, 1975.

Windham, Donald, *Lost Friendships: A Memoir of Truman Capote, Tennessee Williams, and Others*, Morrow, 1987.

Yacowar, Maurice, *Tennessee Williams and Film*, Ungar, 1977.

PERIODICALS

After Dark, August, 1971.

Atlantic, November, 1970; July, 1994, p. 91.

Booklist, September 15, 1995, p. 131.

Choice, February 1996, p. 954.

Detroit News, June 11, 1997.

Esquire, November, 1969; September, 1971.

Library Journal, September 1, 1995, p. 178; October 15, 1995, p. 100.

Modern Drama, Volume 2, 1959; Volume 15, 1972.

Nation, Volume 165, 1947.

New Orleans Magazine, March, 1994, p. 30; July, 1995, p. 34.

New Republic, Volume 112, 1945; June 17, 1996, p. 26.

New York, March 14, 1983; November 28, 1994, p. 75; May 15, 1995, p. 59; October 23, 1995, p. 60; October 30, 1995, p. 137; April 1, 1996, p. 62.

New Yorker, July 18, 1994, p. 68; November 21, 1994, p. 124; December 19, 1994, p. 76; May 15, 1995, p. 100; April 8, 1996, p. 103.

New York Post (interviews), April 21-May 4, 1958.

New York Review of Books, July 19, 1990, p. 12.

New York Times, May 1, 1960; March 28, 1965; November 3, 1975.

New York Times Book Review, May 27, 1990, p. 1.

Observer, May 5, 1991, p. 60.

Opera News, June, 1994, p. 18.

Playboy, April, 1973.

Publishers Weekly, August 7, 1995, p. 447; January 16, 1995, p. 320.

Quarterly Journal of Speech, Volume 61, 1975.

Reporter, Volume 12, 1955.

Southern Living, March, 1996, p. 26.

Southern Review, summer, 1979.

Tennessee Studies in Literature, Volume 10, 1965.
Theatre Arts, January, 1962.
Time, December 5, 1994, p. 94.
Times Literary Supplement, April 19, 1991, p. 8.
Variety, November 21, 1994, p. 43; November 28, 1994, p. 103; May 15, 1995, p. 234; October 16, 1995, p. 105; March 25, 1996, p. 77.
Washington Post, April 4, 1979.
Western Humanities Review, Volume 18, 1964.
World Literature Today, winter, 1992, p. 133.

■ Obituaries

PERIODICALS

Chicago Tribune, February 26, 1983; February 27, 1983.
Los Angeles Times, February 26, 1983.
Newsweek, March 7, 1983.
New York Times, February 26, 1983.
Time, March 7, 1983.
Times (London), February 26, 1983.
Washington Post, February 26, 1983.*

—Sketch by Pamela L. Shelton

Tim Wynne-Jones

Personal

Born August 12, 1948, in Bromborough, Cheshire, England; son of Sydney Thomas and Sheila Beryl (Hodgson) Wynne-Jones; married Amanda West Lewis (a writer, calligrapher, and teacher), September, 1980; children: Alexander, Magdalene, Lewis. *Education:* University of Waterloo, B.F.A., 1974; York University, M.F.A., 1979.

Addresses

Home and office—Rural Route No. 4, Perth, Ontario K7H 3C6, Canada.

Career

Writer. PMA Books, Toronto, Ontario, designer, 1974-76; University of Waterloo, Waterloo, Ontario, instructor in visual arts, 1976-78; Solomon & Wynne-Jones, Toronto, graphic designer, 1976-79; York University, Downsview, Ontario, instructor in visual arts, 1978-80. *Member:* International PEN, Writers Union of Canada, Association of Canadian Television and Radio Artists, Society of Composers, Authors, and Music Publishers of Canada.

Awards, Honors

Seal First Novel Award, Bantam/Seal Books, 1980, for *Odd's End;* I.O.D.E. Award and Amelia Frances Howard-Gibbon award, both 1983, and Ruth Schwartz Children's Award, 1984, all for *Zoom at Sea;* ACTRA Award, best radio drama, 1987, for *St. Anthony's Man;* Governor-General's Award for Children's Literature, 1993, Canadian Library Association Children's Book of the Year award, 1993, and *Boston Globe-Horn Book* Award for Fiction, 1995, all for *Some of the Kinder Planets;* Notable Books for Children citation, American Library Association, and Mister Christie Award shortlist, 1994, both for *The Book of Changes;* Governor-General's Award for Children's Literature, 1995, Young Adult Book of the Year, Canadian Library Association, Mister Christie Award shortlist, and Books for the Teen Age citation, New York Public Library, 1997, all for *The Maestro;* Vicky Metcalf Award, Canadian Authors Association, 1997, for body of work.

Writings

FOR JUVENILES

Madeline and Ermadello, illustrated by Lindsey Hallam, Before We Are Six (Hawkesville, Ontario), 1977.

Zoom at Sea, illustrated by Ken Nutt, Douglas & McIntyre, 1983, illustrated by Eric Beddows, HarperCollins, 1993.

Zoom Away, illustrated by Ken Nutt, Douglas & McIntyre, 1985, illustrated by Eric Beddows, HarperCollins, 1993.

I'll Make You Small, illustrated by Maryann Kovalski, Douglas & McIntyre, 1986.

Mischief City (verse), illustrated by Victor Gad, Groundwood, 1986.

Architect of the Moon, illustrated by Ian Wallace, Groundwood, 1988, published as *Builder of the Moon*, McElderry, 1988.

The Hour of the Frog, illustrated by Catharine O'Neill, Groundwood, 1989, Little Brown, 1989.

Mouse in the Manger, illustrated by Elaine Blier, Viking, 1993.

The Last Piece of Sky, illustrated by Marie-Louise Gay, Groundwood, 1993.

Zoom Upstream, illustrated by Eric Beddows, Groundwood, 1993, HarperCollins, 1994.

Some of the Kinder Planets (short stories), Groundwood, 1993, Orchard, 1995.

(With Amanda Lewis) *Rosie Backstage*, illustrated by Bill Slavin, Kids Can Press, 1994.

The Book of Changes (short stories), Groundwood, 1994, Orchard, 1995.

The Maestro (young adult novel), Groundwood, 1995, Orchard, 1996.

(Reteller) *The Hunchback of Notre Dame*, illustrated by Bill Slavin, Key Porter Books (Toronto), 1996, Orchard, 1997.

(Reteller) Bram Stoker, *Dracula*, illustrated by Laszlo Gal, Key Porter Books, 1997.

On Tumbledown Hill, illustrated by Dusan Petricic, Red Deer College Press, 1998.

Stephen Fair, DK Ink, 1998.

Lord of the Fries and Other Stories, DK Ink, 1999.

Also author of a children's opera titled *A Midwinter Night's Dream* and a musical version of *Mischief City*. Author of regular column of children's book reviews for the Toronto *Globe and Mail*, 1985-88.

NOVELS FOR ADULTS

Odd's End, McClelland & Stewart (Toronto), 1980, Little, Brown, 1980.

The Knot, McClelland & Stewart, 1982.

Fastyngange, Lester & Orpen Dennys, 1988, published as *Voices*, Hodder & Stoughton, 1990.

RADIO PLAYS

The Thinking Room, Canadian Broadcasting Corporation, 1981.

The Road Ends at the Sea, Canadian Broadcasting Corporation, 1982.

The Strange Odyssey of Lennis Freed, Canadian Broadcasting Corporation, 1983.

The Testing of Stanley Teagarden, Canadian Broadcasting Corporation, 1985.

The Enormous Radio (from the story by John Cheever), Canadian Broadcasting Corporation, 1986.

St. Anthony's Man (from his own story), Canadian Broadcasting Corporation, 1987.

Mr. Gendelman Crashes a Party, Canadian Broadcasting Corporation, 1987.

Dust Is the Only Secret, Canadian Broadcasting Corporation, 1988.

We Now Return You to Your Regularly Scheduled Universe, Canadian Broadcasting Corporation, 1992.

■ Sidelights

Tim Wynne-Jones is a British-born Canadian writer whose works range from award-winning adult and young-adult fiction to such popular children's picture books as the "Zoom" series of tales about an adventurous cat. One of Canada's most popular authors among pre-schoolers and primary graders, Wynne-Jones is recognized as the creator of works that capture the mystery, fantasy, and wonder of childhood while addressing such realistic concerns as the conquering of personal fears and the relationship of children with their parents. In addition, his works for young adults have drawn praise from readers and critics alike. Wynne-Jones is known and appreciated for his rich language, zany plots, and a sophistication of theme that does not proclaim itself didactically, but that "reverberates beneath the simple surface of image anddialogue," as Gwyneth Evans noted in *Twentieth-Century Children's Writers*. A scriptwriter and composer, Wynne-Jones is also known for his work as lyricist for the television program *Fraggle Rock*.

The son of an engineer, Wynne-Jones was born in Cheshire, England, in 1948, but grew up in Ottawa, Canada. Attending the University of Waterloo, he began to study children's literature as part of a research project. A group of sociology students secured a grant to study racism and sexism in books for young readers, and Wynne-Jones, studying visual arts at the time, was included in the grant proposal as someone on the creative side

Wynne-Jones received the prestigious Canadian Governor-General's Award in 1993 for this collection of short stories.

of things. In an interview with Dave Jenkinson in *Emergency Librarian,* Wynne-Jones explained that having examined a plethora of children's books and finding fault with many of them, "the group decided that, because they knew what was wrong with children's books, they could then write good ones. It was a great lesson in how you do not write a children's book." While the publishing venture created by the grant was short-lived, it did produce Wynne-Jones's first creative effort, *Madeline and Ermadello,* a "quietly charming story about a young girl's fantasies," according to Linda Smith in *In Review: Canadian Books for Children.*

Wynne-Jones's first book highlighted the elements of fantasy and wonder common to the author's subsequent efforts for children. It was several years, however, before Wynne-Jones published a second picture book. During this time he worked as a designer at a publishing company, as a visual arts instructor at Waterloo University and York University, and as a graphic designer in his own company. He earned an M.F.A. in visual arts and was married. He also wrote and published his first adult novel, a psychological thriller, *Odd's End,* which won him Canada's prestigious Seal First Novel Award and a cash prize of $50,000. Understandably, Wynne-Jones stuck with adult fiction for his next title, *The Knot,* but he returned to children's books in 1983.

Earns Praise for Picture Book Trilogy

"I didn't start writing children's books because I had children," Wynne-Jones told Jenkinson in his *Emergency Librarian* interview. "I'd always had ideas for children's stories." Although a visual artist himself, Wynne-Jones does not illustrate his own books. Rather, he visualizes stories with the illustrations of other artists he respects. One such case was Ken Nutt (Eric Beddows), an acquaintance of his whose artwork Wynne-Jones wanted to see in book form. The direct inspiration for his first successful children's book was the family cat, Montezuma, or Zuma for short. Writing early one morning, Wynne-Jones observed the cat sitting on the kitchen counter batting at water from a dripping faucet. The idea for an adventure-loving and water-loving cat came to the author quickly. "The story, *Zoom at Sea,* was written in 20 minutes," Wynne-Jones told Jenkinson. "I don't quite know how those things happen." In the story, Zoom the cat goes to the home of the mysterious Maria, who helps him realize a lifelong dream of going to sea. Linda Granfield, writing in *Quill and Quire,* noted that the book was a "perfect balance of text and illustration" and served as a reminder to children and adults alike to "live our dreams."

Wynne-Jones initially had no intention of creating a sequel to this first popular "Zoom" title. However, a letter from his mother-in-law suggested further possibilities for Maria's magical powers, and *Zoom Away* was launched. Reviewing both "Zoom" books in *Canadian Children'sLiterature,* Ulrike Walker reminded the reader of Wynne-Jones's theory of thresholds, developmental steps that everyone must take or risk to reach maturity, and placed the books in the context of mythic test or quest tales. The critic concluded: "These

In this 1995 novel for young adults, fourteen-year-old Burl runs away from his abusive father and befriends Nathaniel Gow, a talented music composer.

that genre. He has also written juvenile and young adult fiction, including short story collections and young adult novels. The award-winning *Some of the Kinder Planets* consists of nine stories which tell of children making encounters with other worlds, both metaphorically and realistically. Deborah Stevenson commented in *Bulletin of the Center for Children's Books* that the writing "is thoughtful, inventive, and often humorous," while a *Publishers Weekly* reviewer noted that "ordinary moments take on a fresh veneer in this finely tuned short-story collection."

With *The Maestro*, Wynne-Jones again broke new ground for himself. The story of fourteen-year-old Burl and his struggle for survival, *The Maestro* was Wynne-Jones's first young adult novel. Fleeing his

remarkable works . . . bear eloquent witness to the complex levels of realization which all of us must undergo before we reach that stage we label 'adult.'" In 1993 Wynne-Jones published *Zoom Upstream*, "a book of reunion and probably a book about death, but I don't think any child will read that into it," the author explained to Jenkinson in *Emergency Librarian*.

Pens Tales for Young Adults

Wynne-Jones has written several other picture books for young readers, including *I'll Make You Small*, *Architect of the Moon*, and *The Last Piece of Sky*, all of them well received, but the "Zoom" books remain his most popular achievement in

Readers encounter a number of surprises in Wynne-Jones's 1999 collection of short stories.

brutal father, Burl seeks shelter in a remote cabin by a Canadian lake. The cabin is inhabited by Nathaniel Gow, a musical genius and himself in flight from the mechanized world. Gow, patterned after the real-life Canadian musician Glen Gould, takes Burl in for a time. He also allows Burl to stay at his cabin when he returns to Toronto, and when Burl learns of Gow's subsequent death, he tries to claim the cabin for his, then goes on a mission to save Gow's final composition, confronting his father along the way. Roderick McGillis, writing in *Canadian Children's Literature*, noted that the book is "redolently Canadian," but that it also offers much more. "Its prose is dense and its themes move into challenging areas for young readers," McGillis remarked. Stevenson concluded in a *Bulletin of the Center for Children's Books* review that "Wynne-Jones has displayed a knack for the unusual made credible in his short story collections" and that it was "nice to see that skill expanded into a well-crafted and accessible novel." Writing in *Quill and Quire*, Maureen Garvie commented that *The Maestro* is "tightly and dramatically scripted" and that this first young adult novel is a "peach."

In 1993 Wynne-Jones published a second collection of short stories, *The Book of Changes*. Told from the point of view of their male narrators, the seven stories "hold wonder and fascination for inquisitive readers," according to *School Library Journal* reviewer John Sigwald. "Wynne-Jones deals in moments, and these are carefully chosen and freshly realized," Sarah Ellis remarked in *Horn Book*. In "The Clark Beans Man," for instance, a boy uses a Donald Duck impersonation to fend off a schoolyard bully; in "Dawn," a teenager on a bus trip develops a brief friendship with a tough-looking older girl. Nancy Vasilakis, also writing in *Horn Book*, concluded that "Wynne-Jones tells his readers in these perceptive short stories that we all have the power to create the music of our own lives." Wynne-Jones published another collection, titled *Lord of the Fries and Other Stories*, in 1999. A reviewer in *Bulletin of the Center for Children's Books* observed that the author's "creative plotting and faith in the power of imagination . . . keeps events sparking along in absorbing and unpredictable ways."

Wynne-Jones turned to psychological suspense with *Stephen Fair*, a 1998 novel about a fifteen-year-old plagued by nightmares. With the support of his friend Virginia, Stephen begins to question

---

If you enjoy the works of Tim Wynne-Jones, you may also want to check out the following books and films:

Robert Cormier, *I Am the Cheese*, 1977.
Robin Klein, *Came Back to Show You I Could Fly*, 1990.
Budge Wilson, *The Leaving*, 1992.
What's Eating Gilbert Grape, a film starring Johnny Depp, 1993.

---

his troubled family life, including his mother's erratic behavior and the disappearances of his father and older brother. *Stephen Fair* received strong praise. "Wynne-Jones is an impressive stylist," remarked a critic in *Bulletin of the Center for Children's Books*, "and his depiction of Stephen's family, friends, and thoughts are unforcedly deft. . . ." A critic in *Kirkus Reviews* noted that the author reveals his characters' feelings "through quick, telling details and comments, or heavily symbolic background events," and a *Publishers Weekly* reviewer declared that Wynne-Jones "maintains the suspense while Stephen slowly unveils family secrets."

Wynne-Jones has proved himself a versatile and perceptive writer on many levels. Whether writing children's picture books, young adult titles, or adult fiction and plays, his message of the power of fantasy and fiction comes through loud and clear. As he once commented, "I like to tell stories—to entertain and instruct—about ordinary people in extraordinary circumstances or extraordinary people in very ordinary circumstances." Regarding his efforts for children, Wynne-Jones commented: "I write for children out of the child I was and am. I cannot write for an audience— where children's books are concerned, I am the Selfish Giant, shooing my audience away in order to reclaim the garden for myself!"

■ Works Cited

Ellis, Sarah, review of *Some of the Kinder Planets* and *The Book of Changes*, *Horn Book*, January-February, 1995.

Evans, Gwyneth, "Tim Wynne-Jones," *Twentieth-Century Children's Writers*, 4th edition, edited by Laura Standley Berger, St. James Press, 1995.

Garvie, Maureen, review of *The Maestro, Quill and Quire,* December, 1995, pp. 36-37.

Jenkinson, Dave, "Tim Wynne-Jones," *Emergency Librarian,* January-February, 1988, pp. 56-62.

Review of *Lord of the Fries and Other Stories, Bulletin of the Center for Children's Books,* March, 1999, p. 260.

McGillis, Roderick, review of *The Maestro, Canadian Children's Literature,* Number 81, 1996, pp. 58-59.

Sigwald, John, review of *The Book of Changes, School Library Journal,* October, 1995, pp. 141-42.

Smith, Linda, review of *Madeline and Ermadello, In Review: Canadian Books for Children,* Winter, 1978, p. 70.

Review of *Some of the Kinder Planets, Publishers Weekly,* May 1, 1995, p. 59.

Review of *Stephen Fair, Bulletin of the Center for Children's Books,* April, 1998, pp. 301-2.

Review of *Stephen Fair, Kirkus Reviews,* April 1, 1998, pp. 503-4.

Review of *Stephen Fair, Publishers Weekly,* March 16, 1998, p. 65.

Stevenson, Deborah, review of *Some of the Kinder Planets, Bulletin of the Center for Children's Books,* May, 1995, p. 328.

Stevenson, Deborah, review of *The Maestro, Bulletin of the Center for Children's Books,* October, 1996, p. 81.

Vasilakis, Nancy, review of *The Book of Changes, Horn Book,* February, 1996, pp. 76-77.

Walker, Ulrike, "A Matter of Thresholds," *Canadian Children's Literature,* Number 60, 1990, pp. 108-16.

Wynne-Jones, Tim, *Zoom at Sea,* HarperCollins, 1993.

■ For More Information See

BOOKS

Children's Literature Review, Volume 21, Gale, 1990, pp. 226-31.

PERIODICALS

Booklist, April 15, 1993, p. 1524; January 1, 1994; June 1, 1994, p. 1846; March 1, 1995, p. 1241; October 1, 1995; December 15, 1996, p. 724.

Books for Young Readers, October, 1988, p. 10.

Canadian Children's Literature, Number 70, 1993, pp. 22-33; Fall/Winter, 1998, pp. 141-42.

Canadian Literature, Spring, 1987, p. 160.

Canadian Materials, January, 1994, p. 4.

Horn Book, May-June, 1987, pp. 378-81; May, 1990, p. 332; January, 1995, p. 99; May, 1995, p. 334; May-June, 1999, pp. 293- 300; July-August, 1999, pp. 475-76.

Publishers Weekly, April 12, 1993, p. 61; October 30, 1995, p. 62; October 14, 1996, p. 84; January 25, 1999, p. 97.

Quill and Quire, March, 1984, p. 72; August, 1985; October, 1986, p. 16; December, 1986, p. 15; December, 1989, p. 22; November, 1992, p. 33; October, 1993, p. 38; November, 1993, p. 38.

Reading Time, August, 1997, p. 35.

School Library Journal, August, 1990, p. 136; February, 1994, p. 92; August, 1994, p. 148; April, 1995, p. 138; October, 1995, p. 141; May, 1998, p. 150.

Signal, September, 1998, pp. 160-66.

—Sketch by J. Sydney Jones

Laurence Yep

■ Personal

Born June 14, 1948, in San Francisco, CA; son of Thomas Gim (a postal clerk) and Franche (a homemaker; maiden name, Lee) Yep. *Education:* Attended Marquette University, 1966-68; University of California, Santa Cruz, B.A., 1970; State University of New York at Buffalo, Ph.D., 1975.

■ Addresses

Home—921 Populus Place, Sunnyvale, CA 94086. *Agent*—Maureen Walters, Curtis Brown Agency, 10 Astor Place, New York, NY 10003.

■ Career

Writer. Part-time instructor of English, Foothill College, Mountain View, CA, 1975, and San Jose City College, San Jose, CA, 1975-76; University of California, Berkeley, visiting lecturer in Asian-American studies, 1987-1989, University of California, Santa Barbara, writer-in-residence, 1990. Writer of software, *Alice in Wonderland*, Spinnaker,

1985, and *Jungle Book*, Spinnaker, 1986. *Member:* Science Fiction Writers of America, Society of Children's Book Writers.

■ Awards, Honors

Newbery Honor Book award, Children's Book Award from American Library Association, International Reading Association award, and Carter A. Woodson Award from National Council of Social Studies, all 1976, Lewis Carroll Shelf Award, 1979, and Friend of Children and Literature award, 1984, all for *Dragonwings;* Boston Globe-Horn Book awards, 1977, for *Child of the Owl,* and 1989, for *The Rainbow People;* Jane Addams Award, Women's International League for Peace and Freedom, 1978, for *Child of the Owl;* Silver Medal, Commonwealth Club of California, 1979, for *Sea Glass;* National Endowment for the Arts fellowship, 1990.

■ Writings

FOR CHILDREN AND YOUNG ADULTS

Sweetwater, illustrated by Julia Noonan, Harper (New York City), 1973.
Dragonwings, Harper, 1975.
Child of the Owl, Harper, 1977.
Sea Glass, Harper, 1979.
Kind Hearts and Gentle Monsters, Harper, 1982.
The Mark Twain Murders, Four Winds Press (New York City), 1982.

Dragon of the Lost Sea, Harper, 1982.

Liar, Liar, Morrow (New York City), 1983.

The Serpent's Children, Harper, 1984.

The Tom Sawyer Fires, Morrow, 1984.

Dragon Steel, Harper, 1985.

Mountain Light (sequel to *The Serpent's Children*), Harper, 1985.

The Curse of the Squirrel, illustrated by Dirk Zimmer, Random House (New York City), 1987.

Age of Wonders (play), produced in San Francisco, 1987.

(Reteller) *The Rainbow People* (collection of Chinese-American folk tales), illustrated by David Wiesner, Harper, 1989.

Dragon Cauldron, HarperCollins (New York City), 1991.

The Lost Garden, Messner (Englewood Cliffs, NJ), 1991.

The Star Fisher, Morrow, 1991.

Tongues of Jade (short stories), HarperCollins, 1991.

Dragon War, HarperCollins, 1992.

(Editor) *American Dragons: A Collection of Asian American Voices,* HarperCollins, 1992.

Butterfly Boy, Farrar, Strauss, 1993.

Dragon's Gate, HarperCollins, 1993.

The Shell Woman and the King, Dial Books (New York City), 1993.

The Man Who Tricked a Ghost, Troll, 1993.

Ghost Fox, Scholastic (New York City), 1994.

The Tiger Woman, Troll, 1994.

The Boy Who Swallowed Snakes, Scholastic, 1994.

The Junior Thunder Lord, Troll, 1994.

Hiroshima: A Novella, Scholastic, 1995.

Later, Gator, Hyperion (New York City), 1995.

Tree of Dreams: Ten Tales from the Garden of Night, pictures by Isadore Seltzer, BridgeWater Books (Mahwah, NJ), 1995.

Thief of Hearts, HarperCollins, 1995.

City of Dragons, illustrated by Jean and Mou-Sien Tseng, Scholastic, 1995.

Ribbons, Putnam's (New York City), 1996.

The Khan's Daughter: A Mongolian Folktale, illustrated by Jean and Mou-Sien Tseng, Scholastic, 1997.

The Dragon Prince: A Chinese Beauty and the Beast Tale, HarperCollins, 1997.

The Imp That Ate My Homework, illustrated by Benrei Huang, HarperCollins, 1998.

The Cook's Family, Putnam, 1998.

The Amah, Putnam, 1999.

"CHINATOWN MYSTERY" SERIES; FOR CHILDREN

The Case of the Goblin Pearls, HarperCollins, 1997.

The Case of the Lion Dance, HarperCollins, 1998.

The Case of the Firecrackers, HarperCollins, 1999.

FOR ADULTS

Seademons, Harper, 1977.

Shadow Lord, Harper, 1985.

Monster Makers, Inc., Arbor House, 1986.

Pay the Chinaman (one-act play; produced in San Francisco, 1987), in *Between Worlds,* edited by M. Berson, Theatre Communications Group (New York City), 1990.

Fairy Bones (one-act play), produced in San Francisco, 1987.

Work represented in anthologies, including *World's Best Science Fiction of 1969,* edited by Donald A. Wollheim and Terry Carr, Ace, 1969; *Quark #2,* edited by Samuel Delaney andMarilyn Hacker, Paperback Library, 1971; *Protostars,* edited by David Gerrold, Ballantine, 1971; *The Demon Children,* Avon, 1973; *Strange Bedfellows: Sex and Science Fiction,* edited by Thomas N. Scortia, Random House, 1973; *Last Dangerous Visions,* edited by Harlan Ellison, Harper, 1975; and *Between Worlds,* Theater Communication Group, 1990.

Contributor of short stories to periodicals, including *Worlds of If* and *Galaxy.* Also author of theatrical adaptation of *Dragonwings,* 1991.

■ Adaptations

Dragonwings was produced as a filmstrip with record or cassette, Miller-Brody, 1979; *The Curse of the Squirrel* was recorded on audiocassette, Random House, 1989. *Sweetwater* is available in braille and on audiocassette.

■ Sidelights

The author of such award-winning novels as *Dragonwings, Child of the Owl,* and *Dragon Steel,* novelist and playwright Laurence Yep is noted for penning fiction that brings the history and culture of Chinese Americans into realistic view, exchanging the exaggerated, stereotyped images of Dr. Fu Manchu and Charley Chan for portraits of the real-life men and women who have enriched the United States with their own labor and willingness to share their cultural heritage. As essayist Joe Stines noted in the *Dictionary of Literary*

Biography, "Yep provides the reader with a new way of viewing Chinese-Americans, not as yellow men [and women] living in white society but as ordinary as well as extraordinary people." Noted Yep in his own afterword to his 1975 novel *Dragonwings,* "I wanted to show that Chinese-Americans are human beings upon whom America has had an unique effect." Best know for his books about children from multi- cultural backgrounds, Yep claims that writing has aided him in his personal search for cultural identity. As he once explained, "In a sense I have no one culture to call my own since I exist peripherally in several. However, in my writing I can create my own."

Yep examines the history of Chinese Americans in this story about eight-year-old Moon Shadow who sails from China to the United States to meet his father, Windrider.

Born in San Francisco, California, in 1948, Yep was raised in an African American neighborhood and attended a bilingual school in the city's Chinatown. Despite being of Chinese descent, he fulfilled diverse cultural roles during his childhood. Within his family, he learned both about Chinese culture and about the American society that was now his home. Describing his family's approach to living in a new land, Yep once commented in *Horn Book* that "my mother's family's solution was to juggle elements of both cultures. Though they stayed Chinese in some central core, they also developed a curiosity and open-mindedness about the larger white culture around them." Outside the family home was another story. As Yep once explained in *Literature for Today's Young Adults,* "I was the all-purpose Asian. When [my friends and I] played war, I was the Japanese who got killed; then, when the Korean war came along, I was a North Korean Communist." The fact that Yep did not speak Chinese made it difficult for him to feel totally at home in Chinatown, and he felt equally at sea when he began attending a predominantly white high school.

It was in high school that Yep discovered science fiction, and he began writing stories in the genre and submitting them to magazines. A published sci-fi author by the time he was eighteen years old, Yep would explore the genre further in the novels he would write in later years. Fornow, though, it was off to college, first at Marquette University, which Yep attended from 1966 to 1968 and where he became totally immersed in "white" culture for the first time.

Suggestion of Friend Spark's Yep's Career

Leaving Marquette to finish up his bachelor's degree at the University of California at Santa Cruz in 1970, Yep went on to earn a Ph.D. at the State University of New York at Buffalo in 1975. In the midst of his academic studies in New York, he took the advice of a friend regarding his writing; that advice would change Yep's life. "A friend of mine who had gone to work at Harper's asked me to think about writing a science-fiction book for children," Yep recalled to WNYC radio interviewer Barbara Rollock, "and *Sweetwater* was the result."

Sweetwater, published in 1973 while its author was still a student at SUNY Buffalo, focuses on Tyree, a young man who belongs to a group of transplanted colonists called Argans. While among the first groups to settle the planet Harmony, the Argans are now a racial minority within the planet's growing population, and Tyree and his fellow Silkies—half earth-dweller, half amphibian—must scavenge in order to survive. Their struggle for survival in a frequently hostile environment forms the themes of family bonds, individual freedom, cultural traditions, and racism featured in Yep's novel. *Sweetwater* received positive reviews from critics, many of whom concurred with *Vector 78* contributor Brian Stableford that "*Sweetwater* has one powerful thing going for it, and that is the fact that its writing is, in every sense of the word, beautiful." Praising the novel for its concentration upon planetary ecology as well as its discussion of moral choices, Francis J. Molson added in *Twentieth-Century Science-Fiction Writers* that the novel "also concerns the development of an artist, a relatively rare topic in children's fiction of any kind, as Tyree senses within himself a gift for music which his parents disdain. . . . [The] thematic complexity and verbal richness . . . make *Sweetwater* superior."

Yep's second novel would be the first book for young readers in which he dealt directly with his Chinese-American heritage. In preparation for writing *Dragonwings*, he spent six years researching Chinese-American history, uncovering much factual information but little that reflected how immigrant families and individuals actually *felt* upon being confronted by a totally alien culture in the United States. In the course of Yep's research he found two brief newspaper articles from the year 1909, detailing the efforts of a Chinese American named Fung Joe Guey to build and fly his own flying machine. Seeing in Fung Joe Guey's story the basis of a novel, Yep filled in the blanks by creating a rich human story around the newspaper reports. His study of immigrant culture included the bachelor societies that provided a social interchange for Chinese men working to provide for families back in China and planning one day to return to Asia.

Dragonwings takes Flight

Published in 1975, *Dragonwings* tells the story of eight-year-old Moon Shadow, a young boy who leaves his mother in China's Middle Kingdom to join his father in the bachelor society of turn-of-the-century San Francisco. Moon Shadow's father, Windrider, a kite-builder, came to the United States to earn money for his family, but also to explore unknown frontiers. Together father and son fulfill Windrider's dream of flying his own plane. Through recounting the adventures and discoveries of father and son, Yep reveals a slice of Chinese-American history. "The story is narrated with humor and detail," Joe Stines summarized in *Dictionary of Literary Biography*, "blending Chinese folklore, myths, and legends with historical facts, such as the great San Francisco earthquake, the Chinese bachelor community of Chinatown, and the daring biplane flight of Fung Joe Guey." Critics applauded the complexity of Yep's characters and his sensitive portrayal of the prejudice they faced in the United States, Ruth H. Pelmas writing in the *New York Times Book Review* that, "as an exquisitely written poem of praise to the courage and industry of the Chinese-American people, [*Dragonwings*] is a triumph."

Many highly praised novels have since flowed from Yep's fertile imagination and studious research into the Chinese-American past. A winner of the *Boston Globe-Horn Book* Award, his 1977 work *Child of the Owl* is, like *Dragonwings*, set in San Francisco's Chinatown, but this time the year is 1960, as a young girl raised by a gambling father and then a suburban uncle is confused by her dual American and Chinese heritage. Having been exposed only to American ways and therefore having no means by which to identify with her Chinese background, Casey finds new options for living opened to her when she is sent to live with her grandmother, Paw-Paw, in Chinatown. Paw-Paw tells Casey a long legend about an owl which symbolizes family unity and tradition and provides the young girl a new way of communicating her feelings.

Novels Recall Childhood Experiences

Yep's *Sea Glass*, published in 1979, focuses on Craig Chin, a boy whose search for acceptance by both whites and Chinese Americans ends in rejection. Moving from his home in San Francisco's Chinatown to a small town, Craig is dubbed "Buddha Man" by his Anglo schoolmates, then pronounced like "the white demons" by a Chinese neighbor. Pressures from Craig's sports-minded father to go out for the school team do little to help him assimilate into school culture,

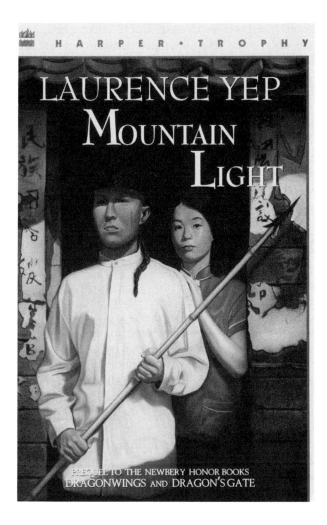

Squeaky Lou and Cassia, member of feuding families in nineteenth-century China, learn to trust each other as they become involved in a revolution against rulers of the Manchu dynasty.

but finally an uncle provides Craig with the key to self-acceptance. Another work with its roots in Yep's personal history is *The Star Fisher*, which the author published in 1991. Based on his parents' life, the novel finds fifteen-year-old Joan Chen moving from the Midwest to a small Southern town in the late 1920s. As the first and only Chinese-American family to arrive in Clarksburg, West Virginia, Joan finds that she must take the first step in building bridges of understanding in her new community, and gradually helps her more traditional parents find a way to assimilate into a community that contains both friends and others whose ignorance makes them bigoted. "Joan's story will appeal to any reader who has ever felt excluded," noted *School Library Journal* contributor

Carla Kozak, the reviewer adding that the "resilience and humor" of Yep's mother and her family "shine through." Finding the novel an equally praiseworthy effort, Alice Phoebe Naylor concluded in her *New York Times Book Review* appraisal that *The Star Fisher* "is a thought-provoking, engaging novel about a fundamental human drama—immigration and cultural isolation."

In addition to historical and fantasy fiction, Yep has also written several mysteries, as well as a number of novels featuring twentieth-century kids in typical twentieth-century predicaments. Two of his mystery novels—*The Mark Twain Murders* and *The Tom Sawyer Fires*—feature nineteenth-century writer Mark Twain as a young reporter in San Francisco who turns sleuth in response to a series of odd occurrences. Mystery again figures in *The Case of the Goblin Pearls*, one of a series of books featuring a group of pre-teens who solve mysteries within their Chinese- American communities while also learning about their varied cultural heritage. In *The Goblin Pearls*, for instance, Lily Lew and her flamboyant actress aunt go in search of a set of pricelesspearls stolen from a local sweatshop owner by a masked robber. Praising the novel's "Snappy dialogue, realistic characterizations and a plot with lots of action," a *Publishers Weekly* contributor added that Yep's spunky protagonist gains a "growing realization of the complexities of her Chinese heritage." And younger audiences are entertained by Yep in books like *Later, Gator*, where Teddy's prank gift of an creepy looking alligator for his younger brother backfires when he realizes that eight-year-old Bobby has actually taken a shine to his new pet, unaware that it will not live long in captivity.

Fantasy Series Draws New Fans

In 1982 Yep published the first of his "Dragon" novels, a four-volume series that *St. James Guide to Fantasy Writers* essayist Gary Westfahl described as "a noteworthy achievement" in the realm of fantasy literature due to the use of Chinese, rather than European, legend as its basis. The series, which begins with *Dragon of the Lost Sea*, introduces readers to Shimmer, a dragon princess who has been exiled from the dragon kingdom of Sambar as punishment for stealing a pearl symbolic of dragon clan leadership. Now disguised as a beggar woman, Shimmer sets out with a young human orphan named Thorn and a monkey wizard called Master of Seventy-two Transformations to restore the Inland Sea, the dragon clan's ancestral home, which was destroyed when the witch Civet stole the sea's water. In the series' second volume, *Dragon Steel*, Shimmer and Thorn are joined by several more companions, including a girl named Indigo, in their attempt to steal a magic cauldron that will allow them to restore the Inland Sea's waters to their proper location. Meanwhile, Shimmer attempts to settle her own accounts to rights when she petitions her uncle, the High King of Sambar, for readmittance to the kingdom, offering Civet as restitution for Shimmer's own thievery.

The third installment of the Dragon series finds Shimmer once again in search of a way to restore the Inland Sea. In *Dragon Cauldron* the magic caul-

In this final book of the "Dragon" series, Shimmer and her friends overcome a number of obstacles to defeat the Boneless King and restore the Inland Sea.

dron has been recovered, but it is cracked, and the only ones able to repair such damage are the Snail Woman and the Smith. Despite numerous obstacles, including an evil magician and a troop of soldiers determined to stop the group, Shimmer and company repair the cauldron, only to lose it again during a flood. It is only in *Dragon War*, the last volume in the series, that the group recovers the cauldron from the hands of the evil Boneless King, who had used it to destroy the dragon clan. Escaping the king's clutches, the group rallies an army of Shimmer's dragon allies and, with the use of shape- changing courtesy of the monkey wizard, defeats the Boneless King and his minions, restoring the Inland Sea in the process.

Reviewers applauded Yep's characters and their comical bantering, his accounts of high adventure, and the ability of each volume in the Dragon series to stand independently and be understood by readers unfamiliar with the rest of the series. Calling the four-volume work "an allegory of perseverance and loyalty," *Voice of Youth Advocates* reviewer Frank Perry added that "the variety of characters, continuity of plot, and incongruence of dragons [disguised] as humans hold fast the reader's attention." In *Washington Post Book World*, contributor Jane Yolen noted that Yep's "adventures are full of imagination and there is a kind of breezy zestiness . . . that will appeal to younger young adults." Noted Stines in *Dictionary of Literary Biography:* "Thematically, the story is characteristic of Yep's writing in its exploration of the ideas of identity, good versus evil, friendship, and loyalty."

Explores Facets of Chinese History

Many of Yep's books provide readers with a window onto both Chinese and Chinese- American history. His 1984 book, *The Serpent's Children*, is set in nineteenth-century China amid the Taiping Rebellion. In its pages readers meet Cassia, a young girl who, along with her family, joins a revolutionary Brotherhood working to eliminate the corruption brought by the rulers in the Manchu dynasty and the wealthy landowners in the now-impoverished Kwangtung Province. The group seeks only an enlightened peace for China. In the novel's sequel, 1985's *Mountain Light*, Cassia and her father, who are returning from a trip through China's Middle Kingdom, meet up with a young man named Squeaky Lau during their journey. On the eventful trip, taken on behalf of the revolution, the clownish Squeaky finds that he possesses his own inner strength and is able to bring out good in others. Although he and Cassia fall in love, Squeaky joins the mass migration to the western United States, "the land of the Golden Mountain," where he faces the chaos brought about by the California gold rush. And in 1994's *Dragon's Gate,* the story of the revolutionary family continues with Otter, Cassia's fourteen-year- old adopted son, as he too travels to America and works on the Transcontinental Railroad as part of a Chinese work crew carving a tunnel through a portion of the Sierra Nevada mountain range during the 1860s. Readers experience firsthand this often-overlooked period in history, as Otter "must struggle to survive racial prejudice, cold, starvation, the foreman's whip, and the dangers of frostbite and avalanche while trying to reconcile his ideals and dreams with harsh reality," according to Margaret A. Chang in her appraisal of *Dragon's Gate* for *School Library Journal.* Although some reviewers found the storyline of the series less compelling than in *Dragonwings, Booklist* contributor Ilene Cooper praised *Mountain Light* in particular as containing "a rich blend of action, moral lessons, and complex characterizations" and recommended the work for "advanced readers."

Other historical novels by Yep include *Hiroshima: A Novella,* a fictional portrait of the events surrounding the U.S. decision to drop an atomic bomb on Hiroshima, Japan, on August 6, 1945, thus accelerating the end of World War II. Focusing on one of the "Hiroshima Maidens"—girls and women who survived the bombing and who were eventually sent to the United States for reconstructive surgery—Yep describes both the actual bombing and its tragic and devastating long-term aftermath. Praising Yep for composing his factual story using "unadorned prose suiting its somber subject matter," *Washington Post Book World* contributor Elizabeth Hand wrote that Hiroshima "should be required reading in every classroom in [the United States] and beyond."

Short Fiction a Treasury of Chinese Folklore

In addition to full-length fiction, Yep has also compiled several volumes of short stories based on folktales and legends of China. In 1989's *The Rain-*

If you enjoy the works of Laurence Yep, you may also want to check out the following books and films:

Hadley Irwin, *Kim/Kimi,* 1987.
Toshi Maruki, *Hiroshima No Pika,* 1982.
Paul Yee, *Tales from Gold Mountain: Stories of the Chinese in the New World,* 1990.
A Great Wall, a film by Peter Wang, 1986.

bow People, he included twenty stories adapted from the recollections of Chinese immigrants living in Oakland, California's Chinatown that were recorded by a U.S. government-sponsored program during the 1930s. Many of the stories, which are divided into sections according to their theme, have their origins in southern China, the birthplace of many of Oakland's immigrant Chinese. Another story collection, *Tongues of Jade* includes both stories and background information that puts each tale, whether it be a ghost story or a love story, into sociological and historical perspective. Including such titles as "The Little Emperor" and "The Rat in the Wall," Yep's retellings "are liberally dosed with magic, and all praise the qualities . . . necessary to succeed in a foreign and often hostile land," according to a *Publishers Weekly* contributor.

During the 1975-76 school year, the year his first novel, *Dragonwings,* was published, Yep taught at San Jose City College. With the novel's success— it would win numerous awards—he decided to leave academia and pursue his writing full time. Although Yep would return to the college environment in 1987 to spend two years as a lecturer in Asian-American studies at the University of California at Berkeley, he has continued to devote most of his time to his fiction. While at the University of California, Yep had recognized the scarcity of anthologies appropriate as course material, and set about to construct his own. In 1993 he would publish this work as *American Dragons: Twenty-five Asian American Voices.* Containing stories, essays, and verse, the anthology contains works by such well-known authors as Maxine Hong Kingston and William F. Wu. Grouped according to such themes as the search for identity, the Japanese experience during World War II, and relationships with Asian-born parents and grandparents, Yep focuses in particular on works relevant to young people attempting to live between two cultures.

Yep, who also occasionally writes for adult readers, is an avid proponent of the power of children's literature. "I enjoy writing for children because you can get back to old-fashioned storytelling rather than inflating a text with material about existential crises and whatever are the latest aesthetic and philosophical fads," he once noted in *Twentieth-Century Children's Writers*. "Stories have to be told in concrete, vivid terms and relationships between characters are basic human bonds and therefore more universal." Calling Yep a "bridge builder," Karen Ferris Morgan concluded in her essay for *Twentieth-Century Young Adult Writers* that through his novels and short stories young readers "look . . . through a window to greater understandings of the worlds of differences and similarities that co-exist in life. Vivid images, complex characters, and well-plotted action" continue to be trademarks of Yep's unique fiction.

■ Works Cited

Review of *The Case of the Goblin Pearls*, in *Publishers Weekly*, December 16, 1996, pp. 59-60.

Chang, Margaret, review of *Dragon's Gate*, in *School Library Journal*, January, 1994, p. 135.

Cooper, Ilene, review of *Mountain Light*, in *Booklist*, September 15, 1985, p. 141.

Kozak, Carla, review of *The Star Fisher*, in *School Library Journal*, May, 1991, p. 113.

Molson, Francis J., "Laurence Yep," in *Twentieth-Century Science-Fiction Writers*, 3rd edition, St. James Press (Detroit), 1992, pp. 895-96.

Morgan, Karen Ferris, "Laurence Yep," in *Twentieth-Century Young Adult Writers*, 2nd edition, St. James Press, 1999, pp. 724-25.

Naylor, Alice Phoebe, review of *The Star Fisher*, in *New York Times Book Review*, October 13, 1991, p. 31.

Pelmas, Ruth H., review of *Dragonwings*, in *New York Times Book Review*, November 16, 1975.

Perry, Frank, review of *Dragon Steel*, in *Voice of Youth Advocates*, August, 1985, p. 195.

Stableford, Brian, review of *Sweetwater*, in *Vector 78*, November/December, 1976, p. 30.

Stines, Joe, "Laurence Yep," in *Dictionary of Literary Biography*, Volume 52: *American Writers for Children since 1960: Fiction*, Gale (Detroit), 1986.

Review of *Tongues of Jade*, in *Publishers Weekly*, September 20, 1991, p. 135.

Westfahl, Gary, "Laurence Yep," in *St. James Guide to Fantasy Writers*, St. James Press, 1996, pp. 637-38.

Yep, Laurence, *Dragonwings*, Harper, 1975.

Yep, Laurence, "The Green Chord," in *Horn Book*, May/June, 1989, pp. 318-22.

Yep, Laurence, in *Literature for Today's Young Adults*, 2nd edition, edited by Alleen Pace Nilsen and Kenneth L. Donelson, Scott, Foresman, 1985.

Yep, Laurence, taped interview with Barbara Rollock, on *The World of Children's Literature*, WNCY Radio, November 1, 1976.

Yep, Laurence, in *Twentieth-Century Children's Writers*, St. James Press, 1989, pp. 1074-75.

Yolen, Jane, "Fantasy Novels: Of Wizards, Whales and Worlds Beyond," in *Washington Post Book World*, May 12, 1985, pp. 13-14.

■ For More Information See

BOOKS

Children's Literature Review, Gale, Volume 3, 1978, Volume 17, 1989.

Contemporary Literary Criticism, Volume 35, Gale, 1985.

Huck, Charlotte S., *Children's Literature in the Elementary School*, 3rd edition, Holt, 1979.

Johnson-Feelings, Dianne, *Presenting Laurence Yep*, Twayne (New York City), 1995.

Norton, Donna E., *Through the Eyes of a Child: An Introduction to Children's Literature*, 2nd edition, Merrill, 1987.

Something about the Author Autobiography Series, Volume 1, Gale, 1986.

Twentieth-Century Children's Writers, 5th edition, St. James Press, 1999.

PERIODICALS

Booklist, April 15, 1992, p. 1524; July, 1995, p. 1880; January 1, 1997, pp. 846-47; February 1, 1997, p. 940; July, 1997, p. 1817.

Bulletin of the Center for Children's Books, April, 1989, p. 211; March, 1991, p. 182; July/August, 1991, p. 279; June, 1995, p. 365; September, 1995, p. 34.

Christian Science Monitor, November 5, 1975, p. B7; May 4, 1977, p. 29; October 15, 1979, p. B11.

English Journal, March, 1982, pp. 81-82.

Horn Book, April, 1978; March/April, 1994, p. 208; July/August, 1995, p. 463; March/April, 1997, pp. 208-9; September/October, 1997, pp. 594-95.

Interracial Books for Children Bulletin, Volume 7, numbers 2 & 3, 1976; Volume 11, number 6, 1980, p. 16.

Junior Bookshelf, February, 1977, p. 48.

Kirkus Reviews, June 15, 1993, p. 794; April 15, 1995, p. 564; May 1, 1995, p. 642; January 15, 1997, p. 148.

Lion and the Unicorn, Volume 5, 1981, pp. 4-18.

Locus, March, 1992, p. 64.

New York Times Book Review, May 22, 1977; January 20, 1980, p. 30; May 23, 1982, p. 37; November 6, 1983, p. 44; July 23, 1989, p. 29.

Publishers Weekly, May 18, 1992, p. 71; June 14, 1993, p. 72; March 4, 1996, pp. 66-67; August 25, 1997, p. 71.

Reading Teacher, January 1977, pp. 359-63.

School Library Journal, June, 1991, p. 114; December, 1991, p. 132; June, 1992, p. 144; March, 1997, pp. 194-95; October, 1997, p. 125.

Voice of Youth Advocates, December, 1985, p. 323; June, 1991, p. 116; December, 1991, p. 320; February, 1996, p. 380.

Washington Post Book World, May 1, 1977, pp. E1, E8; January 9, 1983, pp. 11, 13; November 6, 1983, pp. 17, 22; November 10, 1985, p. 20; May 7, 1995, p. 14.

Wilson Library Bulletin, June, 1995, p. 120.*

—Sketch by Pamela L. Shelton

Acknowledgments

Acknowledgments

Grateful acknowledgment is made to the following publishers, authors, and artists for their kind permission to reproduce copyrighted material.

EMMA BULL. From a cover of *Finder,* by Emma Bull. Tor Books, Tom Doherty Associates, Inc., 1994. Reproduced by permission of St. Martin's Press, Inc. / "Episode des journees de Septembre 1830 sur la Place de l'Hotel de Ville de Bruxelles," detail from painting by G. Wappers. From a cover of *Freedom & Necessity,* by Emma Bull and Steven Brust. Musees royaux des Beaux-Arts de Belgique, Bruxelles-Koninklijke Musee voor Schone Kunsten van Belgie, Brussel. Reproduced by permission. / Bull, Emma, photograph by Will Shetterly. Reproduced by permission.

JOHN FEINSTEIN. Duvoisin, Jacqueline, photographer. From a cover of *A Good Walk Spoiled,* by John Feinstein. Little, Brown and Company, 1995. Reproduced by permission of Warner Books, Inc. / From a cover of *A Civil War,* by John Feinstein. Little, Brown and Company, 1996. Reproduced by permission of Warner Books, Inc. / Baptist, Bill, photographer. From a cover of *A March to Madness,* by John Feinstein. Little, Brown and Company, 1998. Reproduced by permission of Warner Books, Inc. / Feinstein, John, photograph by Robert Crawford. Little, Brown, and Company. Reproduced by permission.

FRANZ KAFKA. "Family Picture," 1920, oil on canvas, 25 5/8" x 39 3/4", painting by Max Beckmann. From a cover of *The Metamorphosis,* by Franz Kafka. Bantam Books, 1986. Collection, The Museum of Modern Art, New York. Gift of Abby Aldrich Rockefeller. © The Museum of Modern Art, New York, 1986. Reproduced by permission of Bantam Books, a division of Random House, Inc. / From a cover of *The Castle,* by Franz Kafka. Cover photograph Culver Pictures. Schocken Books, 1998. Reproduced by permission of Culver Pictures, Inc. / Perkins, Anthony, in the movie "The Trial," 1963, photograph. The Kobal Collection. Reproduced by permission. / Kafka, Franz, photograph. AP/Wide World Photos. Reproduced by permission.

VICTOR KELLEHER. Voevodin, Craig, photographer. From a cover of *The Beast of Heaven,* by Victor Kelleher. University of Queensland Press, 1984. Reproduced by permission.

PAUL KLEE. "Aphrodite's Vases," 1921, painting by Paul Klee. From *Klee.* Edited by Jose Maria Faerna. Cameo/Abrams. © 1999 Artists Rights Society (ARS), New York/VG Bild-Kunst, Bonn. Reproduced by permission of Artists Rights Society, Inc. / "Cat and Bird," 1928, painting by Paul Klee. From *Klee.* Edited by Jose Maria Faerna. Cameo/Abrams. © 1999 Artists Rights Society (ARS), New York/VG Bild-Kunst, Bonn. Reproduced by permission of Artists Rights Society, Inc. / "Insula Dulcamara," 1938, painting by Paul Klee. From *Klee.* Edited by Jose MariaFaerna. Cameo/Abrams. © 1999 Artists Rights Society (ARS), New York/VG Bild-Kunst, Bonn. Reproduced by permission of Artists Rights Society, Inc. / Klee, Paul, photograph. Corbis-Bettmann. Reproduced by permission.

DEAN R. KOONTZ. From a cover of *Watchers,* by Dean R. Koontz. Berkley Books, 1988. Copyright © 1987 by Nkui, Inc. Reproduced by permission of The Berkley Publishing Group, a division of Penguin Putnam Inc. / From a cover of *Lightning,* by Dean R. Koontz. Berkley Books, 1989. Copyright © 1988 by Nkui, Inc. Reproduced by permission of The Berkley Publishing Group, a division of Penguin Putnam Inc. / Brautigam, Don, illustrator. From a cover of *The Bad Place,* by Dean Koontz. Berkley Books, 1990. Cover illustration copyright © 1990 by Don Brautigam. Reproduced by permission of The Berkley Publishing Group, a division of Penguin Putnam Inc. / O'Toole, Peter, with Rose McGowan in a scene from "Phantom," 1997, photograph by John P. Johnson. The Kobal Collection. Reproduced by permission. / Koontz, Dean R., photograph by Jerry Bauer. © Jerry Bauer. Reproduced by permission.

NORMAN MAILER. From a cover of *The Naked and the Dead,* by Norman Mailer. Cover photograph Corbis-Bettmann. Owl Books, 1998. Reproduced by permission of Henry Holt and Company LLC, and Corbis-Bettmann. / Jones, Tommy Lee, with Rosanna Arquette in a scene from "The Executioner's Song," 1982, photograph. The Kobal Collection. Reproduced by permission. / O'Neal, Ryan, with Isabella Rossellini, in a scene from "Tough Guys Don't Dance," 1987, photograph. The Kobal Collection. Reproduced by permission. / Mailer, Norman, photograph. Archive Photos, Inc. Reproduced by permission.

RICHARD MATHESON. From a cover of *I Am Legend,* by Richard Matheson. Orb Books, Tom Doherty Associates, Inc., 1997. Reproduced by permission of St. Martin's Press, Inc. / Crofut, Bob, illustrator. From a cover of *Somewhere in Time,* by Richard Matheson. Tor Paperbacks, Tom Doherty Associates, Inc., 1999. Reproduced by permission of St. Martin's Press, Inc. / Grant Williams in a scene from "The Incredible Shrinking Man," movie still. The Kobal Collection. Reproduced by permission. / McDowell, Roddy, with Gayle Hunnicut and Clive Revill, in the film "The Legend of Hell House," 1973, photograph. The Kobal Collection. Reproduced by permission. / Williams, Robin, with Cuba Gooding, Jr., in a scene from "What Dreams May Come," 1998, photograph by Frank Masi. The Kobal Collection. Reproduced by permission. / Matheson, Richard, photograph. Tor Books. Reproduced by permission.

JEAN DAVIES OKIMOTO. Bacha, Andrew, illustrator. From a cover of *Take A Chance, Gramps!*, by Jean Davies Okimoto. Tor Books, Tom Doherty Associates, Inc., 1996. Reproduced by permission of St. Martin's Press, Inc. / Atkinson, Janet, illustrator. From a cover of *The Eclipse of Moonbeam Dawson*, by Jean Davies Okimoto. Tor Books, Tom Doherty Associates, Inc., 1997. © 1997 by Jean Davies Okimoto. Reproduced by permission of St. Martin's Press. / Okimoto, Jean Davies, photograph by Peggy Washburn. Reproduced by permission of Jean Davies Okimoto.

KATHERINE PATERSON. Deas, Michael, illustrator. From a cover of *Bridge to Terabithia*, by Katherine Paterson. HarperTrophy, 1987. Cover art copyright © 1987 by Michael Deas. Cover copyright © 1995 by HarperCollins Publishers. Reproduced by permission of HarperCollinsPublishers. / Mak, Kam, illustrator. From a cover of *Of Nightingales That Weep*, by Katherine Paterson. HarperTrophy, 1989. Cover art copyright © 1989 by Kam Mak. Cover copyright © 1989 by HarperCollins Publishers. Reproduced by permission of HarperCollins Publishers. / Mak, Kam, illustrator. From a cover of *Jacob Haved I Loved*, by Katherine Paterson. HarperTrophy, 1995. Cover illustration copyright © 1990 by Kam Mak. Cover copyright © 1995 by HarperCollins Publishers. Reproduced by permission of HarperCollins Publishers. / Dodge, Bill, illustrator. From a jacket of *Jip, His Story*, by Katherine Paterson. Lodestar Books, 1996. Jacket illustration © 1996 by Bill Dodge. Reproduced by permission of Lodestar Books, an affiliate of Dutton Children's Books, a division of Penguin Putnam Inc. / Paterson, Katherine, photograph by Jill Paton Walsh. Reproduced by permission of Jill Paton Walsh.

ELLIS PETERS. Bascove, illustrator. From a cover of *The Heretic's Apprentice*, by Ellis Peters. The Mysterious Press, 1990. Reproduced by permission of Warner Books, Inc. / Bascove, illustrator. From a cover of *A Morbid Taste for Bones*, by Ellis Peters. The Mysterious Press, 1994. Reproduced by permission of Warner Books, Inc. / Toelke, Cathleen, illustrator. From a cover of *Fallen into the Pit*, by Ellis Peters. The Mysterious Press, 1996. Reproduced by permission of Warner Books, Inc. / Bascove, illustrator. From a cover of *Dead Man's Ransom*, by Ellis Peters. The Mysterious Press, 1997. Reproduced by permission of Warner Books, Inc.

RODMAN PHILBRICK. Thompson, John, illustrator. From a cover of *The Fire Pony*, by Rodman Philbrick. A Scholastic Apple Signature Edition Book, 1997. Illustration copyright © 1997 by Scholastic Inc. Reproduced by permission. / Shannon, David, illustrator. From a cover of *Max The Mighty*, by Rodman Philbrick. A Scholastic Point Signature Book, 1998. Illustration copyright © 1998 by Scholastic Inc. Reproduced by permission. / Culkin, Kiernan, with Elden Henson, in a scene from "The Mighty," 1998, photograph by Kerry Hayes. The Kobal Collection. Reproduced by permission. / Philbrick, Rodman, photograph by Lynn Harnett. Reproduced by permission of Rodman Philbrick.

ARTHUR RACKHAM. Rackham, Arthur, illustrator. From an illustration in *Gulliver's Travels into Several Remote Nations of the World*, by Jonathan Swift. J. M. Dent, 1900. / Rackham, Arthur, illustrator. From an illustration in *A Midsummer's Night Dream*, by William Shakespeare. Heinemann, 1908. / Rackham, Arthur, c. 1910, photograph. Source unknown.

CHAP REAVER. From a cover of *A Little Bit Dead*, by Chap Reaver. Laurel-Leaf Books, 1994. Copyright © 1992 by Herbert R. Reaver, Jr. Reproduced by permission of Random House Children's Books, a division of Random House, Inc. / From a cover of *Bill*, by Chap Reaver. Yearling Books, 1996. Copyright © 1994 by the Estate of Herbert R. Reaver, Jr. Reproduced by permission of Random House Children's Books, a division of Random House, Inc. / Reaver, Chap, photograph by Scott Reaver. Reproduced by permission of Scott Reaver.

R. A. SALVATORE. Easley, Jeff, illustrator. From a cover of *Exile*, by R. A. Salvatore. TSR, Inc., 1990. Reproduced by permission. / Ciruelo, Cabral, illustrator. From a cover of *The Dragon King*, by R. A. Salvatore. Warner Books, Inc., 1997. Reproduced by permission. / Salvatore, R.A., photograph. TSR, Inc. Reproduced by permission.

DANA STABENOW. From a cover of *A Cold Day for Murder*, by Dana Stabenow. Berkley Prime Crime Books, 1993. Reproduced by permission of The Berkley Publishing Group, a member of Penguin Putnam Inc. / From a cover of *Breakup*, by Dana Stabenow. Berkley Prime Crime Books, 1998. Reproduced by permission of The Berkley Publishing Group, a member of Penguin Putnam Inc. / Stabenow, Dana, photograph. Reproduced by permission.

MEGAN WHALEN TURNER. Smith, Jos. A., illustrator. From a jacket of *Instead of Three Wishes*, by Megan Whalen Turner. Greenwillow Books, 1995. Jacket art © 1995 by Jos. A. Smith. Reproduced by permission of Greenwillow Books, a division of William Morrow & Company, Inc. / Gaffney-Kessell, Walter, illustrator. From a jacket of *The Thief*, by Megan Whalen Turner. Greenwillow Books, 1996. Jacket art © 1996 by Walter Gaffney-Kessell. Reproduced by permission Greenwillow Books, a division of William Morrow & Company, Inc. / Turner, Megan Whalen, photograph by Alex Madonik. Reproduced by permission of Megan Whalen Turner.

TAD WILLIAMS. Whelan, Michael, illustrator. From a cover of *The Dragonbone Chair*, by Tad Williams. DAW Books, Inc., 1989. Reproduced by permission. / Whelan, Michael, illustrator. From a cover of *Stone of Farewell*, by Tad Williams. DAW Books, Inc., 1991. Reproduced by permission. / Whelan, Michael, illustrator. From a cover of *To Green Angel Tower, Part I*, by Tad Williams. DAW Books, Inc., 1994. Reproduced by permission. / Whelan, Michael, illustrator. From a cover of *Otherland*, by Tad Williams. DAW Books, Inc., 1998. Reproduced by permission. / Williams, Tad, photograph by Jerry Bauer. © Jerry Bauer. Reproduced by permission.

TENNESSEE WILLIAMS. From a cover of *The Glass Menagerie*, by Tennessee Williams. New Directions Publishing Corporation, 1949. Copyright © 1945 by New Directions Publishing Corporation. Reproduced by permission. / From a movie still of Tennessee Williams' "Cat On A Hot Tin Roof" with Burl Ives, Elizabeth Taylor and Paul Newman, MGM, 1958, photograph. MGM. The Kobal Collection. Reproduced by permission. / From a production still for "The Glass Menagerie" by Tennessee Williams. Archive Photos, Inc. Reproduced by permission. / From a production still for "A Streetcar Named Desire" by Tennessee Williams. Archive Photos, Inc. Reproduced by permission. / Williams, Tennessee, 1955, photograph. AP/Wide World Photos. Reproduced by permission.

TIM WYNNE-JONES. Temertey, Ludmilla, illustrator. From a jacket of *The Maestro*, by Tim Wynne-Jones. Orchard Books, 1996. Jacket illustration copyright © 1995 by Ludmilla Temertey. Text copyright © 1995 by Tim Wynne-Jones. First published in Canada by Groundwood Books/Douglas & McIntyre. Reproduced by permission of the publisher, Groundwood Books/Douglas & McIntyre. In the U.S. and Philippines by Orchard Books, New York. / Drury, Christian Potter, illustrator. From a cover of *Some of the Kinder Planets*, by Tim Wynne-Jones. Puffin Books, 1996. Copyright © 1994 by Tim Wynne-Jones, text. Copyright © 1994 Christian Potter Drury, cover. Reproduced by permission of Puffin Books, a division of Penguin Putnam Inc. / Brooker, Kyrsten, illustrator. From a jacket of *Lord of the Fries*, by Tim Wynne-Jones. DKInk Books, 1999. Jacket art copyright © 1999 by Kyrsten Brooker. Reproduced by permission of DK Publishing, Inc. / Wynne-Jones, Tim, photograph by Larry Ostrom. Reproduced by permission of Tim Wynne-Jones.

LAURENCE YEP. Himler, Ronald, illustrator. From a cover of *Dragonwings*, by Laurence Yep. HarperTrophy, 1975. Cover copyright © 1995 by HarperCollins Publishers. Reproduced by permission of HarperCollins Publishers. / Dodge, Bill, illustrator. From a cover of *Dragon War*, by Laurence Yep. HarperTrophy, 1992. Cover art copyright © 1994 by Bill Dodge. Cover copyright © 1994 by HarperCollins Publishers. Reproduced by permission of HarperCollins Publishers. / O'Brien, Tim, illustrator. From a cover of *Mountain Light*, by Laurence Yep. HarperTrophy, 1997. Cover art copyright © 1997 by Tim O'Brien. Cover copyright © 1997 by HarperCollins Publishers. Reproduced by permission of HarperCollins Publishers. / Yep, Laurence, photograph by Kathleen Yep. Reproduced by permission of Curtis Brown, Ltd., for Laurence Yep.

Cumulative Index

Author/Artist Index

The following index gives the number of the volume in which an author/artist's biographical sketch appears.